STRAIGHT
AND TRUE

STRAIGHT AND TRUE

A
SELECT
HISTORY
of the
Arrow

HUGH D. H. SOAR

WESTHOLME
Yardley

Frontispiece: North American Atsina Indians ritually shooting arrows into the sky. (*Library of Congress*)

Westholme Publishing, LLC
904 Edgewood Road
Yardley, Pennsylvania 19067
Visit our Web site at www.westholmepublishing.com

First Printing July 2012
10 9 8 7 6 5 4 3 2 1

ISBN: 978-1-59416-147-6

Also available as an eBook.

Printed in the United States of America.

In memory of my son
CAPTAIN HUGH RICHARD SOAR RAMC TA
1950–2009

Contents

Introduction

Subordinate to the bow, its charismatic companion, but purposeful in its intent, the arrow epitomizes both silent death and joyous recreation. With origins lost in time, it is obedient to all who use it, but respectful of none. It is synonymous with both the wayward vagaries of Cupid and the esoteric practices of a divining shaman. It is equally at home in the quiver of Artemis the huntress, in the hands of a formidable English or Welsh bowman on a bloody medieval battlefield, or those of a beguiling Victorian maiden on a dew-soaked vicarage lawn.

Although it is a means of simple pleasure, it has a dark side too, since it was the instrument and symbol of their martyrdom for Saint Edmund, king of Saxon East Anglia; Saint Sebastian of Milan; and Saint Ursula of Cologne.

Whether fashioned from man-made or natural materials, each shaft relies ultimately upon the skill of its creator; its various profiles adopted for purpose, with each supple shape the product of trial and error by arrow-makers across the centuries.

The poet Henry Wadsworth Longfellow reflected the prosaic Western concept of the arrow's task in his epic *The Song of Hiawatha*. His ancient unnamed arrow-maker, sitting with demure daughter Minnehaha at the door of his tepee, reminisces,

> Thinking of the great war-parties
> How they came to buy his arrows,
> Could not fight without his arrows.

And yet again he writes, as Hiawatha prepares to dispatch a deer,

> To his bow he whispered, "Fail not!"
> To his arrow, whispered, "Swerve not!"
> Sent it singing on its errand,
> To the red heart of the roe-buck.[1]

Sadly, Longfellow had no direct knowledge of Indian culture; his romantic epic was a rose-colored fantasy based upon the observations of others. However, fortune favors us, for with Ishi, the last California Yana Indian—who died in 1916 and whose Stone Age knowledge of bow and arrow making added so much to our understanding of early hunting man— we have in intricate detail the minutiae of a Stone Age Indian's life. Reflecting Longfellow, Ishi said, in paraphrase, anyone can make a bow, but it takes skill and experience to make an arrow.[2] These properties he possessed in full measure, and later I will discuss the method he used to make the hunting shafts he called *sa wa*.

Among the traditions, legends, and history of Islam, where archery is a sacred activity, it is believed that the Almighty Creator sent down to Adam, by means of the angel Gabriel, one bow made of a single piece of timber from a tree of Paradise, one bowstring, and two arrows. Upon these arrows were written the names of the five prophets: Noah, Abraham, Moses, Jesus, and Muhammad. In recognition of this, senior Muslim archers habitually shot five arrows at the Great Spring Festival of the Orient, held annually in Turkey for many years. Thus, in Islam, does the arrow embody spiritual authority.[3]

In Japan, archers practicing the subtle art of *kyudo* equip themselves with two sets of paired arrows. One pair they call *haya*, the other *otoya*. The curvature of feathers of each pair differs from the other so that when a *haya* is followed by an *otoya*, the second should not hit the first and by damaging its feathers thus harm its soul.

Longfellow's artless concept, untrammelled by symbolism and devoid of spirit, typifies the secular way we Westerners view the arrow. To us it is a lifeless subordinate tool, a mere adjunct to the revered bow, and for this we are spiritually diminished.

Within the limitations of space, it is the intention of this book to speculate upon the origin of the arrow and its development, both as an indiscriminate killing weapon and as a means of gentle relaxation; to meander through its varied facets, the better to balance its arcane Eastern mystery and symbolism with its prosaic Western purpose.

Read of the *atlatl* used by Aztec warriors and of the poisoned arrows found in Brazilian jungles; of the grey goose wing, victor at Agincourt, and the slim shafts crafted for shooting at target, butt, and clout; of fire arrows, sprites, and Gypsy arrows. Read of Japanese symbolism and Chinese precision; of Indian myth, and of the unfettered joy of Bhutanese archery; of crow bills, cross-nocks, and the black reddendo. All await you within.

It has been a difficult task to decide what should be selected for inclusion in this book and what, through limitations of space, has had to be omitted. I am aware that I will not have pleased all by my selection but I hope that there is sufficient within to satisfy most.

Although this is not a book for academics, I hope my readers will find it an informative and sometimes enjoyable ramble through the history of the arrow, while the bibliography will, I trust, go some way towards whetting the appetite of those who wish to extend their knowledge of the arrow and archery further.

The Arrow

It may be helpful, before we move further, to introduce the general reader, unfamiliar with archery, to the component parts of an arrow, since they will meet these in later pages. An arrow consists of a self shaft (that is, of only one wood), sometimes called a stele, of which the shaftment, also called the little shaft, is that portion of the arrow that carries the feather fletches, or fletchings, which steady it in flight. It will have a nock (notch or groove) for the bowstring. Alternatively, a shaft may have either a foreshaft attached or a footing spliced in at the forward end. In either case it has two essential attachments: feather fletchings (usually three) spaced at equal distances around the shaftment, and a head (or pile). It can also have one desirable but not essential addition: a sliver of animal horn called a nockpiece, which is set into the end of the shaftment and is designed to strengthen the string groove against pressure from the bowstring. The arrow can also be marked to distinguish its ownership either with runes, painted symbols, or cresting; and its profile, or contour, may be to one of five distinct shapes, which we shall examine in more detail later. Both its shape and its overall length will be suited to the style of shooting for which it is intended.

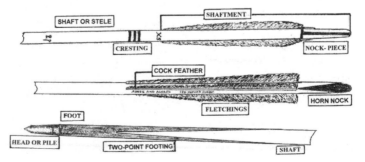

Parts of an arrow. (*Author*)

ORIGINS

To UNDERSTAND THE RELEVANCE OF THE ARROW, WE SHOULD first consider its precursor, the spear, for at some time in the dim and distant past, a random hominid picked up a sharpened stick and with it dispatched his unsuspecting prey. It is a matter for pensive reflection that, in the course of millennia, from this obscure event emerged the arrow, and eventually, through exponential experiment, the intercontinental ballistic missile.

The wooden spear has been known since at least the Paleolithic era some four hundred thousand years ago, while those ancient ancestors from whom modern man has evolved are believed to have combined this standoff weapon with a throwing device since at least the Upper Paleolithic period, between forty thousand and ten thousand years ago. Known today by its Aztec name of *atlatl*, or spear thrower, and by certain Australian aborigines as *woomera*, it was the first mechanical device developed to aid the hunter. The earliest known spear or dart thrower is a fifteen-thousand-year-old object made of reindeer antler of the late Upper Paleolithic period (16,000–10,000 BC) recovered from an excavation in France.[1]

The *atlatl* is a simple device that uses mechanical leverage to achieve greater velocity when a spear, dart, or arrow is thrown. It consists essentially of a wooden shaft, one end of which has an integral cup into which the butt end of the object to be thrown is securely fitted, but with freedom to move forward. When settled, both it and the missile are held at its further end, just above the thrower's shoulder. The missile is then dispatched by a rapid forward movement of the upper arm and wrist, with the *atlatl* as an extension of the throwing arm, adding significant force through increased angular momentum.

One sophistication is believed to have been the addition of a small stone, known today as a bannerstone, at the middle of the *atlatl*. Experiment has shown that this would have improved stability and thus the accuracy of the spear in flight. It has also been said to reduce the initial noise made by the *atlatl* from a "zip" to a "woof," which some consider an advantage in hunting because it does not unduly disturb the prey. Not everyone believes that the two objects are connected with each other, however, and indeed, I can find no reference to these being physically attached to *atlatls* recovered from archaeological sites, although they have been found in close proximity. This has given rise to speculation, notably by professor Snyder Webb (1882–1964), that they were used together. An alternative view, proposed by Robert Berg, proprietor of the American manufacturer Thunderbird Atlatls, is that this stone is merely a spinning whorl from a drop spindle, used for spinning thread.[2] Since so many different shapes have been found, the most plausible popular theory is that they had a number of different uses, just one of which was to stabilize and/or silence the *atlatl*. One modern improvement by those who engage in such throwing today, but which may reflect earlier practice, is the use of thong loops fitted to the throwing fingers.

Modern experiment shows that although an *atlatl* enables the thrown spear to reach considerable distances (over one

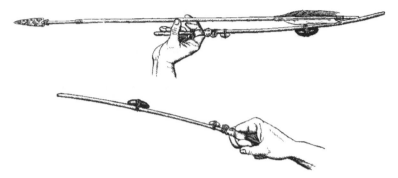

Atlatl before and after the arrow has been thrown. Note the bannerstone secured in position. (*California State Parks*)

hundred yards not being unusual) at an initial velocity of close to one hundred mph, speed plays little part in accuracy at this distance and is not a feature of the system.

It seems likely, therefore, that except in warfare, where massed attack might be made against a large enemy force (witness the Aztec warrior pitted against the Spanish invader), its use by Paleolithic man for hunting would have been confined to comparatively short distances.[3] One might visualize a number of early hunters combining to cast spears and bring down a solitary, slow-moving mammoth, or perhaps aiming at a herd of animals.

Presumed disadvantages of the *atlatl* and its spear or dart when hunting, compared with the comparative stealth of the bow and arrow, are the rapid movement necessary to project the missile and the clear space required to effect this. A wary animal would be instantly alerted, at least in daylight. This presumption has been confirmed by casual observation of a contemporary boar hunt recorded on video in America, when two aspiring hunters failed to strike a watchful boar with their *atlatl*-propelled missile.

The Australian spear thrower, the *woomera*—a name used by the aborigines of New South Wales that has become synonymous with all similar Australian weapons—is shaped in the form of a long narrow bowl and is a multipurpose tool. It can be used to carry food and also wet herbage to be sucked for moisture while on walkabout. Many have sharpened stones at their tips, secured by black gum from the triodia plant, for cutting meat or wood. The *woomera* is still used in some remote parts of Australia.

A late example of the *woomera*, dating from the end of the nineteenth century, is displayed at Pitt Rivers Museum in Oxford, England.[4] Described as a "male spear thrower," this example has thirty-five small notches cut into its edge, suggesting an additional use as a percussive musical instrument. One may visualize an aboriginal audience seated around a campfire at dusk, enraptured by a duet between a didgeridoo and a *woomera*.

Perhaps the most famous spear or dart thrower is that recovered from the French archaeological cave site of La Mas d'Azil in southern France. It is elaborately carved from reindeer antler and has holes in its forward end that are typical of other *propulseurs*, or spear throwers, in that region. Archaeologists believe that the holes enabled the attachment of either loops for fingers or a handle of wood or leather. Dating to the Magdalenian period (Upper Paleolithic) of some seventeen thousand years ago, it is one of the oldest and possibly one of the most beautiful of its kind in the world.

Dorothy A. E. Garrod (1892–1968), Disney Professor of Archaeology at the University of Cambridge from 1938 to 1952 and a leading specialist on the subject of *propulseurs*, draws attention to the recording, in Edouard Lartet and Henry Christy's *Reliquiae Aquitanicae*, of the first identification of the device prior to 1903, by an anonymous individual who, having received an artifact described as a "sculptured reindeer antler," correctly identified its purpose as a "hooked spear thrower of a type well known in Australia."[5] Garrod makes the point that those Paleolithic throwers known to us have been preserved only because they are made of antler. Many more must have perished through being made of wood.

Garrod writes in the *Proceedings of the Prehistoric Society*, "A major area of *propulseur* distribution is southwest France, with an offshoot in what may be described as the Bodensee Magdalenian, that is in the caves northeast of Schafhausen and the Petrusfels rock shelter just across the French/German border."[6] Garrod advises that while the most productive period for the thrower is Magdalenian Period IV (circa 16,000–11,500 BC), the earliest specimens so far recovered date from Magdalenian Period III (circa 11,550–9,000 BC) found in la grotte du Placard, a decorated cave in southwest France. However, Garrod observes that in the scene in the cave at Lascaux, where a dead man is portrayed beside a dead bison, a hooked thrower is seemingly depicted in a drawing that is understood to be pre-Magdalenian and from seventeen thousand to twenty-five thousand years old.

The length of a spear thrower is naturally limited by the source of the material. Although an antler can at most provide a thrower of a little over 13 inches (33.02 centimeters) in length, there is evidence, from those recovered, for a possible extension by hafting in, one supposes, wood. The Australian *woomera* of wood could exceed 48 inches (122 centimeters), while evidence for the Aztec *atlatl* suggests a measurement of somewhere between the two.

The length of the spear thrower evidently varied across the globe, as has the spear used with it. The origin of these aids to hunting is lost in time, although Dr. Hartmut Thieme, who supervised the excavation at an early Paleolithic site close to the city of Schöningen, Lower Saxony, Germany, reports a possible throwing stick associated with eight spears recovered. More than three hundred thousand years old, they are the oldest completely preserved hunting weapons in the world and are regarded as the first evidence of active hunting by early man. The spears are approximately 6 feet to 7 feet 6 inches long (variously 1.8 to 2.5 meters). Thieme records that seven were manufactured from spruce and one from pine. All were made with their maximum thickness at the distal end, resembling, he says, modern javelins. Because they were found together with the butchered remains of fifteen horses, they suggest a degree of foresight and planning by a group of early premodern hominids putatively identified as *Homo heidelbergensis.*

We should now leave the simple spear behind and move to its later and more sophisticated cousin, the stabilized dart, immediate progenitor of the arrow. We have no idea why or when early man decided to stabilize the ballistic trajectory of his spear, but at some time the concept occurred to him, and to the rear end of his trusty weapon were added vanes.

Although feathers may have been added to imbue the shaft with the magic power of flight, the result was a steadier and thus more accurate shot, resulting, we may assume, in an improvement to hunting success and a significant potential to advance social standing within the group. There seems little doubt, though, that the concept was quickly adopted, and in the course of time came shorter and lighter projectiles, from which darts ultimately developed.

Although as a weapon for warfare the dart was used to effect against cavalry and unarmored men, its capability was limited largely by the distance it could be thrown, it being lighter than the conventional spear.

Whereas the *atlatl* can be studied because examples have been recovered from various archaeological sites, the same cannot be said for the alternative method of propulsion, the sling. Invented, so it is said, around 170 BC, this system is known to have been employed to cast darts in early historic times, specifically by the Macedonian troops of King Perseus.

Known as the *kestros* or *kestrosphendone* (alternative spelling: *cestros* or *cestrosphendone*), this device consisted of two thongs, one longer than the other, incorporating a leather cup. More is known of the dart it cast than of the system of propulsion, although it was evidently thrown by an overarm movement.[7]

While dimensions vary, the dart, with its point, is described in one account as being 2 cubits (approximately 36 inches, or 91.44 centimeters) long and consisting of a metal tube into which a wooden shaft, a "span" in length (approximately 8 inches, or 20.32 centimeters) and a "finger's breadth" in diameter was fixed. Into the shaft were inserted three short wooden vanes. Another version suggests a metal point 9 inches (22.86 centimeters) long attached to a wooden shaft of 12 inches (30.48 centimeters), for an overall length of 21 inches (53.34 centimeters). In this account, no mention is made of a metal tube.

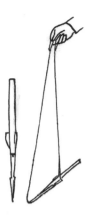

Kestros, a sling system designed to cast darts in early warfare. (T. Dungan)

This type of dart is generally believed not to have been in use for long, being replaced by a lighter version known as the *plumbata*.

Fast forward now to the fourteenth century, to the advent of handguns and the debate as to what ammunition was best suited to them. The presence of darts led naturally to their introduction and use for this purpose. The earliest document concerning this is in French and describes artifacts of iron of some 7 ounces (198.45 grams) in weight with brass vanes attached. When prepared for shooting, they were wrapped in a covering of leather to fit the muzzle bore tightly. Experience is said to have shown them to be unsuited to firearms, although they were certainly used during the late sixteenth and early seventeenth centuries.

On March 30, 1588, Sir Francis Drake added to the record of gunpowder carried on board his squadron, submitting to the Privy Council the following postscript: "Forgett not the 500 musketts and at least 1000 arrows."

Ever concerned with economy, the Privy Council responded by ordering him to be supplied with "muskittes, 200;

arrows for the said muskittes with tamkines for eche, 1000."[8]
These objects are not described; it is, however, relevant to note
that an alternative name for a musket arrow was a sprite.
These were simple in design and made of sharpened wood,
and it was said that they were more effective at penetrating
wood than were their iron counterparts.

Suggesting the use of musket arrows during the English
Civil War, the *Issue Book of the Parliamentary Ordnance
Department* for 1643–1644 has the following entry:

> XXVJ. Aprilis 1644: Deliverd ye day and yeare abovesaid
> out of his Majesty's stores within ye office of ye ordnance
> unto Mr William MOLINS, Comptroller of ye ord'nance
> for ye Militia of London. These arrows etc hereafter
> menc'oned to be imployed for the Service of ye State. By
> warannt from the Lord gen'll ye Earl of ESSEX dat. Ye day
> and yeare above said viz:
> Longebow Arrowes
> Muskett Arrowes

It seems that the musket arrow might also have been
intended for use as an incendiary device. The seventeenth
century version appears to have consisted of a metal shaft
wrapped in fabric containing a flammable mixture, one end
terminating in a broad arrowhead, the other screwed into a
wooden rod. When, or indeed whether, these were ever used
in warfare is open to conjecture. For those concerned about
such matters, a sixteenth century recipe for certain fiery con-
stituents appears in a later chapter, where the contemporary
fire arrow is examined in greater detail.

Where the dart was employed in warfare, as in medieval
Ireland, it was a subsidiary weapon used largely by the kerns,
troops of ill-disciplined men armed with dart and sword. The
kerns were subordinate to the professional gallowglass and
were generally employed as lightly armed skirmishers.
Although the kerns were adept with the dart and their skill
was generally recognized, nevertheless they had an unsavory
reputation, being largely responsible for looting, burning, and

generally harassing the civilian population. In contrast to the gallowglass, who were respected by the English, the kerns were considered scum. The term "kern" became synonymous with loutish behavior. Those who are familiar with the contemporary English word "oik" are well equipped to understand the medieval Irish kern.

The gallowglass also used the dart on occasion, these being carried for them by young men or boys who accompanied them into battle.

A curious reference to the dart occurs in the seventeenth century manuscript *The Bowman's Glory*, an account of the great archery event of 1583 overseen by the "Duke of Shoreditch," an assumed, fanciful name reflecting the earlier naming of a successful archer by Henry VIII as a mark of his appreciation of the fellow's skill. A detachment of Prince Arthur's Knights, an important contemporary archery society, when paying homage to the "Duke" rode up on horseback, "accompanied by Irish lackeys bearing darts," suggesting that the kerns may have accompanied the Irish cavalry in warfare.[9]

It is relevant here to mention the presence among the personal archery equipment of Henry VIII of a "boxe of Irysh arrows."[10] The reference is enigmatic but might be explained if these were Irish darts. Whether they were mere curiosities, or whether Henry, whose interest in archery is well known, would have used them for recreation is a matter of conjecture.

The method of propulsion of the Irish dart seems not to have been recorded. In close combat, however, the power of the arm alone would no doubt have sufficed.

Although we properly associate the dart with medieval warfare, it has a modern connotation as a weapon, for during the early days of aerial warfare, both the Royal Flying Corps and the German and French air forces were given box loads of metal darts to drop on enemy forces. These darts, or *flechettes*, as they became known, were some 9 inches (20.86 centimeters) long, pointed, and had integral metal vanes for stability. They were dropped from around one thousand feet (304.8

meters),[11] and it was said that in early practice, one went straight through a cow—although this tale may well be apocryphal.

Some readers may be familiar with the myth of German soldiers being admitted to hospitals with arrow wounds, attributed, by romantics, to the ghosts of long-dead English archers. If the hospital recorded a wound as being caused by a *flechette*, then it would be but a short step to visualize wounding by an arrow. Of such innocent accounts are myths made. Later, more sophisticated versions were produced, including incendiary darts, one of which is said to have destroyed a German zeppelin.

During World War II, needle darts with poisoned tips are alleged to have been developed by the Allied forces, to be dropped by bombers over enemy territory as retaliation in the event of a German gas attack upon the civilian population. In the event, they were, of course, not used.

Finally, and as an aside, the early forerunner of the modern game of darts was called puff and dart, a nineteenth century parlor pastime from which developed dart and target, also known as dartelle, in which crude darts fashioned from dowels with a pin for a point and paper flights were thrown at a soft-wood board.

We have noted above the Middle Eastern sling known as the *cestros*, but it seems that there may have been earlier usage of this form of propulsion. An erudite if rather wordy paper by artist/sculptor Leon Underwood, "Le Baton de Commandement," in the September/October 1965 issue of *Man*, published by the Royal Anthropological Institute of Great Britain and Ireland, redefines certain artifacts from Upper Paleolithic sites in Europe previously known as "Batons de Commandement" as "Perforated batons," and thus as propelling devices for arrows or darts. We are, however, indebted to an archaeologist and archery historian, Dr. Alf Webb (1924–2011), for a more pragmatic paper, published in 1995 in the *Journal of the Society of Archer-Antiquaries*, in which he takes the matter further, suggesting that a cord passing through the perforations, and thus to the shaft of the arrow, with the baton held in the throwing hand, would provide the means for propulsion. It is interesting that the illustrations of artifacts chosen by Webb show that they have scratched representations of animals on them, lending emphasis to their presumed purpose as hunting weapons.[12]

In modern times, many young boys have made throwing arrows, for no other purpose than to throw them for fun. These were (and still are) known colloquially as either Swiss, Dutch, Yorkshire, or Gypsy arrows. This last name may suggest a more utilitarian purpose, perhaps being used by traveling gypsies to kill rabbits for the cooking pot. Often fashioned from a bamboo garden cane, with the rear split to take a feather and a headless nail inserted, this boy's toy is propelled overhand by a knotted length of cord, the knot loosely fastened within a notch cut into the shaft below the feather. These shafts can fly for considerable distances, to the occasional consternation of passersby, since for young lads at play, distance rather than accuracy is the object

The modern throwing arrow, lineal descendant of spear and dart alike, has a strong following in the United States, and a world association of enthusiasts has been formed.[13] This association has a European element, and, like its American counterpart, it holds competitions for both distance and accuracy against defined criteria. Drawing on this source, it seems appropriate to end a brief exploration of the early arrow and its origins with a discussion of the modern art of spear and arrow throwing.

The experimental use of such throwers, styled "shooting with prehistoric weapons," takes place periodically at tournaments held throughout the United States and adjacent to prehistoric sites in France, and at times in Belgium, Spain, Germany, and Italy. Experimenting "prehistorians" who wished to test the effectiveness of the *atlatl* first began a European spear-throwing event and championship in 1990.

Subsequent meetings proved popular, and many attracted large entries.

A typical European meeting might consist of forty throwers, formed into groups of five to seven people. These groups, which include children, walk around a diverse course of forest, hill, plain, rocks, and the like, among which are placed animal targets representative of those that would have been prey in earlier times.

Throwing distances (distance de tir) are between 28 feet and 84 feet 6 inches (8.53 and 25.76 meters), with the size of the animal varying according to distance. Each animal has on it five concentric circles, strategically placed and varying in value, points being awarded for hits and score. Children under twelve throw at shorter distances. By observing techniques and successes, this "practical archaeology" has made it possible for students to assess the potential of the weapon for early hunters, and it continues to be a valuable aid to studies.

Let us now leave the misty world of these early missile launchers, be they *baton et corde*, *atlatls*, or *cestros*, and turn to the arrow proper.

THE EARLY DAYS

IN THIS CHAPTER WE WILL CONSIDER THE DEVELOPMENT OF the arrow, focusing on a new means of propulsion—one that, from simple beginnings, would come to dominate all others.

We can have no idea when, how, or why the first bow was created; when early man grasped the concept of storage and release of potential energy; how he transferred this concept into practice; and indeed why, with other tried and tested methods of propulsion at his disposal, he did so at all.

However, we can speculate. The essential quality of the bow lies in its *modus operandi*: it is virtually noiseless, both it and its arrows may be easily carried, and it is suited to the stalking of prey in situations where the *atlatl*, or baton and cord, would be difficult to employ. Each is reason enough for its use, and from whatever likely or unlikely source its invention came, it is clear that early man adopted it with enthusiasm—and perhaps for another reason. Where the spear was best employed by a number of hunters acting in unison on an open plain, the bow was ideally suited to the lone hunter; for in a close environment of trees and bushes, where stalking of prey was necessary, its subtle character was fundamental to success.

As the use of the bow grew, so the arrow developed. Whereas the shaft propelled by the *atlatl* was not influenced by its *propulseur* and could within reason be of any manageable length, the missile associated with the bow would be influenced by the arc within which it was drawn and cast. In simplistic terms, the distance between the apex of the angle of the string in a drawn bow, and the center of its belly is broadly equal to half its length. Reflecting this rule of thumb, we may expect early shafts to have been significantly shorter than spears and darts, and this was so.

Because they are thin sticks, arrow shafts are vulnerable to breakage, and complete examples from prehistory are few. However, a complete arrow shaft has been discovered at Vinkel Mose, a bog near Viborg, Denmark, and is now in the National Museum, in Copenhagen.[1] This shaft is of *Pinus sylvestris*, or Scots pine, a popular material for the manufacture of arrows in modern times. It is 40 inches (101.6 centimeters) long, and its maximum diameter is one-half inch (1 centimeter). It has a nock, or notch, to take a bowstring, and is slotted to take a microlithic arrowhead. Sinew binding is still in place, extending for 6.5 inches (16.51 centimeters) below the nock, suggesting feather fletching of a little over 6 inches in length. Pollen analysis has dated this find to the Early Boreal period (8,000 BC).

While complete arrows are exceedingly rare from prehistory, broken shafts are far more numerous. Large quantities have been recovered from the excavations at Stellmoor, Schleswig-Holstein, Germany, where parts of over one hundred have been found.[2] Included among these were many foreshafts. The foreshaft was a separate piece, inserted and glued to the main shaft, into which the flint arrowhead was affixed. The advantage of separate foreshafts was their potential replacement in the event of breakage, thus saving the main shaft—much the same as the footing arrangement on traditional arrows today.

The Stellmoor arrows were of *Pinus silvestris*, a wood favored as much by the men who made them as it is today for

Main and foreshaft arrow fragments from excavations at Stellmoor, Schleswig-Holstein. (After Rust, A., *Die alt- und mittelsteinzeitlichen Funde Stellmoor*, 1943)

the straightness of its grain. But not all prehistoric arrows were of pine: yew (*Taxus baccata*), guelder rose (*Viburnum opulus*), and ash (*Fraxinus*) have also featured among finds at other prehistoric sites.

Heads were of flint, mostly barbed and tanged, or leaf shaped, and fastened into slots at the terminal of either the foreshaft or the shaft proper, being held in place by resin (perhaps birch pitch). Some were bound by animal sinew or gut.

A variation among heads comes from excavations in Denmark: at Eising in Jutland and at Muldbjerg, Sjaelland, where chisel-shaped heads have been found.[3] Not uncommon among recovered shafts is the bolt head, a blunted, thickened terminal suited perhaps for shooting small game or birds—an early bird bolt, in fact. Shafts with microliths fastened have also been uncovered.

We are fortunate to have direct knowledge of arrows used by one particular Neolithic hunter, following the recovery in 1981 of the frozen remains of a corpse, carbon-dated to between 5,300 and 5,200 years old, in the Ötztal area of the Alps.[4] Initially there was much speculation as to how he died, but when a flint arrowhead was found in his shoulder, it became generally accepted that he had been shot from behind. Accompanying this deceased Stone Age gentleman, known now to the world as "Ötzi" and thought to have died when he was twenty-five to thirty years old, was his entire archery equipment, including his arrows, thus providing the opportunity for a detailed assessment of Neolithic hunting gear.

Fourteen shafts lay within the iceman's quiver; two complete but fractured arrows (of which more later); and twelve unfinished staves. Of these twelve, eleven were in good condition and undamaged, the twelfth either missing its lower third or perhaps intended to have a foreshaft fitted. All shafts were of the wayfaring tree (*Viburnum lantana*), using the long, straight, tough sapwood shoots characteristic of this tree. The unfinished shafts were partially rounded but lacked the neat finish of the completed arrows. Other archaeological finds indicate that rounding was generally achieved by the use of sandstone rubbing blocks, two pieces of stone, each with a longitudinal concave groove. Holding these together with the wood between the grooves and drawing and turning it could achieve a circular shaft.

Each of the two finished arrows was fractured, and thus unable to be shot, a curious thing in view of the fact that the accompanying unfinished shafts were whole. Were these deliberately or accidentally broken? The shorter of the two was a self arrow 33.5 inches (85.09 centimeters) long and three-eighths of an inch (9.52 millimeters) in diameter for most of its length, thickening slightly from a point 4 inches (10.16 centimeters) from the foot. The shaftment, where the feathers were set, tapered slightly toward the nock, and within this taper it was fletched with three black feathers, each 5 inches (12.7 centimeters) long, secured by birch tar and bound with thread. The nock was one-half inch (12.7 millimeters) deep and three-sixteenths of an inch (4.76 millimeters) wide. The arrow was armed with a tanged flint arrowhead 1.5 inches (3.81 centimeters) long and three-quarters of an inch (1.90 centimeters) wide, held in position by birch tar and secured by thread.

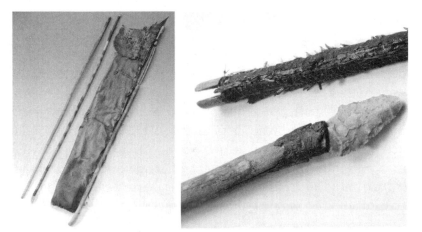

Left, the quiver and two arrows recovered with the body of the iceman Ötzi. Right, a close up of the nock and stone head. (*Courtesy of the South Tyrol Museum of Archaeology*)

The second finished arrow was longer than the first, at just over 35.5 inches (90.17 centimeters), and of a different construction, consisting of a main shaft to which a 4.25-inch (10.79-centimeter) foreshaft made of wood from the cornel tree had been added. This had been sharpened to a point and pushed into the hollow end of the main shaft, where it had been secured by a liberal application of birch tar.

Of parallel (untapered) profile, and approximately seven-sixteenths of an inch (11.11 millimeters) in diameter throughout its length, it had a string notch a little over one-half inch (12.7 millimeters) deep. The leaf-shaped arrowhead fastened to the foreshaft by birch tar was 3.5 inches (8.89 centimeters) long, five-eighths of an inch (15.87 millimeters) wide, and three-sixteenths of an inch (4.76 millimeters) deep. The fletches on this arrow, while glued and bound as on the first, were also slightly longer.

Of the twelve unfinished shafts, eleven were whole but one was broken, with the broken end missing. Lengths vary from 33.25 inches (84.45 centimeters) to 34.5 inches (86.99 centimeters). Some people see significance in the number of arrows, drawing attention to the fourteen arrows found as grave goods of a distinguished Celtic ruler. One enigma concerns the incomplete shafts. Clearly it was intended that these be finished, yet although the iceman's archery paraphernalia was complete in many respects, the rubbing blocks, so useful in rounding shafts, were not present. Neither, it seems, were there any spare arrowheads or fletches. We thus have a man hemorrhaging from an arrow wound, seriously weakened, with no means of securing food, and condemned to die amid ice and snow on a mountain. It is for others to ponder the circumstances. We will pay him our respects and move on.

We move, in fact, to the twentieth century, to 1911 and to California, for it is from there—through the humanity and wisdom of the great Saxton Pope, archer extraordinaire, who recognized the significance of what could be learned from a frightened and emaciated Yana Indian discovered on the outskirts of Orville—that we have come to learn a little of early hunting practice.[5] When professor T. T. Waterman, of the Department of Anthropology at the University of California, learned of this man, he was able to converse with him and took him from the jail where he had been placed (possibly for his own protection) to San Francisco. It was Pope who befriended him and ensured that this simple man, whom we know today as Ishi, was given respect and protection. Ishi lived happily in San Francisco for five years, during which time he showed Pope his hunting skills and much else. It is through the guidance of this modern stone-age man and his instructions that we can, among other matters, gain some idea of how the iceman may have made his shafts.

Ishi was a hunter who used a bow and arrow. By observation and through his careful teaching, we know how he made both. The bow we will leave to others to consider and replicate, for we are concerned with arrow making.

Ishi called his arrow *sa wa*, and the first thing he did was assemble his shafts. He preferred the long, slim, straight stems of witch hazel (*Hamamelis*) about three-eighths of an inch (9.52 millimeters) in diameter at the base, and these he cut to initial lengths of 32 inches (81.28 centimeters). He then peeled away the bark and, after tying a number together, put the bundle away to dry out. (In passing, the word "witch" in "witch hazel" has nothing to do with the occult; it derives from *wice*, the Anglo-Saxon word for "bend.")

After due time, preferably months, Ishi picked out the better of the shafts and straightened them through heat. He held them over the glowing embers of a fire with both hands, and when he deemed them sufficiently warm, he used either his big toe or the base of his thumb to even out individual bends.

He then rounded the straightened shafts using two pieces of grooved sandstone, as we presume the iceman and his contemporaries would have done some five thousand years earlier. This smoothing reduced the diameters to about five-sixteenths of an inch (0.8 centimeters). He then cut the shafts into lengths of 26 inches (66.04 centimeters), bound the ends with a rawhide thong to prevent splitting, and bored a hole to take a foreshaft. This he did by taking a long, sharp piece of bone, holding it between his toes, and revolving the upright shaft between the palms of his hands to drill a hole about 1.5 inches (3.81 centimeters) deep. Here we may note that the iceman's quiver contained a sharpened piece of antler, which, although slightly curved when found, could have originally served a similar purpose to Ishi's bone.

Ishi created the foreshaft using a denser and thus heavier wood, partly perhaps to provide against breakage, partly to give forward weight and thus improved stability in flight. He chose a wood taken from an exceptionally hardy shrub or small tree that Pope calls mountain mahogany (*Cercocarpus montanus*), known colloquially as hard tack.

Of similar circumference to the main shaft and tapering a fraction toward the terminal, this foreshaft added around 6 inches (5.2 centimeters) to the arrow's overall length. The upper 1.5 inches (3.81 centimeters) of this foreshaft were fashioned into a spike or spindle and carefully pushed into the drilled hole in the shaft, and resin and chewed sinew were used to hold it in position.

Pope tells us that to measure his arrows, Ishi placed one end of the completed shaft with its foreshaft on top of his breastbone and, extending his left hand (presumably to the side, as in shooting), measured the other end to the tip of his left hand. The distance was about 32 inches (81.28 centimeters), and he cut the shaft accordingly. We may note that the iceman's arrows were a little longer, seeming to indicate a greater length of arm if measured in a similar manner. Ishi, however, was five-feet-eight-inches tall, while the iceman is thought to have been five feet two (1.73 meters and 1.57 meters, respectively). This suggests that if the iceman customarily drew to the head of his arrow, his measurement would have been made rather differently.

We know from observation that Ishi drew his arrow to his breastbone to shoot; we may speculate from the additional length of the iceman's shaft that his draw was different, and made perhaps to the eye. However, rock drawings from eastern Spain depicting hunters with their bows fully drawn invariably have the arrow protruding beyond the bow, suggesting that, particularly where foreshafts were in position, arrows were never drawn to the head.[6]

To complete his arrow, Ishi notched the end to receive the bowstring. He did this using a small piece of sharp obsidian, notching the foreshaft similarly to receive the arrowhead.

Ishi decorated his arrows quite deliberately, with green and black concentric rings, or with small, circular dots and snake-like lines. The longer of the two completed arrows found with the iceman had marks on it; whether these were for decoration is for others to say.

Ishi called feathers *pu nee*, and he gathered them from eagles, buzzards, or hawks, each a predatory bird and therefore presumably suited to the purpose of guiding a hunter's shaft to its destination. His method of separating feather

Ishi drawing his bow. Note the method employed, using his index finger and thumb, and the position of the arrow on the right hand side of the bow. (*Author*)

from quill was as ingenious as it was dexterous. He grasped a feather between the heels of his palms, carefully separating the vane from the stiff central spine, or rachis, with his fingers, working from the tip of the feather downward. Holding one end of the feather on a rock with his big toe and taking the other end between the thumb and finger of his left hand, he then scraped away the pith from the rachis with a piece of obsidian, until the rib was thin and flat.

After thoroughly wetting each flight, he gathered them together into groups of three before beginning to fletch his shafts. Unlike the iceman, who glued his fletches to the shaft, Ishi chose merely to hold them with sinew binding at both ends and in the middle. Again, unlike the iceman's 5-inch (12.7-centimeter) fletches, Ishi's were seldom more than 4 inches (10.16 centimeters) long.

It may be instructive at this stage to divert a little and consider the bows for which these arrows were made. The iceman's bow was of yew, 71.75 inches (182.25 centimeters) long, and of a proportion and cross section recognizable today as a traditional longbow. There has been considerable debate about its condition and whether, in fact, it was a finished weapon and its possible strength, or draw weight. Based on comparisons with similar bows, both modern and historic, informed consensus is that in the state it was found, its draw weight would have exceeded the tensile strength of the (putative) bowstring of bast found in the iceman's quiver, which it is thought would have been more suited to a bow of some sixty pounds in draw weight. It is therefore considered that while it may have been possible to shoot this bow in the state it was found, it would have put the string severely at risk. For this reason, informed opinion is that the bow was unfinished.

We have direct knowledge of Ishi's bow, which he called *man-nee*, and the way it was constructed. It was short, of a flat rather than plano-convex (longbow) section, and made of mountain juniper (*Juniperus scopulorum*) backed with sinew, and 42 inches (106.68 centimeters) long, measured from his horizontally extended hand to the opposite hip.

The handgrip was 1.25 inches (3.17 centimeters) wide, three-quarters of an inch (19.05 millimeters) thick, and of ovoid section. The bow itself was of elliptical section 2 inches (5.08 centimeters) broad and one-half inch (12.7 millimeters) thick at the center of each limb. Toward its tips it was recurved. The limbs terminated in a pin one-half inch (12.7 millimeters) in diameter and 1 inch (2.54 centimeters) long, serving to hold the string.

Ishi used the outer layer of wood from the juniper tree, shaping it with obsidian and finishing it with sandstone. The recurved tips he made by bending the wood over a heated stone. He left it for some months to season, and then backed it with chewed sinew, which he fastened to the wood with salmon-skin glue. During the course of drying, he bandaged the limbs with willow bark. After removing this he smoothed the limbs with sandstone and bound the handgrip with a buckskin thong. Its draw weight when complete was about forty-five pounds.

The nocks of arrows made by the iceman and Ishi were conventional but unprotected by horn, as was later practice. They also lacked that particular notch shape that would hold the arrow securely on the bowstring while being drawn, also a later practice. Thus they had to be held to the string in a form of pinch draw.

We have professor Edward S. Morse to thank for a detailed analysis of ancient methods of drawing a bowstring.[7] He defines these as primary, secondary, tertiary, and Mediterranean. The primary, or pinch grip, relies on holding the arrow between forefinger and thumb while drawing back the string, in order to ensure that they remain in contact with each other. Arrows used this way are furnished with bulbous nocks, providing the drawing fingers with something to get a grip on. It will be apparent that this method works only with comparatively light draw-weight bows, and it is unlikely that the iceman would have used it. He might perhaps have used the secondary or tertiary grips, each of which held the arrow between thumb and index finger, although the three-finger Mediterranean draw, so familiar to Western archers, was at his disposal, and Morse tells us it has been in use for "tens of centuries."

We have no trouble identifying Ishi's draw, since Saxton Pope observed it closely. It should be noted that he tipped his bow to the left when shooting, placing the arrow on the right. After nocking his arrow, Ishi placed his right thumb around the string hooked upward. He then rested his forefinger against the side of the arrow to hold it in position, with the second finger placed upon the thumb to strengthen it. This appears to be a variant of a Mongolian thumb release, but is not among those Morse described. In view of the shortness of his bow, and thus the acute angle of the string at full draw, Ishi's use of his thumb in this way may have helped to maximize cast.

Prior to the appearance of Ishi in 1911, some people had gathered knowledge of Indian arrow culture in the late 1890s, and papers submitted to the American Anthropological Society by anthropologists interested in native archery were printed in the January 1891 issue of *American Anthropologist*. A summary of these papers, *Arrows and Arrow-Makers*, was subsequently published. Although through Ishi's instruction we have excellent knowledge of arrow making using the shoots from a tree, not all primitive Indians used this method. Anthropologist Walter Hough, one of those whose papers appeared in the January 1891 issue of *American Anthropologist*, observed a member of the Apache nation completing an arrow he had prepared from the hollow stem of a tule reed and recorded his observations. It is necessary to prepare a foreshaft when using reed since it is not suited to the direct attaching of an arrowhead. A foreshaft having been made, with a diameter suited to insertion within the reed, and pushed into position, the maker then cut a slot in its end and into this inserted a blob of gum. This he set on fire, allowed it to burn for a few moments, then extinguished it. He then slid the flint or obsidian head into the notch, lined it up, and smoothed down the still malleable gum. A thin strip of sinew was carefully bound around the join, and all was ready for use.[8] Ishi mentioned that heads for warfare were habitually larger and more barbed than those used for hunting.

The author knows of no absolute typology of lithic heads, although we should note a late nineteenth century classification suggested for native Indian arrowheads within the Department of Prehistoric Anthropology of the US National Museum.[9]

It may be of interest at this point to briefly mention the use of poison in hunting and perhaps also in warfare. Although we will discuss the preparation and use of poisoned arrowheads in more detail in a later chapter, it is worth noting that the North American Indian was not averse to their use. In another paper in the January 1891 issue of *American Anthropologist*, Dr. W. J. Hoffman records that in 1871, examination of arrows recovered from members of the Apache nation showed "the presence of blood corpuscles and a crystalline substance seemingly identical to either viperine, or crotaline, the acting principle peculiar to the venom of the western diamond back rattlesnake (crotalus atros)," while other tribes also knew about poisons and almost certainly used them.[10]

The varied use of the arrow in prehistoric times may be gauged by examining rock paintings. The painting at the Cueva de los Caballos, Castellon, in eastern Spain, indicates an ambush of deer: arrows lie on the ground, and the archers have clearly awaited the arrival of the unsuspecting

Cueva de los Caballos. Note arrows on the ground, suggestive of an ambush of unsuspecting animals. (*Author*)

prey. In contrast, the painting at the Cueva de la Arafa, Valencia, shows spare arrows held lengthwise against bow limbs as a group of bowmen surround and kill a group of animals. Modern hunting archers will be familiar with the technique of holding their arrows thus. A third painting, from the rock shelter of Las Dogues, Castellon de la Plana, in eastern Spain, shows the arrow used not for hunting but for combat, as one group of bowmen have seemingly surprised another by rushing at them.

That the arrow was used for personal protection there is little doubt; that it was used for aggression is beyond question. The presence of arrowheads in many prehistoric skeletons is evidence enough, while the discovery of a flint arrowhead deep within the iceman's shoulder is tangible proof of some long-forgotten event.

Although hunting *par force* by groups of men was seemingly a way to stock the early tribal larder, we are indebted to Ishi for demonstrating his particular style of the sophisticated art of stalking, a style of hunting more appropriate to certain types of terrain. Ishi was a past master at this form, and Saxton Pope carefully recorded his methods.

He used two types of arrow when hunting prey. For small game he had shafts with blunt ends bound with sinew, but for larger animals he used a flint head with barbs for greater damage. Besides arrows contained in his quiver, when hunting, Ishi always carried several tucked between his right arm and his body, ready for immediate use.

Ishi's method was to lure. He would squat, for hours at a time if necessary, behind a small bush. From this vantage point he would call rabbits by producing a squeak similar to that of one in distress. This had the effect of bringing others to its aid, and when they were within shooting range (some fifteen or so yards), he would loose his shaft and invariably secure a kill. Pope records that Ishi could call squirrels, coyotes, and even the elusive wildcat from cover.

He understood the language of the animals he hunted. He knew when his presence had been revealed by listening to birdcalls. Deer he enticed by means of a stuffed deer head he wore as a cap, bobbing up and down from behind a bush to excite curiosity. Ishi told Pope that in preparation for the hunt he would eat no fish the previous day and smoke no tobacco. He would rise early, bathe in a creek, rub himself dry with aromatic leaves, wash out his mouth, and drink water, but eat no food at all. Clearly this worked to prevent animals from scenting him as he lay in ambush.

He occasionally shot at eagles or hawks, but for these he darkened his shafts with mud, light wood shafts seemingly being easily visible to birds in flight and dark ones being camouflaged by the darker earth as the birds look down. If Ishi realized this, it indicates astute observation on his part. Some modern archers also darken their arrow shafts when shooting at the long distant clout targets, thus enabling the arrows to be seen in flight on their way to the target lying on the ground

180 yards (164.59 meters) away as the archers look up into a light sky.

Ishi was content in the presence of those who had befriended him, but he remained aloof in subtle ways. His world had been dictated by nature, and although now drawn into the sophistication of modern life, he remained true to his past. Accordingly, when he died, it was arranged by his mentors that he be laid to rest as he would have wished. He was sent on his last long journey as a Yana Indian should go. By his side were placed his fire sticks, ten pieces of Indian money, a small bag of acorn meal, a little dried venison, some tobacco, and his bow and arrows. These were cremated with him, and his ashes placed in an earthen jar. On it is inscribed "Ishi, the last Yana Indian, 1916."

With Ishi's death, an epoch ended. Modern man had the opportunity to learn from a Stone Age man, and to his everlasting credit, he grasped it with both hands. We are the richer for this knowledge.

ÖBERFLACHT AND BEYOND

WITH STONE AGE TECHNOLOGY EXEMPLIFIED BY THE ICEMAN in the Alps and Yana Indian Ishi in California behind us, we move forward to the European Iron Age and early historic times.

Although the most complete cache of early arrows is that recovered from Nydam Moor in southern Jutland, Denmark, before we consider these and their implications, we will examine the similarly aged examples recovered by excavation among graves of the Alaman people at the village of Öberflacht in Baden-Württemberg, Germany.[1]

And before we discuss the arrows, it is appropriate to mention the type of bows found with them, since these are of considerable interest to archer antiquarian and working bowyer alike. Made of yew, they were unusual, almost unique, for the period in that they had nonworking handles and each limb would have therefore bent individually. This would have limited the working lengths of the limbs, thereby dictating the length of arrow used and, *inter alia*, the method of drawing and releasing it, of which more later.

In an archaeological report published in 1847, Dr. Wolfgang Menzel describes the arrows recovered from the

Öberflacht graves as all being 24 inches (60.96 centimeters) long. However, there would appear to be some doubt as to the actual measurement used. Reference is made to the "Württemberger Foot," an archaic local variant measurement in force before Germany adopted the standard metric measure. By modern measurement, the length seems to have been 22 5/8 inches (55.905 centimeters). The woods from which they were fashioned were viburnum and birch.

The shafts were thicker at the point than at the nock—in archery terms we would say they were bob-tailed—and, from a drawing of a shaft in Menzel's report, we know they had a cup, or bulbous, nock. In the drawing, a cone to which the head was fitted appears to have had two small holes drilled into it, possibly for spikes that would presumably have secured the missing head in position. A vermillion color noted as being present on the cones when found is believed to have resulted from a reaction between the glue (thought to be birch pitch resin) that held the heads and the resinous wood—a reaction observed particularly between hide glue and the resinous sapwood of yew, when a backing is bonded to a bow.

Also recovered were two arrow fragments 7.5 inches (19.05 centimeters) long. These fragments did not appear to be tapered, and we would say they are parallel.

If Menzel's drawing of the arrow shaft is accurate in its portrayal of binding by thread on the shaftment, then the Öberflacht fletchings were secured by glue and thread. There was certainly evidence present of the glue used to secure the fletchings. A quill line at right angles to the nock groove appears on the drawing, suggesting a conventional three-fletch shaft.[2]

No feathers survived, but an illustration of the arrows used by an Alaman archer that appears in the *Stuttgarter Bilderpsalter*, a thirteenth-century German book of psalms, clearly shows feathers of trapezoidal, almost rectangular shape, with a high profile, and one may speculate that this was the style used on the arrows described.

The bulbous nock on the alamanic arrow is representative of those associated with other Germanic cultures. Besides providing a stronger nock wall, the shape helps with a secondary or tertiary draw.

The construction of the alamanic bow, with its stiff handle and short working limbs, significantly limits its draw length, thus determining both the form of draw and the effective length of the arrow used with it. It would have been impractical, and unwise, to attempt to draw an alamanic bowstring to the side of the face or the ear, since it would almost certainly have fractured the bow—a circumstance supported by experiment with modern replicas. Indeed, one replica made could not be drawn beyond a little under 10 inches (25.4 centimeters). Although the draw weight of these bows is assessed at between thirty and thirty-five pounds and would be an exceptionally low weight for a conventional longbow, the short limb length does compound the cast.

While the bow is known to have been among the alamanic armory, and the alamanic tribes were constant thorns on the borders of the northern Roman Empire, it is difficult to see how short arrows shot under such limitations could be properly effective in warfare. It is possible, therefore, that these were hunting weapons. As a relevant aside, early illustrations of archers frequently show bows partially drawn to the chest, suggesting that this was a common form of shooting. In this respect, it should be noted that in hunting, once the arrow is notched, or nocked, the bow is invariably held partially drawn ready to be fully drawn and released when the prey is close enough to be shot, and this may be what is shown in these illustrations.

There is evidence, in early illustrations, for bows of similar dimension to those mentioned above, that is, 67 to 71 inches (170.18 to 180.34 centimeters), but without built-up handles. These would have formed one complete curve when drawn, or, as we say, "come around in full compass," and, if properly tillered, would have accommodated arrows 29 to 30 inches (73.66 to 76.2 centimeters) long, allowing a full draw to the face rather than a restricted draw to the chest and the consequently shorter arrow necessitated by the stiff-centered weapon. The alamanic cavalry is known to have used the bow and arrow, a practice derived perhaps from association with Near Eastern mounted warriors, and weapons of this nature, without built-up handles, may have been those which were carried.

We turn now to a second and equally productive archaeological find: the cache of Germanic weaponry found at Nydam in Schleswig-Holstein.[3] The site, to the south of present-day Denmark, is in Oster Sottrup, Sundeval, about five miles (eight kilometers) from Sonderburg. It is now a bog but is believed to have once been a sacred lake, and it marks the place where pagan sacrifices of a number of boats and much military equipment, perhaps material accumulated from battle victims, took place in the mid-fourth century,

The site was discovered in 1830, when a local farmer uncovered swords and shields, which he gave to his children as playthings. It was professionally excavated between 1859 and 1863 by archaeologist Conrad Engelhardt. Sadly, much of his painstaking work was destroyed in 1864 when Denmark and Germany were at war. German soldiers broke up one carefully excavated ship and used the wood for fuel.

Nevertheless, the finds at Nydam, whose owners predate the Anglo-Saxons and their invasion of Britain, provide us with a picture of the type of arrows used by their Germanic successors.

A report made in 1912 by a visiting archer, Mr. E. Mylius, is explicit about the arrows, which he describes as of "coniferous wood," perhaps the fir *Abies pectinata*. He considered the shafts to have been cleft from the wood rather than sawn, because the grain was long and straight, and they were 29 to 37 inches (73.66 to 93.98 centimeters) long. Because of their length, he considered it likely that they would have been drawn to the ear.

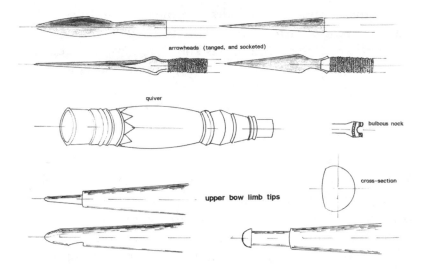

A selection of archery material from the Nydam excavation. Note ferrous arrowhead designed to penetrate mail. (*Author*)

Mylius reports that the Nydam arrows are thickest in the center of the shaft. We would call this barreled. The string grooves were wide, three-eighths of an inch (9.925 millimeters), evidently to contain a thick string, while the nock was large and bulbous and not tapered, as was the later practice. The shaftment was narrow, tapering toward the nock, offering a good grip for the fingers when the arrow was drawn.[4]

At another moor excavation, among other finds was a bundle of arrows with applied nocks of cast bronze, their string grooves being of the same dimensions as those from Nydam, secured by a conical pin.

Evidence from recovered Nydam shafts is of fletching with four feathers, and from the imprint of their quills, it appears they were 4 to 5.125 inches (10.16 to 12.825 centimeters) long. Great care had been taken to secure the feathers, perhaps with regard to prevailing damp conditions, and shallow longitudinal grooves had been cut to receive the quills. These were filled with a resinous substance, and each fletching was then bound into position using thin thread.

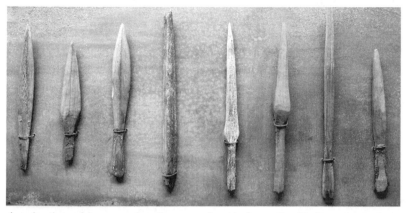

A selection of bone and antler arrowheads from the Nydam excavation. (*Courtesy, Bullenwächter*)

Many of the arrow nocks and shafts were decorated with marks, some of which appear to be runic. If they are, then those represented appear to be the signs for *gebo* (gift-given), *nauthis* (necessity), and *algiz* (protection, or protector), each a relevant message for the arrow's purpose. But here we are guilty of wandering into other realms, and must retrace our footsteps.

Although they were occasionally socketed, the arrowheads were largely tanged and fitted into a slot cut into the foot of the shaft. Traces of pitched wrapping at the foot of the shafts show the method by which they were secured. Head shapes were largely slim and pointed, with a square or rhomboid section of bodkin style for penetration of mail, while others were barbed for hunting. Although heads were mostly of iron, some were constructed of bone and antler. Heads varied in weight, the heaviest being a little more than a half ounce (14.18 grams).

Finally, among the material recovered were a number of small whetstones, a reminder that archers were exhorted to carry one when hunting to refresh cutting edges.

The use of the arrow for warfare is well documented. How it was used, however, is not entirely clear. The Germanic military ethic required hand-to-hand combat following an exchange of missiles, and the preferred Germanic missile was the spear or javelin. The arrow was perhaps no more than a subsidiary weapon, capable of wounding, and less often killing, its victim. The mighty English battleshaft, known poetically as the grey goose wing, was a millennium away.

Where the fifth century arrow had undoubted value as a standoff weapon was in sea fighting. Early Norse sagas are explicit about its virtue, even if it was not always effective. The account of a great ninth century sea battle between King Harald the Fair-haired and King Arnvid records its unsuccessful use: "Against the hero's shield in vain / The arrow-storm fierce pours its rain."[5]

The military arrangements of a Germanic longboat gave pride of place to those in the bow of the vessel, who slashed and stabbed with sword and short spear; while farther down the vessel men stood by either to repel boarders, or in readiness to board themselves, armed with a variety of weapons, including stones and stakes. Those aft of the mast were the archers, ready with their battleshafts

> Steel-pointed spear, and sharpened stake
> Made the broad shield on arm to shake,
> . . .
>
> And stones and arrow quickly flew,
> And many a warrior bold they slew,
> The bowman never twanged his bow,
> And drew his shaft so oft as now,
> And Drontheim's bowmen on that day,
> Were not first tired of this play,
> Arrow and darts so quickly fly,
> You could not follow with the eye.[6]

Scandinavian advice on the use of the bow at sea is to be found in *Speculum Regale*, an early Norwegian educational text containing practical and moral advice on the seafaring trade, warfare, and chivalric behavior.[7]

An explicit report of the arrow's use at sea is the demise, in 1098, of Hugo, Earl of Chester, shot through the eye by no less a person than King Magnus Barefoot of Norway, during an unplanned confrontation on the shores of Anglesey, North Wales.[8] That this feat was achieved from the prow of a ship says much for the skill of the king. Without demeaning the deed in any way, it should be mentioned, however, that both the king and an unnamed archer by his side shot simultaneously. When recording the event, with proper respect for protocol, the skald acknowledges the king's arrow as the fatal shot.

Although the finds at Nydam and their Germanic owners predate the Anglo-Saxons and their invasion of Britain, nevertheless they provide us with a picture of the type of arrows used by their successors and, by reference to their heads, the purpose for which they were intended.

While no early English arrows are known to have been found, the Anglo-Saxons were quite familiar with the arrow in warfare, and although it was not a primary weapon in their armory, its tactical use was recognized. In the epic *Beowulf*, their poetry speaks of the "isernscur," the "iron shower" or "arrow-storm," while the poem "The Battle of Maldon" says "bogan wearan bisige"—"bows were busy"—as a preliminary to the main event.

Whether the English arrows were as finely finished as those of their Norse cousins is perhaps debatable. The Norsemen were seaborne warriors and had damp to contend with on a daily basis. Their fletchings were set in grooves as well as being glued and bound. There would have been less need for this on land; perhaps the English arrows were not so exactly prepared.

The military formation of the Anglo-Saxon army continues to engage the knowledgeable in erudite discussion, and will no doubt do so until other weighty matters intervene. Into which part of the tactical military structure the bowman fitted is therefore debatable.

It is certain that there would have been a battle plan, however rudimentary, and there were protocols to be observed. Thus early confrontations between field armies invariably commenced with an exchange of words and an offer of peace by the aggressor in exchange for goods or *gield* (money). This was occasionally acceptable to the weaker party, and, if so, the confrontation concluded amicably, if expensively. Where it was not approved, then the verbal exchanges deteriorated into taunts and insults until the yelling of fear-inducing battle cries indicated hostilities were about to begin.

Preliminary to the main hand-to-hand engagement would have been a barrage of missiles—light throwing spears and arrows—designed to harass and hopefully to kill or disable the opposition. As we read in "The Battle of Maldon:"

> Bogan waeran bysige: bord ord onfeng (line 110)
> . . .
> Ecglafes bearn, him waes Aescferth nama.
> he ne wandode na, æt tham wigplegan,
> ac he fysde forth flan genehe;
> hwilon he on bord sceat, hwilon beorn taesde;
> aefre embe stunde he seale sume wunde,
> tha hwile the he wæpna wealdan moste.
> (lines 267–272)
>
> Bows were busy, shields, weapon points received.
> . . .
> Ecglaf's son, he was named Aescferth
> he did not hesitate in the work of war
> but he poured forth many arrows.
> Sometimes he shot into shield, sometimes into warrior.
> During this time he wounded some
> while he could wield his weapon.[9]

It is unclear what part the bowman and his arrows played during the ensuing fight. Informed speculation suggests that he left matters to his meatier, better armed, and better protected comrades, although if things were going well, he might

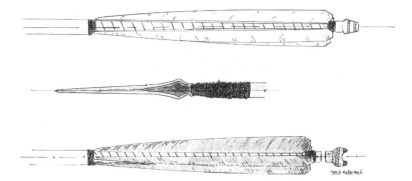

A Viking arrow as it may have appeared. Note bound fletchings, decorated bulbous string groove (nock), and arrowhead capable of penetrating mail. (*Author*)

have joined in the general melee. It is also unclear whether bowmen acted individually or within a structured group, as did that company of archers that was brought to England by Duke William of Normandy in October 1066 and did so much damage at Sand Lake (Senlac) near Hastings, the town that has popularly given its name to the battle.

If the 230-foot-long embroidered history of the events leading to, during, and after the battle near Hastings, known as the Bayeux Tapestry, suggests anything at all about Saxon archery, it is that the Saxon bowman was a slighter individual than the fighting men around him, and it may be that those not as brawny of build, and thus less suited to the main battle line, were selected and trained as bowmen.

Although it is clear that at this time the arrow was not a primary arm, there are tantalizing glimpses of occasional prowess, or lack of prowess, by those entrusted with its use.

A late-twelfth century addition to the *Anglo-Saxon Chronicle*, a collection of important historical events written by and about the Anglo-Saxons, mentions that, prior to the defeat of the Norse army at Stamford Bridge, Yorkshire, in 1066, a solitary Norseman had stood alone defending a bridge, delaying the passage of the English army led by King

Harold Godwinson. Personal confrontation having signally failed, a bowman was brought up to shoot arrows at the defender. "Then one Englishman shot with an arrow but it achieved nothing." A spear thrust from below the bridge finally disposed of the valiant Norseman, and Harold's army passed unmolested over the bridge.[10]

A second and more successful event involving the arrow occurred seemingly during the subsequent battle; this is recorded by a Norse skald and tells of the death of King Harald Sigurdson. That the king died at Stamford Bridge is not disputed, but whether his death was as the saga records may be in doubt. It seems, however, that in the heat of battle, Harald had advanced beyond his troops and was laying about him with a battle-axe when a Saxon bowman shot at him and pierced his windpipe with an arrow. His *huscarls* (housemen, or bodyguards) then gathered around him in what they called a corpse ring and fought to the last.

We will stay with King Harald briefly since the poem of his death presents a potential enigma. The *Anglo-Saxon Chronicle* does not provide details of his demise, so we have no comparison, but we are told by the Norse skald that, "The king whose name would ill-doers scare, / The gold-tipped arrow would not spare."[11]

If Harald fell to a chance arrow shot by a lowly bowman aiming into the melee, then we have no problem. It is debatable, however, whether this was so. The king was eminently visible, and if, as the Norse records have it, he had indeed ventured beyond his men to engage in personal combat then he would have offered a clear target. If the reference to a "gold-tipped" arrow is not merely poetic license but an accurate description of the weapon, then this is not a run-of-the-mill battleshaft but something rather more special.

To carry speculation further, might the bowman have been a man of quality, equipped with a gold-tipped shaft, fit to kill a king, and capable of doing so? If so, who could he have been? We do not know; we may only note that many of the nobles in the royal house of Harold Godwinson were familiar with the bow, and this undoubtedly would have included the king himself. But such is speculation, and we must end it and return to examination of the arrow.

The heel of the shaftment, into which the nock is cut, is variable among cultures and is perhaps reflective of the type of draw. Thus, the thinning of the shaftment terminating in the bulbous nock of the Germanic tribes is associated with a form of light pinch hold (Edward Morse's secondary and tertiary releases), providing the fingers with suitable non slip grip to hold the arrow against the bowstring when drawn.

But examination of the arrows associated with another primitive culture, that of the North American Indian, suggests a preponderance of untapered shaftments with shallow grooves and, once again, the need for that essential pinch grip. An exception to these are the shafts of West Coast Inuit arrows, where the nock end of the shaftment is flattened and the string groove cut at right angles to the flattened terminal. The day of the bell nock groove so familiar to modern archers was half a millennium away.

I am indebted to editor Jim Hamm for his reproduction of illustrations by Steve Allely of certain American Indian shafts that accompanied his article "Western Indian Bows" within *The Traditional Bowyer's Bible, Volume 3*. Notable is the care that has been taken in fletching, and the variations observed. Also, the addition of personalized markings on the shaftments, symbols perhaps of spiritual significance. In common with many so-called primitive people, the American Indian had a spiritual rapport with the animals that, of necessity, he killed to feed and clothe his family. Whereas in today's more worldly society, there are some for whom primitive necessity has given way to "harvesting" for trophies.

Philosophical comment apart, fletching generally consisted of three feathers placed equidistant around the shaftment;

one, which we would call the cock (or leading) feather, was set conventionally, at right angles to the nock groove. Varying from the norm was an unusual four-fletch version with feathers set on the shaftment above and below the nock groove, each rachis joined to its neighbor. A two-feather variant, with feathers tangentially placed adjacent to the nock groove, provided a neat arrangement that would have enabled the shaft to pass the bow limb without damaging the fletches.

Feathers were usually secured fore and aft by sinew strip, and occasionally by additional resinous material. Allely notes particularly a wrap of sinew toward the foot of the shaft, although with no apparent purpose. His view that this is a draw-length check is viable.

Compound arrows, as Allely calls them, had foreshafts of wood or of bone slotted into the shaft and held in position by sinew. Arrowheads were of many materials, with obsidian predominant, and also iron, invariably tanged, and in many cases barbed to hasten death by hemorrhaging. Saw-toothed examples made of bone by people of the Northwest United States were up to 7 inches (17.78 centimeters) long.

For the main shaft, coniferous wood was often used: split staves from Port Orford cedar (*Chamaecyparis lawsoniana*), well known to modern traditionalists, featured largely, as were those made from red cedar (*Juniperus virginiana*), the fir family (*Pinaceae*), and spruce (*Picea*). Self shafts were taken from *Phragmites* reed (*Phragmites australis americanus Saltonstall*) and from many local woods. For the foreshafts, mountain mahogany (*Cercocarpus montanus*) was used, among other material. Profiles were largely parallel, although some of the better-made shafts were barreled, indicating that varied flight patterns were known and understood.[12]

We noted earlier how the California Indian Ishi prepared his shafts prior to completion, and this system would have been common. When completed, just as modern European traditionalists and their forebears identified their arrows by painting particular cresting rings, or occasionally more elabo-

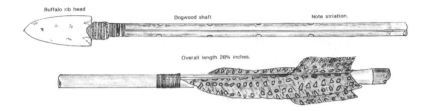

A North American Woodland Indian arrow of dogwood with bone head. Note the use of two, rather than three, fletchings. (*Author*)

rate designs below the fletches, so the American Indian did likewise. To a native people, the hunting arrow was an almost sentient thing, functional, but imbued with symbolism and significance; an object to be cherished, and used again and again.

A shaft in the style of a short Eastern Woodlands Catawba Indian hunting arrow is in the possession of the author— courtesy of Mr. Rod Parsons. Made by Tony Kaczmarek of Toledo, Ohio, it is constructed from a dogwood shoot, with a head from a buffalo rib bone, and two fletchings taken from a guinea fowl. This is a working arrow and has been used to take small game. It is 29 inches (73.66 centimeters) long and parallel in profile.

While most arrows were perhaps nonspecific, and appropriate to various prey, Allely notes two with particular purpose. One was a *Phragmites* reed arrow with a hardwood foreshaft, attached to which was a small sinew-and-resin-gum ring. When shot at a swimming duck, this ring caused the shaft to skip along the water for a short distance, almost guaranteeing a successful strike.

A second arrow, made by Ishi with a crisscross of four small twigs secured to the foreshaft, was used with flu-flu type fletches to bring down birds.

Although many Indians owned guns, and hunting was the main purpose of the arrow, it was also a weapon of war and featured as such with significance during the eighteenth and nineteenth centuries, when the American Indian took up arms against the US Army.

Foremost among the many engagements between the US trooper and his native opponent was the one at the Wabash River in 1791. It signaled lasting respect for the fighting qualities of men previously regarded by some as ignorant savages; and it undoubtedly included their use of the arrow.

The Battle of the Wabash, also known as St. Clair's Defeat, took place on November 4.[13] A force of over one thousand men under the command of General Arthur St. Clair had been dispatched to destroy resistance by the Northern Indian peoples. Opposing St. Clair were the combined forces from eastern Michigan of the Miamis, led by Little Turtle; the Shawnees, led by Blue Jacket; the Delawares (Lenape Sioux), led by Buckongahelas; and others, together totaling one thousand men.

With many raw troops staying in their tents refusing to fight and others deserting, St. Clair was short of manpower, tactically outmaneuvered, and forced into ignominious retreat. Of 920 fighting men, 632 were killed and 264 wounded. Many of the more seriously wounded were left behind in camp, together with two hundred wives and camp followers, all of whom were subsequently massacred. With bayonets fixed, St. Clair and his bedraggled remnants eventually reached safety; with him were just twenty-four unscathed men. At this battle, through cohesive and aggressive tactics, the native Americans had wiped out one quarter of the US Army.

While the Indians undoubtedly had, and used, muskets during this brief campaign, it is certain that the war arrow joined the bullet to good effect. A matter for conjecture and debate, however, is the use of poison by Native Americans in warfare. That it was used in hunting is certain, and many were the concoctions derived from local plants. Thus, among many other sources, the Lakota Sioux spread distillations of poison hemlock (*Conium masculatas*) and meadow death (*Zigademus venenosus*) upon their arrowheads, and the Cheyenne used shrubby cinquefoil (*Pentaphylloides floribunda*) upon theirs.

Most poisons would have been effective against the unprotected flanks of cavalry mounts, but the Indian braves had a special respect for the horse, and I feel that perhaps they would have concentrated their shots on the riders, leaving the horses unscathed to become spoils of battle. The reader wishing to know more about this subject should consult David E. Jones's *Poison Arrows: North American Indian Hunting and Warfare* (Austin: University of Texas Press, 2007).

The preparation and use of poison by South American Indians will be discussed in the following chapter.

4

OF INDIANS AND INDIA

THE PREVIOUS CHAPTER CONCLUDED WITH A BRIEF LOOK AT the poisoned arrow as used by North American Indians. The subject merits greater consideration, however, and in this chapter we will examine in more detail the preparation and potency of the poisoned arrow, this time by the native Indian peoples of South America and others.

Although most poisons were prepared separately and applied to the arrowhead, shafts and points made from particular types of bamboo were poisonous in themselves. One of the rarest arrows, used especially in war, was called *bixo* by the Indians. Its point was shaped like a blade, and it was made of a small poisonous bamboo. Official records quoted in E. G. Heath and Vilma Chiara's *Brazilian Indian Archery* tell of severe symptoms suffered by individuals who had inadvertently been wounded by slivers of a wild bamboo at the botanical garden in the Agua Funda area of Sao Paulo, Brazil. The effects, according to Heath, were the same as those from bamboo points on Indian arrows, causing hemorrhaging through skin, eyes, nose, and ears, and this was confirmed by the director in 1946. Unfortunately, the source does not include the botanical detail nor the date of the incident.[1]

Chief among the poisons used was curare, a corruption of the Carib word *wurali*, or *wurari*, a substance whose potency is undeniable. An animal hit by a curare-smeared arrowhead would lose muscle function by degrees, beginning at the neck, followed by the head and legs. Death would eventually be caused by asphyxiation as breathing became impossible. It is uncertain whether curare was ever used in warfare. Although it is recorded that, by taboo, Indians were forbidden its use for belligerent purposes, how closely this worthy ethic was followed remains a matter for conjecture.

Several plants were used in the production of this poison. Those indispensable to the process were Loganiaceae (*Strychnos*) or Menispermiaceae (*Chondrodendron*), each rich in necessary alkaloid. Many, although by no means all, poisons have antidotes, and curare is apparently no exception. Brazilian Indians are said to apply the starch of the aptly named arrowroot plant (*Maranta arundinacea*) to a wound affected by curare in order to counteract the effect.

The production of poison, so fundamental to hunting success, was the province of the older women in the tribe. The process was dangerous, for a drop of poison contaminating a scratch could mean death. It would be charitable to believe that, in the twilight of their years, these ladies were selected for their knowledge and expertise, and this may well have been so; however, the more cynical might say that of the tribe's human resources, they were perhaps the most expendable. It would also appear that if the batch produced was not up to scratch (literally and metaphorically) and did not meet with the approval of the men, then the old women were severely beaten.

While there has been much comparatively recent interest in the production and the effects of native hunting poisons, the subject has attracted the attention of European amateur scientists since the eighteenth century. We are fortunate to have an account of practical experiments, provided by aspiring archery historian, author, and raconteur Walter Michael

Moseley. Moseley records that Monsieur de la Condamine, an eighteenth century French adventurer who sailed up the Amazon River and visited the Brazilian jungle en route, brought back some poisonous substances derived, Moseley tells us, from plants used by the Lamas and Ticuna Indians.[2] Some of these substances he gave to an English country gentleman, a Mr. Hetissant, whose capacity for practical experiment seems to have been unbounded. Understanding that the correct way to create the arrow poison was to dissolve the substances in water and then evaporate it to produce a resinous substance, he proceeded accordingly. Unfortunately, the fumes given off were so noxious that he was severely affected and recovered only by drinking a large quantity of sugar dissolved in wine.

Having survived this setback, he tried again, putting the result into a bottle and leaving it for a while. When he was ready to begin his experiment, he retrieved the bottle, at which time the cork blew off, spraying his hand with poison. Fortunately, his hand was unblemished, and nothing got into his system.

Undeterred by these setbacks, he began his experiments, meticulously recording the results. On June 6, 1748, he made a small incision in the rear leg of a rabbit and put a piece of cotton moistened with the poison of the Ticunas on the wound. The rabbit died at once, without a sound.

On June 7, he repeated the experiment on some cats, the unfortunate animals dying within three minutes. The following day, having acquired another cat, he tried a mixture of Ticunas and Lamas poisons, with, predictably perhaps, the same result.

On June 9, he experimented on fish, reptiles, and insects, all of which survived.

All told, in the course of his experimenting, Hetissant's curiosity terminated the lives of six horses, one bear, one eagle, one hawk, two wolves, one pig, one lamb, thirteen rabbits, fifteen dogs, nine cats, and a seemingly endless number of rats, mice, polecats, and guinea pigs.

He records that the flesh of these animals was not affected, and that to prove this he had them cooked and "made several other persons eat them." These were presumably his servants, although any invitation to dinner with Hetissant was evidently something of a challenge.

Moseley, who relates the account, was quite rightly appalled by the carnage, remarking, "Had the gentleman possessed less curiosity and more compassion, he might have established his facts with equal firmness."[3]

The arrow, shot conventionally from a bow, was the prime means for delivering poison to kill prey, but Indians within the Amazonian system were also adept with the blowpipe, and these were used to bring down monkeys from the higher branches of trees. Arrow missiles used for this purpose were fashioned from cane, their fire-hardened points smeared with poison paste or liquid. The rear of the shafts had a plug of cotton wound around to lightly seal the interior diameter of the pipe. The pipes varied in length, some being over 9 feet (2.74 meters) long, with arrows/darts appreciably shorter. The effective blowpipe shooting distance seems not to have exceeded thirty yards (27.43 meters), quite far enough to hit and bring down a monkey in a tree.

Although the light arrow and blowpipe are primarily associated with Amazonian Indian cultures, many others used the weapon, including the North American Cherokee Indians. Their arrow/dart was 6 to 22 inches (15.24 to 55.88 centimeters) long, made of locust wood (black locust or honey locust, the genus is unclear), and fletched with bull thistle down to provide an air seal.[4]

Blowpipes also appear in Japanese culture, where their use, known as *fukiya*, after their name, was included in the martial arts. Armed with a poisoned point, the *ninjutsu fukiya* was recognized as a weapon, although one of restricted value, used perhaps for distraction. A typical *fukiya* was about 19.5 inches (49.53 centimeters) long and made of bamboo or hardwood. Its darts, or *fukibari*, were of a wedge or conical shape, with fur, feather, or soft down at their ends to provide an air seal. The modern practice of *fukiya*, employing a pipe of 4 feet (1.22 meters) and darts of 8 inches (30.32 centimeters), has, interestingly, an international following, and the International Fukiyado Association in Japan is pressing for standardization of rules so that it might become an Olympic event.[5]

Here we must leave the blowpipe and its deadly poisoned missile and return to the more conventional Amazonian arrow. Although hardwood is occasionally used when a more substantial shaft is required, arrows are largely fashioned from three types of reed, of which the principal genus is *Gynerium*, a true grass, and *guada*, a bamboo. Those Indians with the largest and heaviest bows, however, prefer the thicker and generally more substantial reed *Arundinaria*.

Shaft lengths vary, some seeming exceptionally long by European standards. They are invariably parallel (except where a naturally tapering profile offers opportunity for a breasted or bob-tailed shaft) and with the forward ends prepared in order to take the foreshaft. This is of a similar hardwood to that from which bows are fashioned. A long tang is inserted into the arrow shaft, and with the joint bound it is firmly secured. The heavier foreshaft serves several purposes: it provides forward weight and thus a more stable shot, it protects the shaft from damage, and it provides a substantial and secure mounting for the arrowhead.

The Brazilian Indian's arrowheads are occasionally of stone, although suitable stone is not available in any quantity. Therefore, heads of bone from prey animals and bamboo slivers predominate, each tanged and slotted into the foreshaft to be held by glue and binding. Heads are usually barbed, and in certain cases horizontally grooved, to allow them to break and remain within the prey, thus maximizing the effect of poison if it is used.

Fletchings, in pairs, are about 6 inches (15.24 centimeters) long and are secured by thread. Small bright downy tufts are added for decorative effect and may reflect tribal, or even individual, custom.

Nocks are either shallow or deep, and in many cases protected from splitting by binding. They can be self (a simple notch), or applied as a plug (where a separate piece to accommodate a thick string is prepared and inserted into the shaftment to be held by glue and binding), or consist of two small sides (like ears) held to the shaftment by binding.

Native Brazilian hunter with bow and arrows. Note short bow and long arrows. (*Library of Congress*)

The fashioning of arrows is a sophisticated and demanding task. Among the Brazilian Indians, arrow making is a shared activity, with men and women having specific roles. Thus, preparation of the resin adhesive used in binding, and the binding thread itself, is women's work, while fashioning the arrow shaft, the foreshaft, the fletching, and the head is work for men.

The whole process begins with a piece of well-seasoned reed, which is first warmed over the embers of a fire to be gently straightened. It is then cut to a length approximate to the finished shaft and, if a self string nock is intended, with one end terminating in a node. If a separate, applied nock is to be glued into position, then the end is bound in order to prevent it from splitting as this is inserted. After insertion, the shaftment is neatly tapered to remove any lip between the two. Nodes remaining on the shaft are carefully smoothed. The shaft is then cut to a more exact length.[6]

In Europe this would be a simple business, a single length, dictated solely by convention, for to a European, arrows match exactly in sets. The Brazilian Indian, however, creates shafts individually; arrows that exactly match do so by chance rather than by design. English anthropologist and physician Walter Roth observed that:

> To obtain the correct length of shaft the Indian rests one end more or less horizontally upon his left forefinger, but under the thumb, where it is deftly dipped downwards and inwards with the right forefinger. In response to this the remainder of the shaft will vibrate and by cutting off a few centimetres at a time the vibrations gradually reduce. Once no further movement is observed following the flip of the finger, the proper length has been obtained.[7]

In this way the arrows are matched, but by a different criterion.

The most complex of the Indian's arrowmaking procedures concerns the fletching. Two vanes are customarily used; these may be secured fore and aft, or alternatively bound to the shaft. Where secured at their extremities, the ends of the rachis are stripped of barbs and bound into place. In certain cases the upper end is secured beneath the nock binding and the vane bent back upon itself. When the forward end is bound, this presents an arched effect.

More intricate binding systems are achieved in one of three ways: by sewing, by continuous binding, or by ring binding. When sewn, the shaftment is punctured in several places, and threads are passed through the holes and around the rachis to secure them in position. Continuous binding is achieved by first smearing the shaftment with melted wax, into which the vanes are pressed, with binding then commencing at the nock end. On completion, more wax is applied to cover the thread. The ring variation of binding follows the same principle of preliminary shaft waxing, but with bindings separated in several groups or rings.

In some cases vanes are set deliberately at angles to the shaftment, with the presumed intention of inducing spin during flight—an unnecessary adaptation since the natural composition of a feather will induce spin.

Arrows prepared for fishing purposes are longer than average and remain unfletched.

When shooting, the secondary draw as described by Edward Morse is employed. With this, the thumb and forefinger hold the arrow nock against the string, while the second and third fingers together draw the string.

Leaving the Brazilian jungle and its hunting tribes, we now move across the ocean and into Asia to consider the arrows used by archers of the Indian subcontinent.

As might be expected from so large an area with so many disparate peoples and cultures, the traditional arrow varied by type and purpose. Its significance is demonstrated in the Indian epic poems the *Ramayana* and the *Mahabharata*, while the great battle hymn of the *Rigveda* is explicit. Here is one of its many arrow references:

> Loosed from the bowstring, fly away thou arrow,
>   sharpened by our prayer.
> Go to the foemen, strike them down and
>   let no one be left alive.[8]

The *Mahabharata*, the celebrated story of the Bharatas (an Aryan tribe) and thus the story of India itself, is an epic of some one million two-line couplets, a monumental work three times the length of the Bible, and contained in many books. Books 5 to 10 tell of the great battle of Kurukshetra, in which the arrow plays a significant part. Lasting eighteen days, it was fought between two legendary peoples, the Pandavas and the Kauravas, descendants of the Bharatas.

The parts of the arrow are variously distinguished according to those particular sacred vedas in which its description appears. For instance, the *Atkaveda* identifies six parts: the *salya* or shaft, the *pranadhi* or shaftment, the *sranga* or arrowhead, the *kulamala* or nock, and the *apaskanibha* and *apastha*, the upper and lower sections of the shaft, defined one assumes, by the point of balance.

Ancient Indian literature refers to arrows by many names. The *Rigveda* identifies arrows as missiles, which the veda says may be either mortal or immortal. Their names directly relate to the purpose of the varying heads. Thus one was designed to split other arrows apart, and another had the characteristics of a spear.

Indian arrowheads were many, and functions varied. We turn once more to a veda, the *Dhanurveda*, an illustrated manuscript, for definitions, of which there are ten:

1. *Aramukha*. Serrated and suited to cutting through hide, leather, and flesh.

2. *Ksurapra*. Chisel-shaped and razor sharp, used for cutting the enemy's arrows and hands.

3. *Gopuchchha*. Leaf-shaped and used for general purposes.

4. *Suchimukha*. Needle-shaped, thin, and pointed, used for piercing mail. The Asian equivalent of the English medieval needle bodkin point.

5. *Bhalla*. Triangular, with a broad head, as of a spear. (We will meet such a description later during an inventory of English medieval arrows and their heads.)

6. *Dvibhalla*. With a two-pronged head, said to be used for "entangling" the arrows of the enemy.

7. *Batsadanta*. Sharp and described as being like "calf's teeth." The drawing of this curious object gives no real indication of its purpose.

8. *Ardhachandra*. Crescent-moon shaped, said to be used in warfare for aiming at the forehead and throat. The English equivalent—the forker—would have been used against birds or as a poaching weapon. An Indian forked arrow used specif-

Indian arrow heads. From left to right, a barbed head (with one barb broken), butt head, leaf head, Crescent head (Ardhachandra), leaf head, broadhead (Ghera), butt head, oval head with decorative cut. (*Author*)

ically against birds was the *tir-giz*, a short arrow probably fletched flu-flu style.

9. *Karnika*. With a "flower head," its use is not specified. A head best left to the more imaginative.

10. The *Kakatundu*. With a globular head terminating in a point, it is said to have been used to penetrate mail.[9]

There are variants in other historic Indian manuscripts, but it is time now to leave the arrowhead and examine the rest of the arrow. We will begin by considering the shaft.

The length of arrows in India varied considerably, from 16 inches (40.64 centimeters) to a surprising 9 feet (2.743 meters), although the latter were rare and apparently carried in long bags dangling from the sides of elephants. I can find no commentator who has any idea of their use, and I cannot even speculate. To shoot such a monster must have proved difficult to say the least; but it seems that some foot soldiers did so, since the *Sukraniti* (an important compendium of teachings on different subjects including the king's duties and warfare) describes soldiers equipped for war with a bow of equal length to the man who carried it. This they rested upon the ground and, "pressing against it their left foot, thus discharge[d] the arrow, having drawn the string far backwards." The shaft that they used, we are told, was "little short of being three yards long, and there is nothing which can resist an Indian Archer's shot—neither shield nor breast–plate, nor any stronger defense if such there be."[10]

Vedic prescription for the arrow was that it should normally be half the length of the bow. (By comparison, an approximate rule of thumb for British longbows would be two-and-a-half times the arrow length.) Because the maximum length of an Indian longbow was 6 feet (1.83 meters), it follows that many Indian arrows were 3 feet (0.91 meters) long. The diameter was to equal that of the small finger or, one assumes, about three-quarters of an inch (19.05 millimeters)—a substantial weapon.

Made of wood or of reed, unarmed shafts were divided into three categories. Those heavier toward the foot were denoted "female" (if defined by profile, these would equate to English bob-tailed shafts). Those heavier toward the nock were called "male" (comparable to the English breasted shaft). The ones that balanced evenly (which in England might be called straight or parallel) were dismissed as "impotent"—a curiously Asian designation that one might guess to mean not very effective. There seems to have been no equivalent to the English barreled shaft.

Certain Indian arrows in the author's possession are of cane. They measure 28.5 inches (72.39 centimeters) long and are three-eighths of an inch (9.52 millimeters) in diameter. They have applied bulbous nocks that are plugged into the shaftments and secured by binding. There is evidence for decoration, while the base of the nock groove is colored red. They are unfletched, although there is evidence for the conventional three fletches, 5 inches (12.7 centimeters) long. Each fletch would have extended to the nock groove. Heads, which are tanged and bound, are leaf-shaped and without barbs. The foot of each shaft is decorated with alternating green and brown spirals, encircled by broad red rings.

Other examples, although of similar material, length, and diameter, are crudely formed and are undecorated. They have blunt heads and may have been intended for small game.

It is questionable whether Indian archery employed poison to any great degree in warfare. For those concerned with ethical protocol, there is conflicting advice. The *Rigveda* commanded "wherever you see the devils kill them with your poisoned arrows," while another ancient text, *Nitiprakasika*, offered the injunction "no-one should strike in combat his enemy with poisoned arrows."[11]

Lord Rama sketched in 1816 with a full quiver and holding a bow and a single arrow in his hands. (*British Museum*)

Notwithstanding this ethical dilemma, the technique for creating poison is described. "The bark of the peepul tree should be ground in a cow's urine and a paste made. This paste should be smeared over the arrowhead and then heated in a fire. It will then become blue like the colour of the neck of a peacock and poisonous."[12]

The Indian warrior no doubt salved his conscience as best he could, but we must now return to his arrow and to an interesting variant.

While most arrows were conventionally made of natural materials, largely reed/cane, mention is made in historical manuscripts of all-metal shafts. These iron arrows, called *naracha*, are described in the *Mahabharata* as being used only by the strongest and most skilled archers. Made of black iron and sharply pointed, they are said to have been fletched with feathers from the vulture. Their purpose is not exactly defined, but the evidence is that they were used against elephants. No early examples are known, although two dating from the eighteenth century are displayed at the Museum of New Delhi. The heads are of wide crescent shape, but because the shafts have no nock grooves, it is unclear how they were shot.

On reed shafts, string notches were chiefly of two types: the socket or plug type and the sliver type (where thin slivers of wood were secured to each side of the shaft by glue and binding, curiously similar to those of Amazonia).

Fletching generally followed convention, three equidistant feathers being usual, aligned parallel to the shaft. In certain cases however, four and even five were used. The ancient manuscripts varied in respect to feather sources, one specifying swan, hawk, peacock, and vulture, another requiring goose, osprey, peacock, vulture, and wild cock, while feathers from parrots and flamingos are also mentioned. There is some contradiction between sources, however; crow feathers are recommended by one, while another proscribes them. It is possible that the proscription relates to a particular genus of crow, with feathers unsuited to fletching. The average length of fletchings was about 5 inches (12.7 centimeters), although 8 inches (20.32 centimeters) was recommended for use with horn bows. The difference related perhaps to variations in the bracing height (string to belly) of the respective bow styles, the deflexed horn bow having the greater of the two.

Compounding the moral quandary of the military archer was a proscribed use of fire arrows by some religious authorities who believed the practice was unfair, a view demonstrably not shared by all, for, notwithstanding pious condemnation, their uses were many and varied. Arrows carrying burning material were recommended against the war elephant, burning oil setting the wooden howdah alight; while in earlier times arrows headed with hollow perforated brass balls filled with combustible material (said to have been naphtha) were regularly used to fire roofs of houses.

Apparently, red hot metal arrowheads were widely used for hunting by aboriginal tribesmen of Bengal and Bihar. We are asked to believe that the hunter had access to the small charcoal brazier in which he heated his arrowhead until it glowed, before loosing it at his prey. An interesting concept, even if logistically difficult, but by so doing, greater success was seemingly assured. This method was said to have been particularly effective against bears.[13]

Before we leave the Indian arrow, we should note one peculiarity: the shaft fletched in such a way that the arrow returned to the sender. In the ancient text called the *Sukranitisara*, a special kind of arrow is described that came back to the shooter, but the essential details are omitted, other than that it was shot from a *nalika*. The reference to a *nalika* is not clearly understood, the word having been used to describe a weapon that discharged a missile by igniting gunpowder.[14] In the *Ramayana*, it is also recorded that arrows shot by Rama never went in vain. If one did not hit its mark it returned to Rama, who replaced it in his quiver.

Quoting from a Turkish source, Thomas Roberts, author of *The English Bowman*, writes, "It is said that if a light shaft is feathered at both ends, the wood being lightest at the pile end and the feather trimmed low at the nock end and high at the pile end and shot against the wind, then it will return. And that a shaft feathered in the middle will in its flight make a right angle."[15]

An interesting experiment performed by Lieutenant Commander W. F. Paterson of the Royal Navy, co-author of *Saracen Archery*, is noted here for the benefit of archery colleagues who may be disposed to create such a returning arrow. Paterson took an aluminum alloy shaft, fitted a nock at one end and a plug at the other; to the latter he glued a small ball bearing, thus providing a little forward weight. Four triangular profile feathers were affixed at the nock end and four at the pile end, set at ninety degrees to each other. The shaftment feathers were 3 inches (7.62 centimeters) long and one-half inch (12.7 millimeters) high, the pile-end feathers one-half inch shorter but of similar height.

The arrow was launched with the bow held not vertically but close to the horizontal, at an angle of twenty degrees and directly into a head wind of some ten to fifteen mph. The arrow described a full circle, and Paterson grasped it as it approached him. The bow used was a conventional longbow of 43 pounds (19.50 kilograms) draw weight, with a bracing height of 7 inches (17.78 centimeters). The experiment was deemed a success.[16]

And so to chapter 5 and the mystic East.

5

THE ASIAN ARROW

WE TURN NOW TO EXAMINE THE ARROW AND ITS PURPOSE IN
what was one of the finest of archery nations: Mongolia,
birthplace of Genghis Khan, surely the greatest of all
medieval warriors, whose mastery of the arrow and ability to
control vast hordes of mounted warriors enabled him to sub-
jugate kingdoms and spread fear from the borders of China
into the very heart of Europe. It was said that the Mongolian
horse archer could shoot accurately at a target 328.04 yards
(300 meters) distant. It would have been a brave opponent
who put that statement to the test. A stone at the Museum of
St. Petersburg, Russia, records the feat of Yessunge, nephew to
Genghis Khan, who in 1266 shot at and hit a target 335 *alds*
distant. (The Mongolian linear measure is estimated to equal
580 yards, or 536 meters.)[1] The achievement, which is well
documented, raises the question of the type of arrow used.
While this is a formidable feat, it may have been achieved
with a more-or-less conventional Mongolian shaft, and it certainly falls some way behind the distance achieved by a
Turkish flight shot of 972 yards (888.8 meters), recorded in
1798 by Sultan Selim. Diverting for a moment, examination
of the arrows customarily used for distance by Turkish archers

Mongol archers with prisoners. Note quivers with arrows. (*Courtesy, Timothy May*)

shows them to have been just 25 inches (63.5 centimeters) long, approximately 190 grains (12.31 grams) in weight, and with a balance point 12 inches (30.48 centimeters) from the nock. Profiles appear to have been barreled, with fletches small and lying close to the shaft to reduce drag.[2]

Stemming from past glories, the practice of archery is an inseparable part of Mongolian culture today. The traditional Mongolian arrow, when armed with a metal head (*zev*) similar perhaps to the English late medieval short bodkin, was shot with deliberation and precision when engaged in battle. When employed for the purpose of hunting, however, a bone or wooden head was fitted, in the manner of the Western horn blunt, killing small game by impact.

Fishing arrows were fitted with forked broadheads; while to take waterfowl, it seems that flat heads were used, to skim along the water when shot, acting similarly to those of North American Indians noted in an earlier chapter.

When engaged in hunting on land, a Mongolian archer would carry two types of headed shaft. Having sighted his prey, a bird or a small mammal, he first loosed an arrow with

An archer shooting a whistling arrow, left, in the 1980s. (*Asian Traditional Archery Research Network*) Right, details of a Mongolian whistling arrow. Note the length of the fletchings and the bulbous nock. (*Grayson Collection, University of Missouri*)

a whistling head. This, it is said, caused the animal to look up in curiosity, and while it was off guard, the hunter quickly notched his second arrow and shot to kill. It is believed that the whistling arrow was also used en masse to disturb and disorient an enemy.

Today, with equal dedication of purpose, shooting is competitive for relaxation, and, from the authoritative accounts available, it seems that the present Mongolian recreational arrow *godle* varies in length from 29.5 inches (74.93 centimeters) to 39 inches (99.06 centimeters), the shorter being an appropriate length for the women who regularly take part. Men's arrows begin at 31.5 inches (80.01 centimeters). Shafts, typically of birchwood, seem always to be of parallel profile. They are three-eighths of an inch (9.53 millimeters) in diameter, but it is unclear whether all are exclusively self, or if some are footed, or have foreshafts fitted. The heads, called *boltsu*, are of wood or bone, and blunt to avoid damaging the targets.

Much care is taken over fletching, with tail feathers always preferred since it is believed, with some reason, perhaps, that wing feathers fly less smoothly. This is in direct contrast to

Mature Mongolian archer in traditional dress, competing at the Naadam archery festival. Note use of thumb lock to draw string, and arrow on the left side of the bow. (*Author*)

archers such as Ishi, who only used tail feathers when obliged to do so. Those from the tail of the crane are used when they are available, but the most prized are feathers from the tail of an eagle. Unfortunately for arrow-makers, the bird is rare, and few are available to be used. Preparing the fletches by size and shape is carried out most carefully, as is feathering the shaft. Accurate positioning is considered vital for correct rotation and for proper balance when in flight.

Mongolian arrows tend to be longer than the draw length one would expect to be appropriate to the bow with which they are used. The reason for this is not immediately apparent, but by the nature of its construction, the Mongolian bow would be susceptible to damage if an arrow were overdrawn by a careless archer. To avoid this, besides their additional length, Mongolian arrows embody draw-length checks that are either visual, employing a painted mark, or by a taped sliver of wood (a *meduuleg*) positioned to touch the bow hand when appropriate.

The practice of Mongolian archery in the form of games is almost lost in time. However, history records that in the tenth and eleventh centuries, "shooting the willow" was a practice in which the better archers indulged. Two lines of willow branches were set in the grounds of a flat field, the archers each choosing one according to their rank and marking it with a piece of cloth. They had first whittled away the bark for a few inches above the ground so that the whiteness of the wood was visible. Then, riding toward the branches at full gallop, each loosed an unfletched arrow fitted with a horizontally mounted blade at their respective branches. An archer who could cut through the branch and catch the cut end at full gallop took pride of place. Next came he who could cut the willow but could not catch it. Those who hit their branch but could not cut it, and those who missed altogether were the losers. One might reflect on the fate of those who missed entirely had they been in battle. During the shooting, onlookers struck drums to encourage the participants.[3]

Although horse archery is still practiced in Mongolia, modern competition takes place on foot at the annual Naadam festival, which involves three "manly games": archery, wrestling, and horse riding, and is open to men and women. Because the arrangements will be unfamiliar and perhaps a little curious to Westerners, we will look at them in some detail.

The Naadam is organized by the Mongolian National Archery Association, formed in 1940.[4] The archery portion consists of three forms of target shooting: *khalkh*; *buryat, or buriad*; and *uryankhai, or uriankhai*. Each is performed by, and restricted to, a separate Mongolian ethnic group having its own history and culture. There is some similarity in the nature of the shooting but a difference in styles and minor variations of rules. Traditional riding boots and hats are common to all, however, worn in honor of the martial traditions of the activity.

In the *khalkh* contest, two types of target shooting take place: *khana* and *khassa* (*khasaa*). First to be set up is the *khana* target. This consists of a wall of hollow cylinders called *sur* made of woven camel hide or sheep gut, 3.15 inches (8 centimeters) wide and high, each upper one resting on two below with a little space between. This target stack is 18.9 inches (48 centimeters) high and extends over the full 4.37 yards (4 meters) of the target area, or *zurkhai*.

In *khassa* events, the cylinders are stacked directly on top of each other, sometimes two and sometimes three cylinders in height. Thirty cylinders are usual within the target area, consisting of a bottom line of eighteen, and an upper line of twelve, in a formation called *dombo*.

To take part, men stand at a distance of 82.02 yards (75 meters), women 71.08 yards (65 meters). Children also shoot, and stand at distances according to their age, which is multiplied by four for boys and three for girls. Thus, ten-year-old boys would shoot at 43.74 yards (40 meters) and ten-year-old girls at 32.8 yards (30 meters) respectively. The archer who hits the most cylinders is the winner.

The *buriad* arrangements differ mainly by requiring men and women to shoot at the same distances. Each looses eight arrows, one at a time. The system is one of elimination. After each archer has shot thirty-two times, those who have hit fewer than half the maximum number possible drop out. Distances begin at 43.75 yards (40 meters), draw in to 32.81 yards (30 meters), and move finally to 16.4 yards (15 meters), cylinders being removed in proportion.

In *buriad* shooting, there are twenty *sur*, eight colored red in the center, with six blue on each side. An extra, thinner cylinder is placed in the middle of the red ones. Points are scored by knocking a *sur* beyond the target line, defined by a trench 2.19 yards (2 meters) to the rear. The number of *surs* diminishes as distances draw near.

Uryankhai is the oldest form and is restricted to men. It derives from an ancient martial practice when Mongolian soldiers held competitions to boost morale, or, in modern terms, to bond. This system has a number of different styles of shooting, including *zus harvah*, or point shooting, in which the archer says what *sur* he will aim at.

Targets are shot at from comparatively short distances: 27.34, 32.81, or 38.28 yards (25, 30, or 35 meters). Two parallel mounds of earth are set up 6.56 yards (6 meters) apart, with the *sur* cylinders lined equidistantly between them. The archer then has to hit a *sur* and knock it 3.21 yards (3 meters) over the rear mound; if two cylinders are knocked over, only one counts. Curiously, in this ancient traditional form of archery, close family members are not permitted to shoot in the same set.[5]

While the arrow is principally a missile, it also has religious significance. From time immemorial, Mongolian shamans and other religious mystics have used it for various purposes. Arrows were sewn into clothing so that they rattled together, frightening demons. They also played a part in supplications to divinities. For example, to invoke the militant spirits called *sulde-genius* (angels or guardians) against war, enemies, thieves, and brigands in general, it was necessary to go to the summit of a high mountain and prepare a pyramidal offering of gold and silver filings, milk, flour, and butter accompanied by a liberal libation of black tea, the whole surmounted by a multipointed arrow. To an Eastern mind, the function of prayer and ritual is endemic and fundamental; it is not for us worldly Westerners to question outcome.

The practice of belomancy, or divination, was, and may still be, widely practiced in the East. It is recorded that when matters of importance required resolution, three unfletched arrows were placed in a quiver. On the first was written "Command me Lord," and if drawn was regarded as a favorable omen. On the second was written "Forbid me Lord." The third was left blank, and if it was drawn the quiver was shaken and arrows drawn again until resolution.

In India, a method called the *Ge Sar mda'mo*, after a mythical king, involved placing numbered arrows in a vessel and rattling them about vigorously until one or two fell out. The numbers on them were solemnly compared with entries in a book of divination, and interpretations made accordingly.[6]

The arrow's mystery was not confined to the East, however, and I am indebted to colleague historian Janet Gendall for drawing my attention to its early and unexplained appearance in the art of the Picts, early inhabitants of Scotland.[7]

Leaving the vast plains of Mongolia, we travel now to a small adjacent country. Nestling amid the foothills and mountains of the Himalayas is the kingdom of Bhutan. Small compared with its giant neighbors India and China but rich in lore, it is a country steeped in archery tradition, a mystic place where the bow is subordinate to the arrow.

A story is recounted of the Lord Buddha, who, while journeying under the pseudonym Phagpa Chharka, one day came across young men competing in the five skills of acrobatics who challenged him to show his skills. Taking five arrows, the Buddha shot four simultaneously, each to one point of the compass. A raven flying past found its way blocked in every direction and was confused by this, so, with his fifth shaft, the Buddha brought it to earth.

Exemplifying divinity in more modern times is an incident said to have occurred during the Duar War between Britain and Bhutan in 1864–65. After prayer and supplication to Yeshey Gonpo, the guardian deity of the country, an arrow was shot from the mountain Yongla Gonpa toward the British position. The arrow is said to have hit the British general on the forehead and killed him. Whether this actually happened seems not to be recorded, or at least not by the British. But the invading army did suffer serious reverses at both Dewngiri and Balla Pass during the war, and the severed hands of a British military officer are located in the sanctuary of Gangty Gonpa.[8]

We will leave the mystic element of the weapon there and turn to today's Bhutan. The country's traditional arrow, the

Traditional Bhutanese archers and target. (*Courtesy, Chhundu Travel & Tours*)

dha, weighs 0.70 to 0.88 ounces (20 to 25 grams), is parallel or straight in profile, and generally 31.5 inches (80 centimeters) long, a length familiar enough to those modern English bowmen who customarily shoot the standard battleshaft. The shaft is fashioned from bamboo acquired from the foothills of the Himalayas, and after preparation and the smoothing of nodes is approximately three-eighths of an inch (9.52 millimeters) in diameter. The head, or *dacha*, pointed for penetration, has the same diameter and is secured into the shaft by sealing wax.

The four fletches extend 4.5 inches (12 centimeters) along the shaftment and are obtained from the primary feathers of the pheasant. In keeping with the traditions of Buddhism, however, the bird may not be killed, the feathers should be taken from the ground, or, presumably, from one having died of natural causes. They are low cut and are placed equidistant, parallel to the shaftment and secured by an animal-hide-based adhesive called *cheyene*. The space immediately below the vanes is painted black, and the cresting, or *pung*, of each arrow usually consists of rings of multicolored thread.

The string nock (*tong*) is a simple cut made directly into the shaftment and is one-quarter inch (7 millimeters) deep. It is bound with thread for protection against splitting. The Mediterranean draw and release is now universal, with the arrow on the bow-hand side, held against the string by the first and second finger, with the third finger being optional, although it seems that at one time the Mongolian thumb draw may have been in use. In this case, the arrow would have been held on the shaft-hand side of the bow.

Essentially a form of target archery, although with some similarity to English clout shooting, Bhutanese archery is somewhat out of the ordinary and worthy of a few words of explanation.

Two teams are involved, each of fifteen members, including two reserves, the reason for which quickly becomes apparent to anyone who has watched the activity.

The object at which the archers aim is made of pinewood and is 3 feet 6 inches (107 centimeters) high, 11 inches (28 centimeters) wide, and 2 inches (5 centimeters) thick. It is rounded at the top and is pointed so it can be embedded in the ground, where it is inclined at a slight upward angle. It is surrounded by frames (*hopsi*) and lined on each side by flags (*dhar*).

Nominal protection is provided by sandbags lined up on either side of the target; although it appears from casual observation that participants customarily risk life and limb while shooting is in progress by dancing about, hurling abuse and advice in equal measure, at a proximity to the target that would give Western health and safety officials heart failure. However this activity seems to be recognized as standard practice, because there are regulations that govern it, and they include the advice that when struck by an arrow, the unlucky recipient should be taken to a hospital with the arrow *in situ*.

The aiming mark is some 2.5 inches (6.35 centimeters) in diameter and placed 12 inches (30.48 centimeters) from the top of the target. The rest of the wood is decorated with clouds and flowers. Shooting is two-way, from one target to the other and back again. A central hit (called *karey*) earns three points, anywhere else on the target scores two points, and an arrow landing on the ground within a shaft's length of the target scores one point. Games are complete when one team has scored twenty-five points.[9]

Influencing the participants and perhaps occasionally the outcome is the *tsips*, a man with religious credentials but dubious scruples. A combination of spiritual mentor and holy terror engaged and paid by the archer, his task is spread equally between endeavoring to ensure success for his man by proactive intercession with his chosen deity, while seriously discomfiting the opposition by fair means or foul. Those regulating the National Archery Federation of Bhutan are understood to officially discourage divine interference with the result, a proscription apparently honored more in the breach than in the observance.

Bhutan is a buffer country, its mountainous regions separating the two cultural giants of Asia, India and China. Since we have considered the arrows of India, we should now turn to the mysteries of Chinese archery. In doing so, we will draw upon a report on arrow manufacture in the provincial city of Chengtu first published in 1951 in Taiwan and reprinted in the Soochow University *Journal of Chinese Art History* in 1981,[10] and also upon the translation of an early treatise, which includes part of a royal ritual and is titled *Examination of Crafts*, by multitalented historian and author Stephen Selby.[11]

The Soochow report was based on the practice of one arrow-maker, Ch'en Ch'uan T'ai, born in 1900 and one of the last of the traditional arrow-makers to have learned the craft from a master, in this case his father. Now long dead, in his later years, with the decline of interest in traditional archery, the old man eked out a precarious living by making and selling tobacco paper and charcoal, fashioning the occasional arrow when required.

In Mr. Ch'en's shop, the arrowmaking section occupied a small area, just one-sixth of the floor space, where his tools were concentrated:

> The *arrow frame*, essentially a work bench, divided into three parts; the top for the assembly of arrows, the middle for the storage of materials, and the lower to hold tools. The *stove*, used to hold the glue pot used to boil the glue and for heating the *fire awl*, used to drill the hole at the foot of the shaft to take the arrow head tang. The stove is fashioned from wood with a clay interior. This is perforated in several places to permit insertion of the fire awl. A *saw*, unbacked and flexible.

Mr. Ch'en used five kinds of doweling planes, each slim and differing in the concave shape of its blade. First was a primary rough plane used for the first preparation of the components and with a slightly concave blade. Second was a secondary rough plane, with a slightly more concave blade. Third was a tip plane used to plane the foot of the shaft. This tool had a smaller and more concave blade. Fourth was an arrow plane, the first of two finishing planes, and fifth, the final finishing plane.

Each plane was 8 inches (20.32 centimeters) long, 4 inches (10.16 centimeters) deep, and just three-quarters of an inch (19.05 millimeters) wide.

A correcting tool was used to straighten crooked arrow shafts. Made from a strip of wood 12 inches (30.48 centimeters) long, 7 inches (17.78 centimeters) wide, and 6.75 inches (17.145 centimeters) deep, with a wide but narrow trough.

Used to taper the exterior of the shaftment to the base of the bulbous nock, the nocking tool was a thin strip of steel, 13 inches (33.02 centimeters) long, with one end sharpened as a blade.

To cut arrow and bow-nock grooves Mr. Ch'en used a nock cutter made of steel and with saw teeth. The blade, seven-eighths of an inch (0.87 millimeters) wide and one-sixteenth of an inch (0.06 millimeters) thick, was held in a wooden

Above, a Manchu arrow. Note the long fletchings and lozenge-shaped head. Left, detail showing the elaborate design and bulbous shape of the nock. (*Author*)

handle. Including the handle, this tool was 17 inches (43.18 centimeters) long.

A steel glue pot, shaped like a barrel and containing a second pot within, equipped with a lifting handle, was used to boil the glue. His scissors were like regular scissors, but with a blunter end.[12]

These, then, were the tools used by a modern Chinese master traditional arrow-maker. For arrow-shaft material he used white poplar or aspen staves. He preferred those cut in winter, and with no knots. If this was not available, he would use wild pepper wood. For fletchings he used eagle or vulture feathers obtained from Yunnan Province, and he preferred those naturally colored green. He used sinew to strengthen and protect both shaft ends, the nock, and the foot where the arrow tang was inserted, finishing off by wrapping soft silk thread around both ends.

Cow-hide and fish-bladder glue were used to attach the arrowhead and feathers and to secure the sinew. Once complete, lacquer was painted over the sinew and silk wrapping.[13]

As with many other Eastern and Far Eastern arrows, the upper shaftment of a traditional Chinese arrow narrows toward the heel, forming a bulbous terminal incorporating the string groove. This narrowed portion is called the neck, and the terminal itself the hat. The foot, or lower shaft, tapers slightly and is called the point.

At this point we may digress a little to examine much earlier advice on certain aspects of arrow making, as set down in the "Rites of Zhou" from *Examination of Crafts*.[14] The commentary concerns cane shafts, and, among other advice, it recommends the following points of balance: heavy military arrows and hunting arrows, "two fifths from the tip," fowling arrows, "three sevenths from the tip." The distinction is slight, but each conforms with the European distribution of forward weight for purpose and maximum effect.

Where the cane was tapered (toward the foot) we are told this should extend over one-third of the shaft, fletching over one-fifth, and that feathers should be no greater in height than the diameter of the shaft itself—a requirement that contrasts with past and present European practice, where deep fletchings were, and are, the norm.

An interesting and relevant operation concerns the position of the nock groove on cane shafts. It was recommended that the shaft be floated in water and the line noted where part of it appeared above the water. The string groove should then be cut at right angles to the flotation line. The theory behind this is interesting. Early craftsmen knew that the cane from which the arrow was created would have grown with one side normally facing the sun. It was believed this side would thus be denser and firmer; accordingly, when floated in water, the sunward side would float underneath.

In deciding the position of the string groove, the suggested advantage is that the flexing of the shaft will be even, enabling a steadier initial passage with less subsequent vibration either around, or past, the bow limb, thus the arrow would be expected to achieve a greater distance. Had the groove been cut along the flotation line, the arrow would tend to steer toward its denser side.

When selecting material for the shaft, canes that are naturally cylindrical are considered best. From among these, those that match by weight are paired. Shafts with nodes far apart and of a good chestnut color are preferred. By its nature the presence of a node will affect the elastic modulus of the shaft, and ideally the selected cane should be without nodes for its effective length. But because the length of the tang of the arrowhead in the foreshaft will adversely affect the elasticity of the forward end, it seems that this would determine the position of any existing node. Clearly the ancient arrow-makers had much with which to contend.[15]

Mr. Ch'en had his own problems when using wood. If staves were sawn, much wood was saved, but the run of grain might be detrimental to the arrow's flight, or even its integrity. If, however, the run of the grain was observed, then the billet had to be split, with consequent loss of much wood. We do not know how arrow-makers of old dealt with the problem. Mr. Ch'en's practice was unequivocal: his staves were sawn.

After this initial preparation, each piece was planed, using one plane and then another, until ultimately a sixteen-sided stave emerged. If the shaft was bent, it was straightened by direct heat from the fire. When the timber had turned yellow it was ready to be corrected, using the straightening tool.

When completed, the shaft was set aside for a while; this was called "setting the character." A second heating would be done if needed. Assuming all was well, the final rounding was accomplished with the finishing plane.

The way was now clear for the hole to be created into which the tang of the arrowhead would be inserted. This was accomplished using the fire awl. When the hole had been made, the foot of the shaft was tapered using the tip plane. Attention now turned to the nock. This was created initially using the nock cutter to prepare two slits, each 0.8 inches (7 millimeters) deep and 0.12 inches (3 millimeters) apart. The material between was dug out using the point of the nocking tool.

That action finished, paring produced a hat, or bulbous nock, by evenly tapering the upper shaftment.

The arrowhead was glued into place, secured with sinew, and covered with pieces of soft silk.

Then came the feathers. Mr. Ch'en would have taken the central portion of the vane and rounded the top. Three feathers would be equally spaced around the shaft, with the "cock" feather colored red.

The way was now open for decoration, and for this both shark skin and ornamental paper were used. A thin strip of the former was glued around the side of the string nock, the hat, while different colored strips of the latter were wrapped around the upper part of the lower foot and the upper part of the shaftment below the hat. Each adornment having been attached by hide glue, the arrow was ready.[16]

Military arrows varied but were typically 39 inches (1 meter) long, durable, and capable of delivering large and heavy heads with great force. Feathers were typically 9.84 to 13.78 inches (25 to 35 centimeters) long, and arrows could be fletched in one of three ways.[17]

Chinese shooting technique is influenced by imagery; the report tells us that the mouth is a flower, past which the string is drawn to a point beyond the ear. The string arm is bent "as if holding a baby," while the bow hand is the moon and the drawing hand is the sun. The thumb and forefinger of the bow hand, within which the arrow rests, form the "crescent of the moon," while the remaining three fingers grasp the bow. The thumb and forefinger of the drawing hand together also describe a circle. The hat (nock) is positioned within the circle and pressed tightly against the string at the nocking point, which is five-sixteenths of an inch (8 millimeters) deep by 0.19 inches (3 millimeters) wide, where presumably it is held by friction. The other fingers draw the string.[18]

If this draw has been correctly described, then it differs significantly from the Mongolian thumb draw defined by Morse, found generally with this form of bow, where just the thumb (with thumb ring) and forefinger are used. Much time has passed, however, and it would be instructive to compare present practice with that of the past.

The Soochow report was prepared in 1942, and Mr. Ch'en has long since joined his ancestors. It is possible today to purchase "traditional Chinese arrows," but to what extent they reflect the old construction ways is a matter for conjecture. The master's gently simmering glue pot with its cowhide contents has long been replaced by some modern resinous substance. The lovingly created individual arrow has given way to the anonymity of mass manufacture. Shafts are artificially straight, subtleties of decoration are no more, and the infantry arrow, the *liang huang* (double signal), and the *teng tzu* training arrow are long since gone, replaced by traditional heads, designed to please the North American buyer.

It is time now to leave the fading memory of Mr. Ch'en the master arrowman and his varied skills and to depart the East, for in the next chapter we examine the Western arrow, its development, and its culture.

WARFARE

WHILE THE AUTHOR KNOWS OF NO SURVIVING EXAMPLES OF native British arrows, either complete or incomplete, their past existence may be inferred from the bows recovered from Somerset and other peat bogs. From an abundance of flint arrowheads it is evident that the arrow was a hunting weapon from Neolithic times. So let us now consider the early English arrow, that coupled with the Anglo-Saxon bow, such consideration being conjectural and based upon what literature survives.

Several Old English words describe the arrow: *flan*, *fla*, *flo*, while *flacor* describes the arrow's flight. S*træl* (or *stræla*) is generic and could equally describe a dart. *Arwe*, *arrew*, and *arruw* are recognizable as our "arrow," as is *sceaft*, from which our "shaft" derives. Fletchings are *feathergearwe* (literally "feather gear"), while the *sceafmund* is our "shaftment."

The Anglo-Saxons were also prone to employ poetical, descriptive names, or kennings, for ordinary objects. The kenning *hildenædre* (literally "battle snake") is specific to a battle-shaft, as is *hyldepilas* ("battle point"). The kenning term *isern-scur* ("iron shower") is a vivid description of the fearful arrow storm, precursor of the massed medieval arrow volley familiar to the student of early warfare and a tactic so devastating to our enemies.

Although not a principal weapon in Anglo-Saxon warfare, skill with the bow was not confined to the lowly peasant.[1] Shooting with the bow and arrow was an essential accomplishment for the ruling class, and the nobility practiced regularly for sport, sometimes with tragic results. The early poem *Beowulf* contains the lines:

> Wæs tham yldestan ungedefelice
> mæges dædum morthorbed stred
> syththan hyne Hæthcyn of hornbogen
> his freawine flane geswencte,
> miste mercelses ond his mæg ofscet
> brothor otherne, blodigan gare.

> For the eldest unfittingly was
> the bed of death laid out by his kinsman's deeds
> once from his horn-bow, Hæthcyn
> killed him with an arrow, his noble loved one,
> he missed his mark and shot down his kinsman,
> his own brother, with a bloody shaft.[2]

The reference to "horn-bow" is enigmatic and suggestive not of the simple weapon found at Nydam but of the heavily recurved and very powerful composite bow used by the Near Eastern horse archer. We are left to guess how the tragedy occurred, but hunting on horseback was common for the nobility and, as an activity, was often fraught with almost as much danger for the hunter as for his prey. The shorter composite bow, acquired by contact with Eastern horse archers, would have been more suited to this activity than the longbow.

As might be expected, Anglo-Saxon arrowheads reflected the purpose of the arrow. Archaeological excavations have uncovered barbed and unbarbed heads, tanged and socketed. It is probable that the former were used primarily, if not exclusively, for hunting, because the head would remain in place, maximizing hemorrhaging. Although there is some debate as to whether certain spear-type heads were for arrows or spears, there is consensus that the shorter and thinner examples were more likely to be arrowheads used for warfare, since it is realistic to suppose that the thinner the blade the more potent its purpose against mail. Lengths of heads varied between two-and-one-eighth and six-and-one-eighth inches (5.11 and 15.27 centimeters).

While arrows were used conventionally in sea warfare, they were also used to launch bags of lime: a caustic dusting of lime powder would have caused considerable confusion to those on an enemy vessel. Fire arrows are also said to have been used against the thatched roofs of villages and were a regular feature of later times.

Little is known of the construction of Anglo-Saxon arrows, but material recovered from excavations at Chessel Down on the Isle of Wight suggests that shafts were of hazel wood, although poplar, birch, and willow are also believed to have been used.[3] It is reported that shafts were between 26 and 27 inches (66.04 and 66.58 centimeters) long, consistent with drawing to the chest. The longer arrow, necessary when drawing to the ear, was yet to come.

Here it is appropriate to discuss this change, for it heralded entry upon the scene of that most deadly of medieval weapons, victor of Crecy, Agincourt, and beyond: the fearsome English battleshaft.

Drawing a bow requires muscular activity. If the body is to be used to maximum advantage, tricep, rhomboid, and trapezius muscles each come into play but must be supported by the latissimus dorsi. Traditional archers today define their correct use within a draw-force line, a straight line from heel of thumb of bow hand to point of elbow of drawing hand. Correctly applied, this maximizes these important muscle groups, providing the opportunity to draw a heavy bow. (The heaviest bow so far drawn by hand to shoot a 31-inch arrow under test conditions is a two-hundred-pound English longbow.)

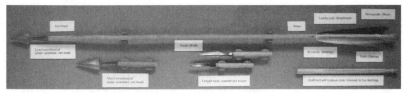

Replica Saxon hunting and battle arrow, c. 900 AD, along with various arrowhead styles. A shaftment on the lower right shows the grooves to take the fletchings and the bulbous nock. (*Author*)

However, early bows drawn to the chest and using a shorter arrow would probably have relied largely upon bicep, tricep, and rhomboid muscles for their effectiveness, "muscled through," as we would say today, and were restricted in their draw weight.

This lighter bow was of no great disadvantage for hunting purposes, or even for warfare where rival armies were within shouting distance and arrows could be aimed directly at an opponent. The virtue of the arrow in warfare, however, is in its use en masse at distance. This is the arrow storm, a feature of the Norman army at Hastings in 1066, where Breton archers standing some distance from the English loosed their shafts high into the air, landing them well beyond the shield wall.[4] The use of massed archery was a successful tactic developed by the Norman military commanders and their later medieval successors, but with it came a transition from the lighter hunting bow to the heavier war bow, and from a 27-inch (68.58-centimeter) arrow to the 31-inch (78.74-centimeter) "clothyard" shaft.

Just when the change took place is conjectural. Although Welsh archers drew heavier bows and presumably longer arrows, and were engaged as paid mercenaries to fight in English armies, clearly it was not politically expedient for this to continue. England needed its own English bowmen, and archery was officially encouraged by King Henry I in the twelfth century by statutes which, among other decrees, gave protection from manslaughter charges if an archer accidentally killed a man while at practice. In 1252, King Henry III required all males fifteen to sixty years old to keep arms, including bows.

For the English archer to be effective, it follows that at some time it was necessary for him to discard the lighter bow, drawn to the chest, and adopt the stronger weapon, drawn to the ear. No one can say when this occurred, but there are clues in perhaps the least obvious of places, the early English folk ballads, for here we find occasional references to the power of bows, and to the need to draw to the ear.

It is beyond the scope of this book to dwell at length upon such archery references; just two will suffice to illustrate conjecture. Each is taken from an early ballad. The first is from *A Lyttel Geste of Robyn Hode* (A Little Tale of Robin Hood), a work that scholars believe dates from the fourteenth century and that may draw from varied oral sources.

In the tale, we learn of an archery tournament to be held in Nottingham, the prize to be a silver arrow. It matters not whether this was a later interpolation; clearly a prize of some value was there to be had. Shooting was to be at a pair of butts set "fayre and longe." The *Geste* tells us that "Many was the bold archere that shuted with bowes stronge." The target appears to have been a willow wand. "Thryce Robin shot about and alway he slist the wand."[5]

So by the fourteenth century and, if scholarship is correct, perhaps even as early as the thirteenth, men using "bowes strong" were engaging accurately in archery competition for awards provided by authority. The lighter English bow had at last given way to its more powerful successor.

A second example comes from *Robin Hood and the Potter*, believed by some to have been set down in the late fifteenth century and perhaps drawing upon an earlier oral tale. Once more we have an archery contest, but this time the emphasis is on the strength of Robin's bow. He is offered the best bow that can be provided, yet he dismisses it with disdain. "Thys is bot ryght weke gere." However, he uses this bow with a "good bolt" (in this context an arrow), which he takes from his "quequer"—an early word for a quiver. After being exhorted by the sheriff and master of ceremonies to "Polle het op to they ner" (pull it up to thine ear), through the excellence of his shooting he "cleffed the pricke in thre" (split the wand in three shots).[6]

With these two ballads we have an inkling of the nascence of early archery with heavy bows matched with good arrows, drawn to the ear. Men were encouraged to draw heavy bows and to shoot well-made arrows for accuracy.

Finally, as reward for his assistance to an impecunious knight, Robin received a parcel of one hundred new bows and the same number of sheaves of arrows, each arrow said to be an ell long.[7] The length of an ell has varied over the years and also in different parts of the country, so in Robin's time it is debatable; 45 inches (114.3 centimeters) is one measure, but that is unrealistic in practical terms and is said to have been a later introduction. Other lengths are 27 inches (66.58 centimeters), which would seem too short to be drawn effectively to the ear, and 37 inches (93.93 centimeters), which was a Scottish measure. There is no known standard for a medieval ell.[8]

One possible clue to the length of the ell in the thirteenth century occurs in the record of a murder in Leicestershire in 1297. The arrow concerned had a head of iron 3 inches (7.62 centimeters) long and 2 inches (5.08 centimeters) wide, while the shaft was of ash "three quarters of an ell in length and one inch in circumference." If an ell were 45 inches in 1297, then here the shaft length would have been a realistic 33.75 inches (85.73 centimeters). The fletchings of this arrow were of peacock.[9]

Let us next take note of the fragment of an arrow 7.5 inches (19.05 centimeters) long, recovered from the moat of Caerlaverock Castle in Dumfriesshire, Scotland, and believed to date from 1300, when the castle was besieged by King Edward I. It is the remnant of an ash shaftment tapering toward a bulbous nock. The nock groove is slight and thus would have been required to have been held against the bow-string. Since Edward used archers from Wales at that time, it may be that the shaft is of Welsh provenance.[10]

Although there is a dearth of artifacts available for study, we are fortunate to possess a substantial inventory of arrows dated to 1422 and once the property of Sir John Dynham, who lived in Cornwall in the fifteenth century.[11] Known as the Arundel Archive, this inventory, which is housed in the county records office in Truro, Cornwall, includes arrows that are almost contemporary with the 1415 Battle of Agincourt.[12] By considering the detailed descriptions of these arrows, it is possible to put together a picture of archery material in use at that time.

Arrows are grouped, like for like, in dozens, in sheaves (presumed to be of twenty-four), and in other varying quantities. It is noteworthy that the term "shaft" is used to distinguish an unheaded arrow. Each group is defined by the type of head, coupled with the source of fletching. Feathers were of grey goose, peacock, peahen, and swan, with peacock predominating. Where nocks are mentioned they are of "full horn." If by this is meant a separate horn wedge dovetailed into the shaftment, then this is an early example of a regular feature of later recreational arrows. The Arundel arrows are occasionally "pouderd," an early term for decorative embellishment, and in many cases are described as "crossnokked"—an enigmatic term not entirely understood in this context.

Of considerable interest are the names that describe the arrowheads. These include "brodhok," "hoke," "byker," and "dokebil." None of these terms is in either curatorial or working traditional use today, and identification with recognizable types recovered from excavations must be speculative.

Thus, "brodhok" and "hoke" may be variants of a general shape (the modern broadhead comes to mind), the distinction being in width, or shape, of barb. It is also possible, however, that these are crescent broadheads, known colloquially as forkers and used in hunting.

Reproduction Medieval military arrowheads. From left to right, Type 8, Type 9, Type 10, Type 16, and Type 7. (*Author*)

"Dokebylled" (duckbilled) is perhaps descriptive of those elongated barbed heads illustrated in medieval battle scenes where archers are depicted.

"Byker" offers a particular challenge. The word "beak" may have some connection, as this was seemingly the name for the pointed end of a war-hammer head. It also describes part of a blacksmith's anvil. The context would broadly suggest the head shape we know today as bodkin.

Interestingly, the verb "to byckar" ("bicker") is first met with as descriptive of an assault with arrows, mentioned in the English ballad *The Hunting of the Cheviot*, where "bomen byckarte vponne the bent, with ther browd aros clear."[13] In this context, "bent" is grass or turf. It would not strain credulity to suppose that these were arrows to be used in an initial assault, but we must be careful of our flights of fancy, for the purpose, or purposes, of this assemblage of over seven hundred arrows is speculative.

Accompanying the inventory of arrows is a small list of bolts, presumably for use with a crossbow, although at that time "bolt" and "arrow" were often interchangeable terms. Once again we are presented with the unfamiliar:[14]

ii perhead boltis of lesse sort of pohen crossenocked with nayllys.
Two pear [?] head bolts of lesser sort of peahen crossnocked with nails.

And again:

> i brodhead bolte tappyd with horn & with I nayl fetheryd
> with pocock the nocke hol horn.
>
> One broadhead bolte tapped [?] with horn and with one
> nail feathered with peacock the nock full horn.

In company with his peers, Sir John Dynham would have enjoyed hunting as a relaxation, his early chivalric training familiarizing him with both longbow and crossbow. If "pouderd" nocks is taken to mean embellished nocks, then many of the arrows were superior to others and appropriate for his hunting use.

Of several enigmas associated with this collection, the term "crossnokked" puzzles with its speculative purpose. For those who may be mystified, it is appropriate here to briefly discuss the word "nock," which is of Dutch origin. Its nautical reference is the grooved terminal of the yardarm of a sail where it meets the mast. An early English equivalent to "nock" when associated with an arrow may have been *streng slitan* (string slit) replaced perhaps by the Anglo-Norman "notch."

Cross-nocking as we know it today requires a second string groove to be cut at right angles to the first, and is used to facilitate the rapid nocking of the arrow during speed shooting because it will fit on the string either way around. For practical effect, however, it is ideally associated with four, rather than three, fletches, to avoid one feather running against the bow.

However, unless the heel of the shaft is bulbous, the effect of cutting two string grooves will weaken the nock walls, and this will have been an evident disadvantage in the robust conditions of battle. It is conceivable, however, that cross-nocks might have been useful in hunting because they would facilitate placing the arrow on the bowstring while maintaining sight of the prey.

Each conjectured use demands special pleading, and it may be that the term merely referred to the practice (now a regular

Replica Medieval hunting arrowheads. Note horn blunt at the far right for small game and Type 15 swallow tail or horsehead in the center. (*Author*)

feature of medieval replica arrows) of supporting a self nock by a sliver of horn, termed a nock piece, set into a slit cut at right angles to the nock. Whatever its meaning, the term "cross-slitting" was recognized by the Worshipful Company of Fletchers, formed in the City of London in the fourteenth century, and was evidently in common use.[15] We will meet with visible signs of the practice of inserting this nock piece in the sixteenth century when we later examine those arrows recovered from the sunken Tudor warship *Mary Rose*, and again in the seventeenth century where, among notes pertinent to the making of arrows, the term "cross-slitting" is used.

Returning to the Arundel Archive, in a number of cases distinctive binding is mentioned:

I brodnoked arwe . . . fetheryd with pococke, crossnokked, bound in iii places with gold
vi arwys of pocoke y bound in ix places with gold in the federys with dokebylhedys, the nokkys holhorn
xii arwys of pocoke y bound with gold and silk with . . . dokebyllhedys of a sort

> One broadnocked arrow . . . feathered with peacock, cross-
> nocked bound in three places with gold
> Six arrows of peacock bound in nine places with gold in the
> feathers with duckbill heads with nocks full horn
> Twelve arrows of peacock bound with gold and silk with
> . . . duckbill heads of the same

Yet others are bound with "gold of Cyprus" and "red and black silk." Clearly these are particular and special, and, unless intended for presentation, were perhaps for Sir John's personal use in hunting. Arrow lengths are not specified, although several groups and one individual arrow are described as "small shooting" and may indicate a shorter length:

> vi smale shutyng arwys of pocoke and pohen the nokkys of
> holhorn iii hedys lake . . .
> vi smale shutyng arwys v fetheryd with whyt way and whyt
> goos crossnokked of a sort

Six small shooting arrows of peacock and peahen, the nocks of full horn, three lacking heads . . .
Six small shooting arrows, five feathered with white way [?] and white goose, cross-nocked, all the same

It is unclear whether "small shooting" relates to their length or to their purpose; it may just define their use at garden butts. The inventory includes "i bowe for a child," and short arrows would thus have been appropriate. Fletches of "whyt way" defy present-day interpretation, although colleague Janet Gendall suggests "way" as an early term for duck. "Wayz" is a Middle English term for stubble, and also for certain geese fed on stubble. The connection is tenuous, however, and the matter is best left for posterity to solve.

The Arundel Archive introduces us to highly decorated arrows; but we turn to Geoffrey Chaucer's translation a century earlier of a poem by Guillaume de Lorris and Jean de Meun for the description of arrows that would truly have caught the eye. In his translation of "Romaunt du Rose" ("Romance of the Rose"), he tells of a *bachelere* who stands observing a dance:

> And ten brode [broad] arowes held he there, of whyche fyve in his right hand were. But they were shawen wel and dyght [made well], nocked and fethered aright. And al they were with gold begon (ornamented) and strong paynted everychon [each one] and sharpe for to hevven. But yron [iron] was there noon [none], ne steel [nor steel] for al was gold, men mighte it se, outtake [except] the fethers and the tree [shaft].
>
> Five arrowes were of other gyse [different], that bean ful foul to devyse [made], for shafte and ende soth for to tell were also blacke as fende [fiend] in Hell.[16]

The original authors are clearly focusing on good and evil here, using readily understood similes for the purpose. The vivid description leaves the reader in no doubt of which they support. How relevant this was to contemporary practice we are left to speculate.

While illustrations of medieval archers abound in representations of battle scenes, it is to a fourteenth century illuminated book of prayers, the *Luttrell Psalter*, that we may turn for a picture of them at practice. Here, with commendable dedication, an instructor is shown taking a group of rustics through their paces as they shoot at a pair of butts. If the arrows are portrayed accurately, then their blunt heads with spikes inserted are such as were then appropriate to butt shafts. Today's coach would stand aghast at the techniques depicted and would also rush to correct the arrow position; but arrows are frequently shown on the "wrong" side of the bow in early drawings, and this representation would not be unusual.

An accompanying drawing of a longbowman illustrates an arrow with a lumpen or blunt head, the only type that would have been permitted to forest dwellers since it could not harm deer. Although by statute all men were required to own and practice with a bow, authority took a jaundiced view of any who were disposed to try their skill against the king's venison. Forest law was uncompromising in that respect, the cabbalistic verse "Dog draw: Stable stand: Back beround: Bloody hand" specifies four situations, any one of which meant that an illicit hunter might be apprehended while in the king's forest.[17]

A Luttrell Psalter drawing of Medieval English archery practice. Note the use of blunt heads. (*Author*)

An entry in the New Forest venison pleas for 1247 is explicit: "It is presented and proved that on the Monday before the feast of St. Nicholas [December 2] John, the son of Edonis de Lyndhurst, and Simon le Theyn were taken by foresters with bows and arrows for harming the deer. Afterwards they were hanged for theft."[18]

In the event a dead or wounded deer was found, any associated arrows were to be collected, impounded, and "enrolled" by the forest official known as the verderer. If the owner were known, or subsequently found, he had some serious explaining to do. Forestry law was quite clear. Those passing through were required to have their bows unstrung and their arrows tied securely to them. Accompanying dogs, particularly greyhounds, were to be knotted, or coupled together, so they could not easily run.

A subject worthy of conjecture is the use of poison in medieval times. An abiding folk myth associates it with those arrows used in warfare being deliberately rubbed with feces before use, and there is little doubt that many casualties of the English battleshaft died indirectly from septicemia. Whether this resulted from unsanitary conditions or was induced by poison is open to question.

It is likely, even probable, that those hunting the king's deer illicitly would have used whatever means they could to succeed. Familiarity with poison acquired from wayside plants would have been within most peasants' understanding.

We learn of one example of the use of the poisoned arrowhead in a curious way. In connection with a coroner's verdict of death by misadventure we read that, in May 1267, one William de Stangate was noticed walking down a Sussex road "with a cross-bow on his shoulder and carrying a poisoned arrow." He was met by a friend, one Desiderata, godmother to his child, who asked him jokingly "whether he was one of these men who were going about the country with crossbows, bows and other weapons to apprehend evil-doers by the king's order," adding that "she could overcome and take two or three like him." Putting out her arm and grasping his neck, then tripping him over her outstretched leg, she fell on top of him; the poisoned arrow pierced her heart, and she died on the spot.[19]

This sad event recorded by a coroner seems to present proof for the use of poison on arrowheads, and it is reasonable to assume the practice was not unheard of.

Although the livery arrows provided for warfare were a matter for the professional fletcher, the peasant archer may well have made his own locally using ash staves, heads of horn or antler, or perhaps of iron if he had the wherewithal to pay the blacksmith. His fletches would have come readily from those dropped by "wayz," or stubble geese, and the glue necessary to affix them from the humble bluebell, for the bulb of this seasonal flower, when boiled with a little water, provided, and indeed still does, a most satisfactory adhesive.

John Gerard's *The Herbal, or the Generall Historie of Plantes*, published in 1597, is equally clear on earlier country lore: "The blew harebell or English Jacinth [hyacinth] is very common throughout England. It hath long narrow leaves leaning towards the ground, among the which spring up naked or bare stalks laden with many hollow blew floures. The root is bulbous. Full of a slimie glewish juice, which will serve to set feathers on instead of glew."[20] Nicholas Culpeper's *The Complete Herbal* of 1653 is equally explicit.

With a bough bow cut from hedge yew and a bowstring of retted nettle, the forest dweller had all the means for illicit hunting at his fingertips.

Although the humble fourteenth century peasant relied upon nature to provide his arrows, the role of arrow-maker had become a profession. On March 7, 1371, in the City of London, the hitherto joint trades of bowyer and fletcher parted company and the Worshipful Company of Fletchers came into being.

From the beginning, quality was their watchword, and this extended beyond ensuring straight and true shafts made of good dry wood, to checking the work of those arrowsmiths living outside the city boundary, seizing and destroying arrowheads that were not correctly "seasoned," or hardened. Working at night was particularly frowned upon, with fines for those caught doing so.

The Fletchers Guild, or Worshipful Company of Fletchers, recognized two fundamental types of shaft in those early days: "bearing," or heavy, used for warfare, and "mark," a lighter version for use in butt shooting. For one hundred best-quality bearing shafts, "well and cleanly cross-notched after the best manner, peeled and varnished," a workman received sixteen pence, and for "ordinary" bearing shafts "of seasonable wood, well and cleanly made, cross-notched, peeled and varnished" fourteen pence. The distinction is not obvious, and the terminology appears to have changed in a succeeding century, as we shall later see. For one hundred mark shafts, the fee was twenty pence, an interesting variation suggesting an altogether better finished arrow.[21]

In later times, shafts were carefully paired, as we will note in a succeeding chapter, and matching arrows would evidently have commanded a higher price.

THE TUDOR ARROW

IN THE PREVIOUS CHAPTER WE CONSIDERED THE FIFTEENTH century arrow in the context of a significant collection gathered together for sport and perhaps warfare by a Cornish nobleman. In this chapter we will look at the arrangements made for the manufacture of these and similar shafts.

Although the makers of arrows had earlier gathered together in an informal group, comprising perhaps those whose apprenticeship had been in that skill, the formal beginning of arrow making or fletching as a separate profession in England can be dated at least to 1371, for in March of that year in London, members of the already extant City Company of Bowyers delivered a petition to the mayor and aldermen asking that bowyers be prevented from working at night, since continuing to do so was proving detrimental to quality.

Simultaneously, a group of those who practiced arrow making petitioned the Aldermanic Court, stating that there had been agreement among themselves that "for the profit and advantage of all the Commonalty," the two trades of bowyer and fletcher should be kept separate, and that no man involved in one trade should become involved with the other in any way.

The matter was duly debated, and it was agreed that those involved in both trades should forthwith decide which they would follow and from thereon keep to that trade. A system of fines, to be paid to the city's chamber of commerce, was proposed in the event this arrangement was not observed.

Both petitions were granted, and thus the Worshipful Company of Fletchers came into being. Unlike other contemporary city companies, it received no formal charter. It was therefore a company by prescription, that is, by title or right.[1]

All seems to have been well with the new arrangement, which was honored by observance in all but one case, that of a Robert atte Verne, whose interests evidently lay in both activities and who, because he had apprentices in each, was disinclined to give up either trade. Pressed to decide, he originally declared that he would become a bowyer. But he was not true to his professed calling and was brought before the mayor, accused of practicing as a fletcher. The mayor duly fined him for the offense and ordered him to keep to bowyery in future. Whether he did so initially we do not know, but in 1386, a year after the first known masters of the fletchers company were sworn in, Robert Verne is recorded as a master fletcher. Evidently, he was a man of independent mind.[2] In 1403, the first regulations or rules (historically known as ordinances) were published, including the understandable proviso that fletchers should not sell their arrows to aliens without special leave of the king.

A principal purpose of the fletchers company was to maintain quality in manufacture, and ensuring this occupied much time and effort. A major problem concerned the regular practice of freemen of the company of employing journeymen to fulfil royal contracts. These men were allowed to work at home and were therefore not subject to proper and adequate supervision. Consequently, many worked well into the evening and at night, producing, it is said, inferior and unserviceable arrows. It was also claimed that they changed dry seasoned wood for green wood and were generally unreliable.

Clearly matters had to be corrected, and in 1432, a petition was prepared and subsequently granted requiring that no freeman should employ a workman other than in his own house where he could be properly supervised. Through avarice the independent journeyman had lost his independence.

While City of London arrow-makers believed they should be separated from those who made bows in order to form their own company, such was not necessarily the view of those in the provinces. Thus, in Bristol, although following disparate trades, bowyers and fletchers came together in 1479 to form a joint guild.[3] The introduction to their ordinances suggest that prior to their guild, their formal attendances at the various festivals were included with those of the hoopers or coopers, a trade that used many of the same tools and whose apprenticeships were perhaps not too dissimilar. The following passage is relevant: "Graunting them and theire Successours under the commen seale of this worshipful Toune for evirmore to contiynue and endure to have as large and Ample libertyies as the craft of the Hopers in this worshipful Toune have . . ."[4]

Included in their ordinances was the requirement that no apprentice serve a term of less than seven years, and that "he be no rebel of Ireland, nor Alien, but liegeman born, to the King our sovereign Lord."

The ordinances end with the curious phrase, "Given in the Guildhall of Bristowe foresaid on the xix day of May, the year of the reign of King Edward the iiijth after the conquest the xixth."[5] It is not clear today what the final five words refer to.

The Bristol guild seems never to have been large, and it is uncertain how long it lasted. In apprentice records for the eighteen years from 1533 to 1551, the names of just four fletchers and five bowyers appear, together with those of two bowstring-makers, one of whom combined the business of stringer with that of barber, and these perhaps reflect the original numbers of each trade. It is of some incidental interest that although no female bowyer is known from early times, it was not uncommon for widow fletchers to assume their husbands' responsibilities and to take apprentices. For example, in 1543, Bristol fletcher John Badnall is recorded as acquiring John Base as an apprentice; four years later, Lucy Badnall, his wife, now has the business and has additionally taken on young John Morris.

Young lads were taken on to learn the trade for varying numbers of years, periods no doubt reflecting their age when indentured. In Bristol, which is likely to have been representative of other major cities, of nineteen accepted for the trade of fletcher from 1533 to 1551, five were indentured for seven years, six for eight, four for nine, one for eleven, and one for twelve. This latter was the son of a mariner who was no doubt at sea for much of his life. The recorded occupations of the fathers reveal an interesting cross-section of sixteenth century urban society. The sons of tinker, tailor, weaver, miller, and sailor rubbed shoulders with those of husbandmen, yeomen, and gentlemen, while their origins are scattered widely, between Wales, Westmoreland, and Ireland.

From these apprentice records we have an indication of the tools of the sixteenth century fletcher on his becoming a journeyman or even achieving the coveted freeman status; for in 1554, after learning the trade from his master, John Wyllyams, for nine years, young Morgan Jones was to begin life as a fletcher with four shaves, two knives, one plane, and a pair of shears. In a later chapter we will examine the arrows made by fletchers at that time.

Sadly, London records of fletcher apprentice indentures are untraceable before 1739 and finish in 1850. Parental occupations of those seeking apprenticeships for their sons from 1739 to 1754 do, however, reflect eighteenth century city life, including six yeomen, five gentlemen, two merchants, a schoolmaster, a goldsmith, an undertaker, and, perhaps surprisingly, a Chelsea pensioner.

From the Bristol Guild Ordinances we have an indication of pay during the late fifteenth century for those casual workmen hired by fletchers. An "able werkeman and a Jurneyman for his hyre by the weke xiid [pence], and his table [food and lodging] without enny other yefftis [gifts] or Rewarde And the holy dayes Abatid [not counted]."[6]

Besides London and Bristol, guilds were well established in other major cities, the importance of their presence reflected in periodic religious plays (called mystery plays, as they still are today) that they performed on large traveling carts which, when they found somewhere they could be seen easily by large numbers of people, they would stop for another performance. Thus in York, the bowyers combined with the fletchers to perform *Peter's Denial: Jesus before Caiphas*, while in Chester the fletchers linked with the bowyers, coopers, and turners to present *The Scourging of Christ*. A surviving manuscript detailing performances of the latter between 1463 and 1477 is at the British Library. The York Mystery Cycle (Corpus Christi Plays) comprises some forty-eight pageants illustrating the Christian history of the world.[7]

Given the importance of archery for national defense and King Henry II's 1252 decree that all males should keep bows and practice archery, it is a little surprising to find that in the thirteenth century, the important city of Coventry could apparently muster just one fletcher and one bowstring-maker. Although two crossbowmen are mentioned, seemingly no bowyer was present, suggesting that locally made bough bows and shafts were perhaps the order of the day.

While in London trades were separate by agreement and decree, north of the border, in Scotland, matters were a little different. In Edinburgh and other large Scottish towns, organized incorporations were formed to accommodate those artisans having a monopoly in their particular trades and occupations. With arrangements in many ways similar to the English guilds, they provided fraternal well being and quality assurance, as well as recording decisions of those overseeing the crafts, where established precedent might affect future policy.

Since there were too few Scottish fletchers to form their own incorporation, it is unclear to which those making arrows belonged, although logic suggests liaison with the bowers (as they were called in Scotland) and hoopers. *Scottish Arms Makers*, by Charles Whitelaw, names just ten makers who appear on the city's Burgess Rolls between 1435 and 1582. These are described variously as "Fletcher" (two), "Arrow maker" (four), and "Bow and Arrow maker" (four).[8] While we may be reasonably certain that making arrows was a principal if not a sole occupation, the same cannot be said of the bowers, who seem to have included either the making of arrows or their vending as part of a normal day's work.

In 1564, arrow-maker Richart Walker, described as an "Inglishman," was (a little strangely, perhaps) required to "remaine in toune for teaching his art." That he duly remained at his post is attested by an entry for 1582, when he took on Robert Spens as an apprentice.[9]

The Scottish kings seem to have enjoyed archery as a pastime; an entry for payment in 1497 reads, "Bertholomo bowar for arrowis to the king at the buttis, at the King's command xiiiis," and another, in 1511, "To Berty Wardlaw for ane quivir for arrowis, vi arrowis, ane dusane of bowstringis, tua [two] furneist [furnished] crosebowis, v genyeis [arrows], ane coffir [case] with ganyeis, ane dussone barrit boltis and ane dussone blunt boltis for the Kingis Grace ix li xiiiis."[10]

This archer king was James IV, whose sad death two years later at the Battle of Flodden was directly due to a surfeit of (English) arrows.

Although those named as fletcher, or arrow-maker, may well have remained true to their calling, it is apparent from examination of wills that the title of bower was rather loosely interpreted. The goods of Alexander Dais, bower of St. Andrews, who "died of the pest," or pestilence, in 1585, illustrates the range of activities in which he was involved: "of bowstrings made and unmade 11 scoir sauld together for £39. 10s [Scots]. 500 arrow schaftis price of the hundred 24s. Certain club heidis and schafts for £5. 8s. Certain lows [?] fedderis estimate to 11s."

A similar will, of bow-maker Donald Baine of Edinburgh, who died in 1635, includes, "thrie hundreth bowis maid and unmaid iiii lb. Clubheids and clubshaftis ane thowsand maid and unmaid xl lb. Arrowis maid and unmaid xx lb. Certane bandit (banded) staiffis [staffs] heids and schaftis xxx lb. Thriescoir speris [spears] maid and unmaid xx lb." It is clear that any object requiring shaping, be it bow, arrow, spear shaft or club was fair game for the Scottish bower.[11] Indeed the independent occupation of fletcher was shortly to vanish in both Scotland and England as more and more erstwhile makers of bows came to practice it with other crafts. Thus, in 1676, the newly formed Royal Company of Archers sent Robert Monro to London to learn the joint skills of bow and arrow making from a bowyer named Egertoun.

We know nothing of seventeenth century arrow making in Scotland; two examples of the early eighteenth century art survive, however, and we will note these in detail in a later chapter.

It is now time to consider the sixteenth century arrow, its use and its making. For this we turn to the Tudor warship *Mary Rose*, which capsized in 1544 while engaging the French fleet off Spithead, Portsmouth, England. The inspired recovery of its remains, supervised by research-directing archaeologist Dr. Margaret Rule following many years of seabed survey by journalist and amateur diver Alexander McKee, has enabled examination of the many hundreds of war arrows that formed part of the ship's armament.

No written explanation of the manufacturing process is known or is likely to exist, since that information was passed verbally from master to apprentice with the sworn proviso that no word of his teaching would be revealed to others.

However, close scrutiny of surviving shafts has enabled much to be deduced, and this, coupled with practical knowledge contributed by modern fletchers accustomed to making shafts in the traditional way, has opened the door to sixteenth century practice.

Before commenting upon the recovered shafts, we will first look at the teachings of a contemporary master archer, Roger Ascham, for in his seminal work, *Toxophilus: The Schole or Partitions of Shootinge*, he devoted a chapter to the arrow.[12] Although Ascham was concerned primarily with recreational archery, at least some of his advice was intended to be helpful for the warrior bowman. He lists fifteen "diverse" woods from which sixteenth century fletchers could, and one presumes did, make arrows: "Brasell, Turkie Woode, Fusticke, Sugarcheste, Hardbeame, Byrche, Asshe, Oake, Servisetree, Hulder, Blackthorne, Beche, Elder, Aspe, Salowe." Although we can recognize some of these, many are unidentified today.

He then comments on the qualities of these woods, reporting that "Brasell, Turkie Wood, Fusticke, Sugarcheste and such like make dead, heavye, lumpishe, hobbling shaftes." Developing his theme, he dismisses Hulder, Blackthorne, Servestree, Beeche, Elder, Aspe, and Salowe, either for their weakness or their lightness as making "holow, starting, scudding, and gadding shaftes." Finally he concedes that "Birche, Hardbeame, some Oake, and some Ashe, being both stronge enoughe to stande in a bow and also light enoughe to fly farre are beste for a meane, [average] shaft for all occasions."

For warfare, however, after practical experiment, he dismisses the contemporary use of aspen, or as we call it, poplar, for shafts "as they be nowadays," recommending ash. "For of all other woods that ever I proved [experimented with], Ashe being bigge is swiftest, and againe hevye to give a great stripe [wound or hit] withall, which Aspe shall not do. What heavinesse doth in a stripe every man by experience can tell, therefore Ashe being both swifter and heavier is more for sheafe arrowes than Aspe, and thus for the best wood for shaftes."

It is now time to look in some detail at those shafts recovered from the seabed grave of the war ship *Mary Rose*, and in doing so we see that Ascham's trenchant observations did indeed reflect practice by contemporary fletchers, for a significant majority of arrows carried on board the warship were of poplar.[13]

It may be helpful here to restate the definition of an arrow. It may be of either two or three component parts: a self shaft (stele) of which the shaftment (little shaft) carrying the fletches is separately defined, and a nock, or bow-string groove; alternatively a stele to which a spliced in footing has been fitted. In either case it has two essential attachments: feather fletchings (usually three) spaced at equal distances around the shaftment, and a head (pile). It can have one desirable but not essential addition: a horn nockpiece designed to strengthen the string groove against pressure from the bow-string. It can also be marked to distinguish its ownership, and its profile may be to one of four distinct shapes. Its standard overall length is suited to the style of shooting for which it is intended, although it may also be shortened to reflect the physical characteristics of the shooter.

The profile of an arrow has an important bearing on its purpose. Ascham distinguishes two such profiles: "little breasted, and bigge breasted." The former he tells us are called "taper fashion, rush grown, or by some mery fellowes, bobtails," and he considers them best for shooting "under hand," for distance, or what he calls "shooting in compass" by those with a "soft loose." The latter he considers suited to "fore hand" shooting at shorter distances since the "bigge breste" is more suited to "beare the great might of the bow."[14]

The term "breasted" is used today, while modern archers, being "mery fellowes" also recognize and use the term "bobtailed." Strangely, however, Ascham does not define or seemingly recognize two other contemporary sixteenth century profiles, the parallel, or straight, and the barreled, each of which is reflected in the two thousand and more shafts recov-

A selection of arrow shafts recovered from the warship *Mary Rose*. Note evidence of binding fletchings. (*Mary Rose Trust*)

ered from the *Mary Rose*, and each of which continues in use today. Although a parallel arrow has no special property other than ease of manufacture, barreling a shaft reduces vibration during initial flight, thus improving distance made, an obvious advantage when shooting long range.

A straight shaft has no taper, beyond that at the shaftment where it meets the nock, while the barreled shaft tapers from its center to both nock and head. In passing, it is appropriate to mention a fifth shape that appears among shafts found in the various *Mary Rose* arrow chests: a saddled, or doubly barreled, profile. It is a complex shape, tapering toward nock and head from two high points, separated from each other by a dip in the center of the shaft. Opinion is divided on the purpose of such a profile; it may have been created as an intended improvement upon the barreled shaft, although it has not survived. Statistically, of 609 examined, 268 were bob-tailed, 168 parallel, 114 barreled, 32 saddled, and 27 breasted.

The length of medieval arrows has long been a point of contention between those who abide by historic references to the clothyard shaft and those who practice archery. There is no exact definition of a clothyard measure, beyond the method by which it is determined: by drawing cloth from a roll using the distance from outstretched arm to ear. We are reminded of the words Shakespeare puts into the mouth of old King Lear, "That fellow handles his bow like a crow-keeper; draw me a clothier's yard"—a clear reference here to the similarity of the actions.[15]

By good fortune, we now have late medieval arrows by the score to examine, and conveniently, they reveal contemporary lengths.[16] Examination of 1,054 taken from four chests recovered from the *Mary Rose* shows there to have been a 6-inch (15.24-centimeter) variation between them. Although a substantial majority (841) were 31 inches (78.74 centimeters) long, 190 were 29 inches (73.66 centimeters), 9 were 32.5 inches (82.55 centimeters), 8 were 28 inches (71.12 centimeters), and 6 were shortest of all at 27.5 inches (69.85 centimeters). These measurements include the cone to which the head would have been affixed, however, and the inconsistent lengths of these contribute to the variables.

Although no fletchings survive, marks on the shaftments indicate they were approximately 6 inches (15.24 centimeters) long. Thread binding common to all appears to have been commenced at the tip of the fletch, working upward toward the nock end, a system traditional fletchers use today.

There is evidence for the use of verdigris on these arrows, mixed with the adhesive used. This suggests an attempt to combat infestation by mites, as constant a problem then as it is today for those archers who choose natural feathers over manmade vanes.

Ascham is explicit about nock shapes,[17] describing a selection then in use but favoring a deep groove for war arrows, which would hold the arrow firmly onto the string, and a shallow groove, which he says was for "pricking" and also shooting "for compass" to ensure the "cleane deliverance of a shoote." He also mentions a "double-nock," which he says is used for "double suertye [surety] of the shafte." The term is enigmatic and seems not to have the same meaning as today, when two grooves, one at right angles to the other, are cut into the shaft and used during speed shooting.

In the context of improving the surety, or safety, of the nock, however, the practice of double-nocking may be synonymous with cross-slitting, a practice we will meet later. Here a slit is made at right angles to where the nock will be and a sliver of horn is inserted; being glued into position, it thus strengthens the nock. This is a regular feature of arrows recovered from the *Mary Rose* and one in use on replica battleshafts today. Whether the practice equates with cross-nocking, as recorded in the Arundel Archive, is surely a matter for earnest intellectual debate.

Ascham is also aware of the practice of boring a hole at the nock end and filling it with lead to manipulate the balance, a feature of sixteenth century European distance shooting which we will examine in a later chapter. While noting that this manipulation happens, he comments dryly that "none of these wayes be anything needful at all," observing that it is the nature of the feather, if properly selected and shaped, to stabilize flight.

Turning now to the other end of the shaft, Ascham is explicit about the spliced addition that today we call footing but in sixteenth-century parlance he termed "peecing." Piecing, or footing, with a heavier wood such as Brazil or holly he accepted as making the shaft end "compasse heavye with the feathers for the stedfaster shootinge," a technical expression we might translate today as "proportionately heavy, for better balance of the shaft when shot." He is dismissive of any more than a two-point piecing, observing that any more would only enhance the danger of moisture loosening the glue and adding that "many pointes be more pleasaunte to the eye than profitable for the use."

He adds (a little sarcastically, perhaps) that when some archers have broken a shaft, they are loathe to lose it, and piece, or foot it. Then, because this makes it "gaye," or good to look at, he says they "cutteth theyr (w)hole shaftes and peeceth them again; a thinge by my judgemente more costlye than nedefull."

Ascham considers the feather carefully in his *Toxophilus*, devoting several pages to source, texture, and color. It is

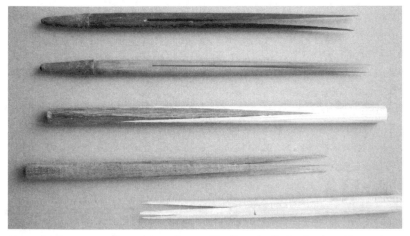

How footings are pieced together with the shaft. A nineteenth century two-point footing is at top, with a modern three-point example below. (*W.E. Searle/Author*)

accepted wisdom today that medieval shafts were best served by feathers from the goose. Few modern fletchers would debate the difference, as Ascham does, between those from an old or a young bird, from a gander or a goose, from what he calls a "fenny" goose or an "uplandishe" goose, terms that are not clear to us today. To these he might have added the "wayzgoose" (from *wase*, an obsolete word for stubble), a goose fattened for the table.

Whether taken from the left or right wing, whether pinion or other, each feather had, and presumably still has, its individual quality. Ascham is explicit about these qualities. The old goose feather is stiff and strong and good in a wind, while a feather from a young goose is weak and should be cut high to compensate for its propensity to flatten. The flesh of a "fenny" goose, he reports, is the darkest and least wholesome of table birds, and this is reflected by its feather which is coarse and rough.

Ascham is not above criticizing where he feels it necessary, and he wags his finger reprovingly at some fletchers who do not always give proper care to the preparation of their feathering, suggesting (probably with authority) that some may only pare down the rachis properly when they have "leysure and heed," adding that "God sendeth us good feathers, but the devill noughtye fletchers," and that they "ought rather to amende themselves for doing ill, than be angry with me for saying truth." Having delivered this informal reprimand, he goes on to discuss the shape of fletchings and their purpose. Essentially these were four: round, saddle back, swine back, and triangular. Of these he seems to favor the triangular shape, a choice borne out through usage across the centuries by many traditional fletchers up to and including the present day.

Although archery still played a part in warfare, its effective use had significantly diminished. The Battle of Pinkie Cleugh, near Edinburgh in 1547, is considered to have been the last occasion when bow and battleshaft were used tactically. While statute still required men to own bows and arrows and to practice with them regularly, this rule was ignored more often than it was followed. Ascham wrote, therefore, at a time when those who did take up their bows and arrows did so largely for relaxation, and *Toxophilus* evidently reflects this. Although he pays lip service to the war arrow, he is mainly concerned with the recreational shaft, and this is nowhere more apparent than in his commentary on arrowheads.

He writes of the recreational arrowhead when he observes that they have either sharp or blunt points. He cautions against the sharp head because men do not draw it fully, to avoid "*settinge it in the bowe,*" although it "*perches quickly through the wind.*" He then draws attention to the activities of some London arrowhead-makers who, having invented and perfected new files and other tools, now create heads with ridges around them that let an archer feel when he has reached full draw, allowing him to use the full length of the arrow without fear of overdrawing. These heads, he says, are termed "Ridged," "Creased," or "Silver-spoon" (the latter because of a likeness to the knob end of certain sixteenth cen-

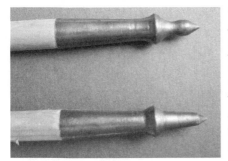

"Silver-spoon" recreational arrowheads, named for their likeness to the knob end of a sixteenth-century style spoon. Top, "silverspoon;" bottom, "ridged" (Ascham: "rigged"). These arrowheads were designed to enable the archer to feel when he has reached full draw. (*Author*)

tury table items), and he is thoroughly in favor of their use. Modern archers will be familiar with the principle, although today the bow-limb-mounted clicker serves this purpose.

We will conclude this chapter on a cautionary note, for drawing the arrow inside the bow was not only dangerous, in one case it was fatal. The incident occurred October 28, 1562, and concerned one Henry Pert of Welbeck, Nottinghamshire. Disenchanted perhaps with the more mundane garden butts, he had decided upon an experiment, to see how high he could shoot. It is not recorded how he attempted this, but in doing so he leaned over his bow with his face directly over the arrow. Upon releasing the string, the arrow (valued at just one farthing, a quarter of an old penny), which had drawn beyond the bow limb, changed sides and traveled upward, striking him over his left eyelid and penetrating his brain. Death was not instantaneous, however: he lasted until 12 o'clock the next day.

How he managed to achieve the feat at all is a matter for conjecture, and the coroner was sufficiently interested to inquire further. It would appear from witnesses that the unfortunate Henry Pert was in the habit of regularly overdrawing his arrow.[18] A salutary tale, and one with which we close this chapter.

SHOOTING FOR DISTANCE

ALTHOUGH ENGLISH LAW WAS EXPLICIT ABOUT LEARNING TO shoot in a bow, and penalties awaited any father whose son had not received bow and arrows on his seventh birthday, it would seem from history that monitoring this activity was somewhat less than perfect. Coroners in their courts regularly considered the fate of sundry small boys who had strayed into the path of an arrow while indulging in archery practice.

Typical is an incident that took place in Nottinghamshire on June 10, 1534. This involved young Thomas Riche of Newark, "who, from inexperience ran between two small targets where Francis Spayning, aged over eight years was shooting arrows with other boys for recreation, and Francis's arrow, worth a halfpenny struck Thomas on the front of his head, giving him a wound half an inch long, half an inch wide, and one inch deep of which he died the next day." The coroner's verdict: "Thomas came to his death by misadventure."[1]

Young Francis would have been using a garden arrow appropriate to his size and that of his bow. Two children's bows, each 40 inches (101.6 centimeters) long and of the same period, have been recovered from an archaeological excavation at Acton Court, a Tudor mansion in South

Gloucestershire; their length suggests an arrow some 16 inches (40.64 centimeters) long.[2] The dimensions of the wound Thomas suffered indicate a simple blunt bullet head. Those familiar with Professor Oliver Jessop's "A New Artefact Typology for the Study of Medieval Arrowheads" (*Medieval Archaeology* 40, 1996) are referred to MP (Multi-purpose) 10, defined as for "Practice Purposes." Lengths varied, but they included one-and-one-eighth inches (2.86 centimeters), and diameters of one-half inch (12.7 millimeters). One recovered from the Castle Green, Hereford, is one-and-one-eighth inches long and has a three-eighths-inch (9.53 millimeters) socket and a three-sixteenths-inch (4.76 millimeters) tip.

Although designated areas were set aside for practicing archery, and each town and village of any size was required to set up butts, this seems not to have concerned some youthful practitioners who set up targets wherever there was space to do so. Inevitably there were accidents.[3]

In June 1562, Alexander Godbye of Lowick, Northamptonshire, was sitting on the churchyard wall watching companions John Fryssby and friends shoot at targets next to the wall. Although warned several times to move, Alexander refused to do so. He was subsequently struck on the head by John's arrow and died the next day. Coroner's verdict: death by misadventure.

Accidental shooting did not always result in a fatality. In Grimsby in 1516, John Atkinson, a "scoler," accidentally shot a girl in the town, although the town surgeon was able to save her. Of some slight relevance, the author can declare a casual personal interest in this particular event, since his grandfather was an Atkinson and lived in Grimsby.

Men were not immune from accident of course. The coroner's report on an incident at Upton, Nottinghamshire, in June 1550 reveals the penalty of carelessness. Shooting at garden butts was a popular activity but one fraught with danger for those without respect for elementary safety:

At about 4 pm, Thomas Lamont the younger, and other honest men assembled together at Upton, were shooting at garden butts. As soon as Thomas had shot, Richard Alott suddenly and unexpectedly ran between the butts, and Thomas's arrow worth one penny struck the left side of his head, giving him a wound 1 inch deep and 1/2 inch wide of which he languished at Southwell from 29th June to 1st July when he died thereof. Thus Thomas in shooting his arrow at the said butts and by Richard's unexpected running, slew Richard by misadventure.

As an aside, Upton's neighbor village is Askham, a poignant name in these circumstances.

Convention, and indeed statute law, required that to qualify for a verdict of manslaughter and not murder, an archer had first to shout "fast" when potential casualties were present. Whether Thomas observed convention is not recorded, but the coroner was satisfied that malice was not intended, and unlike his companion, he lived to shoot another day.

In this case the cost of the arrow was one penny, the contemporary price of a full-sized garden arrow.

Although garden archery was regularly practiced for relaxation in the sixteenth century, authority was more concerned with the distance shooting so necessary in warfare. In furtherance of this, events were held periodically on Finsbury Fields in London, when money prizes were offered for success at shooting three kinds of arrows: the standard arrow, the bearing arrow, and the flight arrow. We will ponder the meaning of their names in a later paragraph. These events were well attended by archers hoping to qualify for the not inconsiderable awards, and by spectators looking for cheap entertainment. Elementary arrangements for the safety of those watching were in place. From a preliminary notice of the inaugural event in 1521 we learn:

> This Proclamacon must be made [by the local Mayor] when my Lord Mayer [of the City of London] and the Aldermen and the Games be assembled. My Lord Mayer

and my Maisters the Aldermen on the behalf of owre Sovraign Lorde the Kyng charge and commaund that any man repayring to this Game of Shotynge kepe the Kyngs peace in his owne persone upon the payn of Imprisonment and farther to make ffyne by the discretion of my said Lord and Maisters and also that no person approche or cume so nere that he shall stand in daunger for hys own ease and others. And for the good and due orderyng of the same no persone be so hardy to stande within xxty yards of any of the Stakes appoynted for a mark upon the perill that will fall thereof. And to the intent that no persone shal excuse hym by ignorance there shal be a Trumpett blown at every shot as well of the Standard, as of the Arowe or flyght that every persone may thereby take warnynig to avoyde the daunger of every of the said Shotts, and God save the Kyng.[4]

Whether twenty yards proved adequate in the circumstances is not recorded, but the author has personal experience of organizing distance shooting at which archers, misloosing shafts or misreading a crosswind, have placed arrows over twenty yards adrift of the mark at just nine-score (180) yards (164.6 meters).

Distances expected to be shot were considerable, particularly those thought feasible for flight arrows. A reward of twenty pence, or a "silver flight" to that value, was offered for anyone making twenty-four-score yards (438.91 meters) of ground; for twenty-two-score yards (402.34 meters) they received twelve pence, and for twenty-score-yards (365.76 meters), eight pence. For purposes of comparison, distances achieved today with contemporary replica heavy draw-weight bows and flight shafts have not yet exceeded twenty-score yards (365.76 meters), suggesting that present longbowmen have literally some way yet to go to reach Tudor standards.

As a matter of record, the sounding of a trumpet or bugle before shooting prevailed for the next three hundred and more years, supplanted by the more prosaic whistle only during the early twentieth century.

So, what of the three arrow styles for which rewards were given. The standard arrow has been the subject of some antiquarian debate because certain references suggest its association with ceremony; but consensus is that it was a well made but largely untouched standard livery shaft such as would have been included in any sheaf provided for a military archer. Today's interpretation, set down some twenty-five years ago, is loosely based upon shafts recovered from the warship *Mary Rose* in 1983 and defines an arrow 31.5 inches (80.01 centimeters) long, preferably of ash, three-eighths of an inch (9.53 millimeters) in diameter, and of parallel profile. It should weigh not less than 52 grams (802 grains) and should have triangular fletchings three-quarters of an inch (19.05 millimeters) high and no less than 6 inches (15.24 centimeters) long. The string groove should be cut into the shaft, with a 2-inch (5.08-centimeter) nockpiece of horn inserted, and it should be armed with a recognized military head. Here we may speculate a little, for no recognizable arrowheads have been recovered from the *Mary Rose* site. It is, however, possible that they were similar to heads recovered from the site of the 1485 Battle of Bosworth Field, where Henry Tudor gained victory to become King Henry VII, suggesting that short, diamond-shaped, armor-piercing points were favored at that time. These arrowheads are known colloquially as Tudor bodkins; examples may be found carved on the Worcester Cathedral tomb of Prince Arthur Tudor.

Sixteenth century contestants were seemingly required to bring their own standard arrows, and this gives rise to some relevant speculation. The Tudor standard arrows so far recovered vary in profile between parallel, bob-tail, barreled, and breasted, and are largely of aspen and ash, with aspen predominating. Was the aspiring competitor allowed free choice of material, profile, and head? Or was there a recognized standard for the "standard" arrow? And did authority inspect each competitor's shafts? Twenty-first-century logic suggests that all shot a similar shaft; statistics from the *Mary Rose* excavations indicate that the most numerous shaft profile recovered was bob-tailed, followed at some distance by parallel. So were all expected to shoot a bob-tailed aspen shaft? Perhaps, even probably. The air is rife with speculation; it is time to tiptoe away.

The bearing arrow also offers something of an enigma. The term has been used and generally understood since the eighteenth century in connection with archery. A bearing arrow, Thomas Roberts tells us, is "an arrow which possesses a steady flight," while a bearing bow is "a bow that casts an arrow well."[5] So far, so good; but is this just an ordinary sheaf or standard arrow that by chance possesses that quality? Or is it an arrow that has in some way been improved? Within a batch of traditionally made arrows there will occasionally be one that, although to all intents and purposes seems identical to its fellows, will, for no apparent reason, fly better and make greater distance than the others. In the postrevival sense this is a bearing arrow; but was that the case in the sixteenth century? Or did "bearing" then have a more specific meaning? Surprisingly, my Middle English dictionary does not include the word, nor does Ascham use it. It may be that the bearing arrow was cut to an archer's particular draw-length with fletchings shortened, and perhaps the point of balance adjusted by the use of a different head. Perhaps it was of a barreled profile instead of the more usual bob-tailed shaft. Speculation, and it gets us nowhere. The distinctive bearing arrow remains a mystery.

The third term, "flight arrow," is understandable today, and we may assume it had similar meaning in the sixteenth century. It is now, and was then, an arrow designed for distance, with one probable difference between then and now: in a contest involving military arrows, it had a military purpose. It certainly would have been lighter in order to fly farther, but prospectively it was armed with a military head, the type of arrow used at the commencement of a field conflict between armies, designed to embarrass the enemy from afar.

We know little or nothing of the construction of English flight arrows. Beyond commenting that sharp, or pointed heads "perch" (cut through) a wind better than blunt ones, Ascham is not explicit about such things. But he does have much to say about weather, particularly about wind and mist. He mentions that once, while shooting at Cambridge on a misty day when the air was "thick," the downwind twelve-score-yard (219.46 meter) mark was overshot by 30 yards (27.43 meters), while when shooting back (one assumes against the wind), the overshoot was "a great deal above four-teen score" (256.03 meters).[6]

Archery generally, and distance shooting in particular, is affected by weather conditions, as Ascham well knew and as we know today; the chance of a Tudor bowman pocketing twenty pence at the sixteenth century flight contest on Finsbury Fields thus rested to a large degree in the lap of Mother Nature.

Although we can learn little from Ascham about the flight shaft per se, we may turn to France and to *L'Art d'Archerie*, a treatise dating from the late fifteenth or early sixteenth century, for information about the French approach to flight shooting. This quite detailed manuscript is the work of an anonymous archer/author whose preface bemoans his inabili-ty to shoot any more, through illness.[7]

He opens his comments on the flight arrow by advising that it should be made of light but stiff wood, and he speci-fies birch *(Betula pubescens)* or cherrywood *(Prunus avium)* as acceptable. He goes on to say that French flight arrows do not perform as well as those made in England, since English wood is lighter and stiffer than any available to French arrow-makers, although he does not specify the wood that is used.

He defines a flight arrow as being slighter (presumably in length and diameter) than any other small feathered arrow. For fletching he recommends primary feathers from a duck or a pigeon. The head might be of horn or metal, the former being lighter than the latter. He suggests the conventional arrangement of three fletches but mentions that some use six feathers and others as many as nine. In all cases they are glued into position. He does not indicate the position of these additional feathers, or, if they are positioned in three groups of three, the size of one group in relation to the other two. It is all rather mysterious, but the use of multiple fletching may be concerned with an attempt at gliding after reaching the apogee of the ballistic curve. Our French author is dismissive of the arrangement, however, observing that this is only for show and worth very little in terms of distance.

The best flight shafts, he tells us, are those conventionally fletched with three feathers, 2 inches (5.08 centimeters) long and sheared close to the shaft. But here we are introduced to the secret world of French flight shooting, for French shafts were of two sorts: the hollow and the solid. The solid shaft is self-explanatory, but the hollow was bored along its length as far as the shaftment and filled either with lead or, in some cases, mercury. This additional weight gave advantage of distance, but because they could not readily be detected, they were considered dishonorable. Thus the author tells us that the solid shaft is "the more honest to shoot." There is an enigmatic reference to the disadvantage of "baking" the wood, which, in the context of translation, may perhaps refer to the overreduction of water content in relation to seasoning of the timber.

Here, then, are the criteria associated with early French flight shooting. Since it is believed from identification of dialect in the original that the manuscript originated from Picardy, an area subject to English influence, it is possible that to some small degree it reflected English practice. It seems unlikely that the use of additional fletchings would have interested English bowmen shooting for distance, but drilling and filling with lead or iron might well have appealed, assuming there was no interference from authority. This is speculation, of course, and we must leave the matter so.

Our French author is informative in other arrow matters, and again we are able to expand our knowledge of fletching practice, for we learn that in France there were two methods of attaching feathers to shafts: with glue, or with molten wax, in the latter case the feathers being secured by silk thread. The wax and thread system was used, we are told, for butt or target shooting but not for flight.

Contemporary French arrow-makers appear to have made a distinction between those feathers used on butt shafts, for which primary feathers were recommended, and those used on target shafts, for which secondary feathers were favored. The distinction perhaps concerned the behavior of the shaft, presumed or otherwise, at varying distances, since butt shooting was conducted at a shorter distance than target shooting. Feathers from a swan or from a gyrfalcon were to be preferred for butt and target purposes. Goose feathers were thought particularly suited to the English battleshaft. The author follows Ascham in advising that if the head is light, then the feathers should be cut low to reduce drag. For both butt and target shooting, aspen wood, a type of poplar, is recommended by Ascham for lightness, preferably seasoned naturally without artificial heat.

Although our French author infers a distinction between arrows to which feathers have been secured by wax and thread and those to which feathers have been glued, it is not apparent whether it was French practice, as it was in England, to also bind the latter. Indeed, the distinction between the individual purpose of glued and waxed arrows is unclear and has perhaps been lost in translation. We are told, however, that "according to the English, every glued and iron headed shaft, whether big or little, is called a sheaf arrow." If this really was so, then it is not helpful in our quest for the "standard" arrow.

We will leave the arrow to itself for now and turn once more to the contests in which it was used. While in England military archery practice was defined by statute, and men over twenty-one were barred from shooting at less than eleven-score yards (201.17 meters), otherwise recorded as 40 x 5.5

yard roods,[8] in France matters were seemingly arranged differently, for *L'Art d'Archerie* introduces us to shooting under the screen, "for it is easier to learn to shoot by shooting under the screen than by any other way."[9]

The screen, which was suspended between two gantry poles, was placed across the shooting range, half-way between the butts, the bottom edge being one foot above the ground for every ten paces there were between the butts. Thus, if the butts were one hundred paces apart, then the screen bottom would be ten feet high. The bottom edge of the screen would have bells fastened to it so that if even the feather of an arrow touched it they would ring. The screen itself was to be of sufficient depth to be fully visible to the archer. The object was to shoot at each butt in turn, the arrow passing beneath the screen. It would have been a challenge to achieve a flat enough trajectory but would have been an excellent way to ensure steady and exact shooting. We are not told the fate of arrows that transgressed the line, but it may be that if in contest, they were forfeited. There is no evidence that shooting under the screen was attempted in medieval England, although an early ballad does speak of "shooting under the line," which may have been a rural equivalent. Here, arrows that missed the target (in this case the rose garland) were forfeit. There is some tentative similarity.

In the early ballad *A Lytell Geste of Robyn Hode*, a verse reads:

> Two yerdes [rods] were up set,
> On every syde a rose garland
> They shot under the lyne,
> Who fayleth of the rose garland,
> His takyll he shall tyne [forfeit or lose].[10]

To what extent this method was practiced in medieval France we have no way of knowing. A club at Doullens in northern France was founded in 1487, while another, at Conde Sainte-Libiaire, also in northern France, is even older, claiming to have been formed in 1302. Archers at Doullens shot at the butts at a distance of 49.21 yards (45 meters), and at Tir a la perche, 38.28 yards (35 meters) high. Those at Conde shot at 54.68-yard (50-meter) butts. Who knows whether members in each of these once practiced shooting beneath the screen to hone their skills?

Whereas Continental archers shot their arrows for pleasure at short-distance butts, or vertically at Tir a la perche, their English equivalents were concerned primarily with distance. The longbow and its battleshaft remained tactical military weapons longer here than elsewhere. The primary purpose of disrupting an advancing enemy over two hundred yards distant by volleys of arrows was far more effective than anything achieved by its ultimate successor, the harquebus or hand gun; and although garden butts had their appeal for some, recreational practice largely reflected military need.

The activities of "roving," which used formal, permanent, long-distance marks such as at Finsbury Fields, and "hoyles," a more casual countryside activity utilizing molehills and other closer natural features as targets, were popular among English archers. Archery per se was encouraged by the Tudor monarchs. Henry VII was fond of shooting, while his elder son and heir to the throne, Arthur, was recognized for his skill with the bow before his untimely death. So expert had he become that, after his passing, a London-based archery society, Prince Arthur's Knights, was formed. Members took the names of Arthurian notables and are believed to have shot on fields at Mile End in East London. Henry VIII shared his father's and brother's enjoyment of archery, and in 1537 granted a charter of incorporation to the Guild or Fraternity of Saint George, and gave it the splendid title of "Fraternitie or Guylde of Artillary of Longbowes, Crosbowes, and Handegonnes."

Although formed as a recreational guild, its primary purpose was for "Better encrease of the defence of this our Realme, and Maynetennce of the Science and Feate of

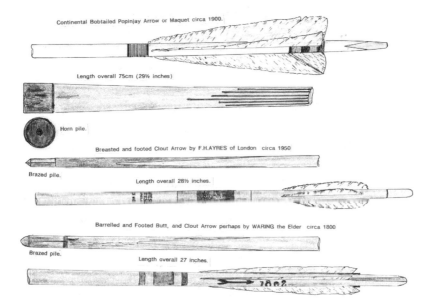

Clout and popinjay arrows. Top, nineteenth century Tir a la perche/Popinjay shaft; center, twentieth century clout shaft; bottom, eighteenth/nineteenth century clout shaft. (*Author*)

Shoting in Longbowes, Crosbowes and Handgonnes at all Marks and Butts and as at the Game of the Popinjaye and other Game or Games as at Fowle or Fowles." It was in effect a society for gentlemen and was intended to develop a knowl edge of weaponry by potential commanders of the nation's forces, within a fraternity of like-minded individuals.[11]

The reference to "Marks and Butts" is understandable, while shooting the "Popinjaye" had some similarity with the Continental practice of Tir a la perche. "Popinjay" is derived from "papageai," the French word for parrot, and was the name given to a medieval version of vertical shooting at a col-ored wooden bird extending from a high pole or tower. It was revived during the late eighteenth century by a London archery society, the Eagle Bowmen, who perched a wooden eagle on a pole some 90 feet (27.43 meters) high to be shot at during Eagle Days.[12]

To the author's knowledge, no examples of medieval English popinjay arrows survive, although it is known that they were headed with blunts of horn or perhaps wood, since the object was to dislodge the "bird" rather than to pierce it; and for another reason, too: for what goes up must come down, and a falling arrow, unless it was blunt-headed, could easily have transfixed either a shooter or a bystander. This form of shooting was not widely practiced in England. In Scotland, however, its survival has been assured by the Ancient Society of Kilwinning Archers, who claim to have first shot the "Papingo" (their interpretation of the word "papageai") in the year 1485. This society continues to this day.

French archers of the nineteenth century used a specially made arrow while engaged in Tir a la perche, and it is possible that this is identical with, or derives from, those in use during medieval times. An example in the author's possession is 29.5 inches (74.93 centimeters) long and bob-tailed in profile, tapering from one-quarter inch at the self-horn string notch to three-quarters of an inch at the foot. The head is circular and of horn, three-quarters of an inch in diameter and length. The shaft is self, possibly beechwood, and is striated 5 inches (12.7 centimeters) from the foot for 12 inches (30.48 centimeters). The three fletchings are conventionally triangular, three-quarters of an inch in height, and 4.5 inches (11.43 centimeters) long. The cock feather is grey, the shaft feathers white, perhaps goose. The shaftment has blue silk thread as decoration below the fletches, and red silk thread above.

Members of the Fraternity of Saint George were permitted to take fowl or fowls, and it would be interesting to know what type of arrowhead was used for this. Hunting venison and other game was also regularly practiced, and two distinct types of arrowheads are known to have been used: conventional triangular broadheads conforming to London Museum Type 14 and 15 (Jessop's Type H3, and H4), and forkers, or crescent broadheads, London Museum Type 6 (Jessop's H1 and H2). Each was used for game. Crescent broadheads are said to have been preferred by poachers since the heads did not remain in the animal. A case concerning a local poacher heard at Marlborough, at the Wiltshire Court's Quarter Sessions on October 2, 1628, is explicit:

> Uppon Sundaie last was a month, between three and ffower of the Clocke in the morninge, Edward Phills, and William Butler came and called at the Widow Emett's house in Melkshame to drincke. Phills had a crossbow and a broad forked headed arrow and a bolt, and the feathers [tips] of the forker were red as though stained with blood.

Although horn blunts (also known as bird bolts) are known to have been used to kill by impact while not damaging the flesh, some knowledgeable archers suggest that crescent broadheads were also used for that purpose, the belief being that the crescent head also killed by impact while bundling the feathers together and thus not damaging the flesh, proved by recent practical experiment.

The crescent head is said by Edward Gibbon to have been used to sever the heads of running ostriches to amuse Roman crowds in the Colosseum.[13] Modern experiment using the head of a (dead) goose shows this to be possible, but for accuracy only from a known distance, since as with all arrows, the fletchings impart spin to the shaft and thus to the head.[14] The suggestion, made by Sir Arthur Conan Doyle in his otherwise excellent fictional account of the White Company of archers, that the forker, or crescent broadhead, could be used to sever mooring ropes on ships may be taken with a large pinch of (sea) salt, although again, modern experiment has shown that if shot from a very carefully measured and precise distance to allow for the natural spin of the shaft, it is possible for a sharp-forked arrowhead to cut into a taut rope.[15]

In the next chapter we will note the demise of military archery and consider the emergence of the true recreational arrow, untrammelled by military needs.

SIGNIFICANT CHANGES

ALTHOUGH THE WAR BOW AND ITS BATTLESHAFT WERE obsolescent by the beginning of the seventeenth century, as we shall see there was considerable continuing interest in the weapons.

During the preceding century, much acrimonious debate had taken place between died-in-the-wool advocates of the "handgonne," such as the cumbersome harquebus, requiring a support, who were influenced by Continental practice, and those whose experience with archery convinced them that the combination of bow and arrow was still viable, albeit in a diminished role. These latter were dismissed contemptuously by the "modernists" as "King Harry Captains," intimating that supporters of the longbow were living in the past. The culmination of one debate, if the vituperate exchanges may be so described, had the proponent of the handgun offering to stand "fully harnessed" (in full armor) for an archer to shoot at him, stating that if he were hurt as a consequence, he would bear the cost of subsequent treatment himself. It is to the credit of his antagonist that the offer was rejected.[1]

Matters simmered on until, in 1625, archer William Neade petitioned King Charles I to allow the arming of companies of pikemen with a combination of both bow and arrow and pike, the separate weapons being coupled together to form, as Neade explained, a "Double Armed Man." Charles was sufficiently impressed by Neade's claims to allow the arrangement, although Neade admitted that having equipped "that Worthy Societie in the Artillery Garden of London [the Honourable Artillery Company] for the Practice of the Bow with the Pike, because many of that worthy Society have not heretofore exercised shooting, it doth not take that perfection yet."[2]

That the system may in fact have been used by at least one local militia, or "trained band," is suggested by a report of an event during the English Civil War when, in August 1642, at the town of Hertford, one Captain Ankle, a commander of the Earl of Bedford's forces, had occasion to pay an official visit. "Upon his arrival at the entry to the town stood the whole Traine Band in a full body placed in warlike equipage. He was escorted to the Court of Guards where he was demanded of the [pass] word, which was 'Prevention': having given it them, he was by them conducted to the second watch, being a Company of Pikes with Bowes and Arrowes: they conducted him to the Captain."[3]

That the battleshaft was still a valid weapon, in the mind if not in reality, is illustrated by an entry in the publication produced by the Parliamentarians, *Mercurius Civicus* (The City Mercury), in September 1643:

> From Oxford the last certain intelligence is to the effect that they, [the King's men] have set up a newe Magazine without [outside] Morgate, onlye for Bowes and Arrowes which they intend to make use of against our horse, which they heare (to their greate griefe) doe much increase; and that all the Bowyers, Fletchers and Arrowhead makers that they can possibly get they imploy and set to worke there for that purpose. It is therefore necessary that no arrow heads be suffered to go from London, or into any parts where the Cavaliers may by any means come to atchieve or surprise them. And it were to be wished that the like provision were

made by the Parliament here to get some Bowes and Arrowes (or at least some for their Pikemen).[4]

How accurate the report was no one can tell; it may have resulted from some clever frightening tactic employed by the Cavaliers, or perhaps been an endeavor to instill general wariness in the army. Although nothing seems to have happened prior to September 1643, in November that year the Earl of Essex issued instructions for the raising of a company of archers for the service of the king. Whether this company was ever formed or, if it was, whether it was used to any effect is unclear. But as a result of external pressure, or of its own volition, in April 1644, the City of London's Court of Common Council authorized the creation and arming of six regiments of the city's auxiliaries, partially equipping them with bows and arrows.

For all the posturing, it was left to the Scots to make the last use of the bow in warfare when, in 1644, at the Battle of Tippermuir, an army led equally by the Royalists James Grahame, Marquis of Montrose, and Alastair MacColla, confronted troops of the Scottish Presbyterian Covenanters outside the city of Perth. Montrose was an archer and knew the power and use of the bow in battle. Accordingly, he placed his bowmen on the flanks to deal with a cavalry attack, his own Atholl and Badenoch Highlanders to the right flank, and those led by Lord Kilmont on the left. The center was composed of the Irish commanded by MacColla.

As it happened, however, events moved rather faster than Montrose had anticipated. It was customary in contemporary pitched battles between field armies for there to be successive exchanges of fire, followed by slow advance and push of pike, with cavalry charges intervening. But this was not how MacColla and the Irish were used to fighting. After an initial discharge of muskets, the whole center charged forward as one man, yelling their fearsome Gaelic battle cries and falling en masse upon those luckless Covenanters who had not turned and fled. The result was a massacre, with the Highland bowmen having little opportunity to use their weapons.[5]

Although the bow and arrow continued in use during Scottish interclan battles until late in the century, Tippermuir is considered to be the last set-piece engagement in which arrows were deployed; so when, in 1662, the bow and arrow were omitted from the statutory list of weaponry, we have arrived at the beginning of true recreational archery and the emergence of the truly recreational arrow.

We are fortunate to possess an account of the process by which these arrows were made in the seventeenth century. It is recorded in the gallimaufry of heraldic information and loosely associated facts assembled in his *Academy of Armory* by Randle Holme III of Chester (1627–1700), an antiquary concerned with heraldry, with explanation where it is thought appropriate.

The account includes a summary of the "severall parts of an Arrow." These are given as the "Shaft"—the wooden part of the arrow. The "Horne." The "Nock slit, or nick where the string goes in." The "Feathers, which sometimes are pieced if they are broken." The "Cock feather which is the highest feather which stands contrary [at right angles] to the nock." The "Footing is the piecing or the setting [splicing] of one part into another." The "Head or pile head, is the iron or steel socket put on the end of the shaft."

Elsewhere he introduces us to the process by which the seventeenth century arrow was fashioned, commencing with the "Staff," the product of first cleaving of the timber, to make the shaft:

> Pointing of it out is the first cutting of it round with a knife out of the rough.
> Ripping it is to give it the first rounding.
> Shaving it is to round with a hollow shave.
> Smooth it is to polish the same smooth with a Fish-skin [forerunner of sandpaper].
> Sliting it. Putting the horn for the nick.

A Crose-slit making the 'nick' of the arrow.
Fitting the head. Cutting the end [shoulder cone] to put on the Pill [pile] head.
Heading the Arrow is gluing it on.

Then came the fletching of the shaft:

Drawing the feathers. Cutting or stripping the feathers of the Quills.
Pareing the feather is to cut the backs to make them lie close.
Ribbing is cutting the side-skirts away [of the rachis].
Cutting them of a length is to cut them to their shapes and breadths.
Pressing the feathers, putting them in a wet cloth to keep them even and straight.
Polishing or Glazing or Varnishing the arrow with glue is to rub it over as far as the feathers with glue before they are set on.
Feathering the Arrow is to glue on the feathers.
Pareing or Cutting them down is cutting the Feathers even and all of a length and breadth.
Poising the arrows is to know whether the pair of Arrows be of an equal weight as they are of a length.
Turning them is to give them a Twerle in one's hand to know whether they be straight.

Holme mentions seven supposed arrow-maker's tools that appear in heraldry. First is the flote [float] "an iron instrument with teeth on the lower side and an iron handle on the top." It was said to be used for rough working of the wood, although in the form illustrated it appears identical with a bowyer's tool of the same name that may be seen within the arms of the Worshipful Company of Bowyers.

Second is a "piercer," a "kind of square head bit, set in a bush and is to be used in a brace (as joyyners use their brace and bit)." It is unclear to the author just how this tool could have been used in arrow making. An accompanying illustration suggests a device for drilling stringing horns for bows.

Third is a "polisher," which is "to set a gloss and brightness upon their work." Once again the illustration seems to show a tool used not by fletchers but by traditional bowyers for boning their finished work

Fourth is a "Framing or slitting saw," a slender saw set within an iron frame with a removable handle. With this the horn slit and the string groove are made.

Fifth and sixth are small, half-round planes, one termed a ripper, used to "make the rough work somewhat fashionable," the other a hollow shave to complete the rounding of the shaft.

Seventh and last is a "graver," a long, smooth, iron file with a handle far more suited to preparing shafts than is a clumsy float.[6]

There is no indication of profiling in the processes, and thus the result would have been a parallel shaft. However, it would seem that arrows were customarily produced in pairs, matched for weight and length.

Holme was based in Chester, southwest of Manchester, and one assumes that his description of processes relates to local makers.

To learn something of the stock-in-trade carried by working fletchers in the seventeenth century, we may turn to their wills. An example that may be typical is Richard Hollister, a fletcher from Bristol who died in July 1625 and at his departure had:

> Item. "iiij [four] sheafe of halfe peny ware at viij d [eight pence]."
> Item. "a sheafe of ordenary ware unheaded."
> Item. "iij [three] sheafe at viij d [eight pence] per sheafe."
> Item. "more, one sheafe of the Better sorte ij s [two shillings]."
> Item. "more of preased [pieced] shaftes over-drawen or Rowe wroughte [rough worked] xii [twelve] sheafe at viii d [eight pence] per sheafe."
> Item. "ij [two] sheafe of cross bow garre unfeathered."

[The term garre is interesting. In context it may just mean gear, a colloquial term for equipment, or it may be a relic word from earlier times since gar is an Anglo-Saxon word for a dart.]
Item. "xij [twelve] sheafe of Rowe Aspe [rough aspen or poplar] undrawen at ij d [two pence] per sheafe." (Undrawen being the basic unworked timber staff.)

Also among fletcher Hollister's stock were:

Item. "xxij [twenty-two] dyssen [dozen] of Rowe timber for to macke Bowing stickes at ij d [two pence] ye dyssen."
Item. "viij [eight] dyssen of Bowes at ij s [two shillings] per dyssen."
Item. "ij [two] grosse of Bowe stringes."
Item. "ij [two] pounds of waxe."[7]

Although there was a traditional distinction between bowyer and fletcher, it is not unusual to find a blurring of the demarcation, less so in England perhaps than in Scotland. The bows and bowing sticks recorded, together with the bowstrings and wax, were doubtless made for the process of felting of wool, which was carried out to some considerable extent within the area. Richard Hollister may also have made strings for crossbows and even longbows. Stringing, as with fletching, was a comparatively sedentary operation and perhaps more suited to a fletcher than a bowyer. Certainly in London, the Worshipful Company of Fletchers retains the existing archives of the Ancient Company of Bowstringmakers (latterly the longbowstringmakers), suggesting a fraternal link at one stage.

In Scotland, as has already been noted, bowyers (or, as they were then called, bowers) habitually made arrows as well. Just two lone arrow-makers are recorded as Edinburgh burgesses during the sixteenth century and none before or after. Richart Walker, described as an "Inglishman" and, one assumes, a bona fide fletcher, was permitted to remain in Edinburgh for the purpose of teaching his art. At his death in 1582, his then-apprentice arrow-maker, Robert Spence, was admitted as burgess on January 30, 1583.[8]

A Scottish contemporary of fletcher Hollister's was bower Donald Baine, who died in November 1635. In his workshop, among other paraphernalia, were three hundred bows, both "made and unmade," and an unspecified number of arrows, also "made and unmade." At least one bow-maker, George Tait of Perth, who died in 1575, appears to have specialized in children's tackle, for among the items remaining unsold, plus a number sold but not paid for, that he left were two dozen children's bows, priced at forty shillings, and six arrows for children of the Lord of Innernethy, for which he was owed six shillings.[9]

Although in theory the war bow still had half a century before its obsolescence, as the sixteenth century drew to a close, recreational archery was becoming increasingly popular, and the first of the true recreational archery societies began to make their appearance. Finsbury and Mile End fields were, with others in London, dotted with permanent marks. Those at Finsbury were formalized in booklets during the latter years of the sixteenth century, although it was not until 1601 that the first truly definitive list of marks was set down. The *Ayme for Finsburie Archers* was published for "the ease of the skilful, and behoofe [on behalf] of the yong beginners in the famous exercise of Archerie." Names of all marks were given together with distances. Shooting advice was also included: "you must shoot 'long ayme' because this is set down by measure of the line," meaning that the distances now recorded were accurate and not approximate as some marks had habitually been. A set of eight simple rules was appended, prime among them being, "First for the finding of your marke, it must be within every man's reach. Also the precise naming of your marke preventeth much cavil [argument]."[10] Updated booklets were issued as the years passed, and it is notable that additional rules appear. One, in 1628, dealt with what must have been a regular occurrence: "if your arrow breaks you may measure at the nearest piece that hath wood and head, or wood and feather."[11]

Rules were created, it was said, not only for observance, but to offer solutions to difficult situations "whereby often arise controversies and discord and at times grow rash and undignified oaths, to the derogation of God's glory."[12] To what extent rash and undignified oaths were thus diminished we do not know, but subsequently oaths attracted fines, which proved useful additions to a society's bank balance.

The seventeenth century was notable for the creation of three important archery societies: the Society of Finsbury Archers, the Royal Company of Archers, and the Society of Archers at Scorton, in Yorkshire.

Although the Finsbury Fields were habitually used, and a loose association of those shooting there may have already existed, the Society of Finsbury Archers is first formally noted in 1652 when two stewards were elected to make arrangements for their shooting during the year. The Society of Archers at Scorton was a gathering of gentlemen archers formed in 1673, and it was followed three years later by the Royal Company of Archers, a body of Scotsmen, many of whom had retired from distinguished military careers.[13]

This last body was awarded the privilege of acting as the sovereign's ceremonial bodyguard during royal visits to Scotland, upon payment by the company, when requested, of a *reddendo*, or tribute, of "a pair" of arrows (traditionally three). This carefully guarded privilege was secured by the company under a charter from Queen Anne in 1704. Nominally, the *reddendo*, of barbed silver arrows, was required every year, although in practice it has been sought only occasionally.

The awarding of silver arrows as prizes was a feature of archery in the seventeenth century. In 1670, members of the Society of Finsbury Archers were presented with two, each 11 ounces and 5 pennyweights, by their stewards, Sir Reginald

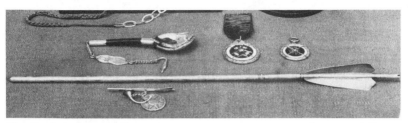

The "Antient Scorton Silver Arrow," with horn spoon award and medallions. (*Society of Archers at Scorton*)

Foster, Baronet, and Warwick Ledgingham Esq. One of these was subsequently lost, a replacement of 12 ounces and 5 pennyweights being provided by Mr. Ellis, a steward, in 1672.[14]

The Society of Archers at Scorton, the oldest continuous English sporting society, was formed in 1673 to shoot annually for the "Antient Scorton Silver Arrow," an event that (wars permitting) has taken place every year since then. There are a number of conundrums associated with this venerable institution, not the least being the origin of the Silver Arrow.[15] It consists of two pieces joined by a ferrule, one piece being slightly older than the other. It was provided by a founder member to whom it was given on the understanding that its origin should never be disclosed. Predictably, stories have grown around it, each more fanciful than the last.

The second mystery concerns the society's rules. These are remarkably similar to those of the Society of Finsbury Archers, and it has been suggested that they derive from that source. There is a problem here, however, since the Scorton rules predate those of Finsbury, drawn up in 1687 and presented to that society by Sir William Wood, its captain general. Herein lies the enigma. Is it likely that an obscure Yorkshire club should provide a London society of age and prestige with its rules? Or is it possible that the Scorton rules are derived from some earlier Finsbury rules replaced by Wood. If this is so, how did the Scorton gentlemen come by them? It is at least arguable that they came with a remnant of the Silver Arrow. So, did the Scorton arrow originate at

Finsbury? Might it have been the arrow lost between 1670 and 1672, or a part of it suitably mended? The presenter was named Wastell, and Wastell is a name familiar to the Honourable Artillery Company, which was closely associated with the Finsbury Archers. The matter must rest there.[16]

We move now to Scotland, where more silver arrows await us. Principal among these is the Musselburgh Arrow, an ancient artifact whose age and origin is unknown. However, the medals that are attached indicate that it has been contested since 1603. It is the oldest of the Royal Company of Archers' trophies and is shot for annually. It is of normal arrow length and may at some time have been gilded. The representative feathers are short and triangular and are described as butt fletches. The earliest extant rules of shooting date from 1709, and include the prescription for "a competent space of at least Thirty Ells square, round every Mark that the Spectators may not sustain Prejudice, nor the Archers Arrows broken." In 1726, it was necessary to add some teeth to this rule: "and, if any Person is found within that space he shall be fined Four Pounds Scots." The distance shot is 180 yards, the same as that for the younger (1709) Edinburgh Arrow.[17]

Let us return to the seventeenth century, and to an important bow meeting held in 1663 on Finsbury Fields under the auspices of the City of London and its aldermen, to commemorate the restoration of the monarchy. The whole occasion was designed to demonstrate the city's loyal acceptance of the royal prerogative of King Charles II. The choice of a bow meeting was particularly apt, since Charles was known to enjoy archery, having indulged in the activity while in exile on the Continent.

The event, recorded as "The Ancient Honour of the Famous City of London Restored and Recovered," followed earlier convention for such displays, with archery, wrestling, and backsword and dagger fighting.[18] It is of particular interest to us since it is in the records of this meeting that we first find the term "Pound Arrow." Thus, the pound arrow, the broad arrow, and the flight arrow were each shot for distance.

So, what was the "Pound Arrow"? Did it replace either the earlier standard arrow or the bearing arrow, neither of which are by now in evidence? The short answer is that we do not know. We can speculate, but that is all. However, there are three possibilities for its name: that it weighed one pound, either avoirdupois or Troy; that it weighed the equivalent of twenty shillings (one pound sterling) against silver coin; or that one pound sterling was the reward for maximum distance achieved when it was shot. Let us examine each of these possibilities.

A Finsbury archer as appearing on the left side of an entry ticket to a seventeenth century Finsbury shooting event. The stave in his hand may be a measuring pole. (*Author*)

To create an arrow weighing one pound would be both difficult and pointless, besides putting the bow at risk if it were to be shot. However, the English are strangely attracted to the odd and unusual, and the possibility cannot be ruled out. What is perhaps more likely is the second notion, that it was an arrow weighing the equivalent of twenty silver shillings (one pound sterling). The author possesses an arrow marked 9*6, which means it was weighed at nine shillings and sixpence, measured against silver coin, and this broadly equates to fifty-six grams. Against silver coin, a "pound" arrow would therefore weigh the equivalent of four ounces, or a quarter of a pound, which would be heavy, but manageable. For comparison, the military arrow shot by members of today's English War Bow Society weighs four ounces.

Finally, there is the award given for success. Monetary awards were customarily offered at such gatherings, and in 1521, for shooting the standard arrow the longest distance the award was one pound. There is, therefore, some reason why the term "pound arrow" might have been used in this context. But was the pound arrow an alternative, later name for the standard arrow? And if so, what was the broad arrow? The matter remains unresolved.

Let us leave speculation and return to fact. Although at this 1663 bow meeting the distances achieved by those shooting pound and broad arrows are not recorded, that for the winner of the flight arrow contest is given, and we are told that a Mr. Girlington achieved twenty-two-score yards (402.34 meters), a distance measured personally and, one assumes accurately, by Mr. Smee, master of the game. This is a considerable distance, exceeding the maximum legitimate distance of nineteen-score yards (347.47 meters) available to those who shot the marks on Finsbury Fields. For this, Girlington received ten shillings. It is interesting to note that a century and a half before, in 1521, for achieving this distance he would have qualified for just one shilling.

Earlier in this chapter we briefly discussed the use of archery in warfare and its decline. A little-known feature of military archery was the fire arrow. A number of the special heads are extant, and the modus was not confined to the United Kingdom or indeed Europe. However, unlike the neat aesthetic appearance of Eastern equivalents, the European versions were crude and workmanlike in appearance, consisting of a strip of metal, at one end of which was a broad head and at the other a socket to fit a shaft. An example, recovered originally from a house in Lincoln and putatively associated with the Civil War, is at Alnwick Castle. It is described as "an iron shaft 10 1/2 inches long of which 5 1/2 inches is occupied by a mass of combustible material wrapped in canvas and with a hole at the fore-end evidently there to receive a fuse. It is armed with a light broadhead, and at the distal end terminates in a socket."

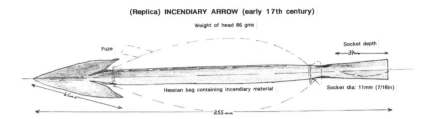

Reconstruction of a seventeenth century incendiary arrow. Note outline of bag (with fuse) containing inflammable material. (*Author*)

Although the combustible element of a fire arrow was essentially gunpowder, saltpeter, and sulfur, it was seemingly necessary to improve this concoction by adding other ingredients. Thus, small parts of rosin, in crystal form, turpentine, linseed oil, verdigris, bole armeniac (an earthy material from Armenia) sea salt (from the Bay of Biscay), and colofonia (a resin formed from distilling turpentine and water) were included, doubtless adding to pyrotechnic advantage. Those eager to know more about the subject are referred to *The Complete Soldier*, a booklet published by Thomas Smith in 1628.[19]

We will conclude by mentioning another booklet, also published in 1628, that similarly intended to influence military progress. The anonymous author, identified only as H. L. and described as "a true patriot," is evidently aware of the combination of bow and pike advocated in the same year by William Neade, and he approves of it.[20]

Although the thrust of his argument points to the disadvantages of the "corslet," or light armor worn at the time, he does eventually concentrate on the fire arrow, opening by suggesting that children might "make their sport with them," a suggestion at which concerned authority may have looked askance.

Warming to his subject, he then suggests that "if at festival times, a Bull, instead of bayting him with dogges were tyed at stake . . . conveniently placed upon a Common or other spacious place; men might make triall with their fire-shafts, a brave and man-like sport where happily the madding of the enraged beast, besides inuring men to conflict would teach some profitable stratagem for warre." Those who quite properly are appalled by this suggestion should recognize that bull baiting was a fashionable occupation for gentlemen and others, even into the early nineteenth century.

H. L. concludes his discourse by explaining how to make and shoot his fire shaft; in the belief that it may be of interest, I give it here verbatim:

> Let the Fire-shafts have one end feathered and shaped after the manner of an ordinary arrow, and the other end fitted with a pipe of latten [a metallic substance], ten inches long or more, at discretion, a bearded [barbed] head of iron fast glued into it with a socket of wood, and a touch hole made close by it, with some little reverse [perhaps a type of back facing barb is intended] to stop the arrow from piercing so deepe into a man's cloaths, the flanques of a horse, or other marke of easie passage as to choake the fire. The shaft may be made fast within the pipe (if men so please) with hard waxe; which melting as the pipe groweth hote, will make it very difficult to draw the arrow from where it [a]lights.
>
> The pipe must be filled with this mixture, bruised very smal and hard ram'd in. Gunpowder and salt-peeter a like proportion, and brimstone [sulfur] half so much, with some small quantity of camphir (if men please) to make it operate more strongly when the mark is wet. If the mixture burne too quicke, add brimstone; if too slowe, adde powder.

The touch hole was stopped up by candlewick cotton, soaked in vinegar and finely ground gunpowder, and left to dry. Once this was completed, H. L. gave instructions to shoot: "Take the Bowe with a match well lighted, into your left hand, then hold the Arrow ready nocked in the Bowe. Lastly give [set] fire, return your match and deliver the Arrow."

I discussed this concept with those knowledgeable about gunpowder confined in small spaces, and the consensus was that when the fuse touched the gunpowder, it would explode, not only setting fire to its immediate surroundings but blowing a large hole where it landed. The result of discharging such a lethal device at a tethered bull may be readily imagined.

Let us leave our patriotic pyrophile to his bovine pleasures, for it is time now to move on.

ROYAL PATRONAGE

The seventeenth century saw the disappearance of archery as a tactical military arm and its emergence as a true recreational activity.

Whereas King James I confirmed the validity of practicing with the bow and arrow through his Book of Sports, it was his grandson, King Charles II, who actively encouraged it. He was a competent archer, with skills developed while he was in exile on the Continent, and his presence at bow meetings attracted a prodigious number of gentlemen archers who demonstrated their various abilities before him. On conclusion of the shooting, those who took part were permitted to kiss the king's hand. One supposes that this was a major attraction, since after Charles's death in 1685, interest in archery and bow meetings declined significantly.

The huge assemblies of bowmen meeting in Hyde Park and elsewhere now ceased. However, principal among the archery groups that survived were the City of London Society of Finsbury Archers and the Royal Company of Archers in Scotland. Distance shooting at marks on Finsbury Fields was a prominent activity of the day, and flight arrows would have been the choice. Although portable targets may have been erected on occasion, butts and butt shafts seem not to have been in use, becoming a permanent feature of shooting only when, in the eighteenth century, responsibilities for the fields and the marks were assumed by the Honourable Artillery Company.

The Finsbury society seems to have developed a wish for short-distance shooting, and in 1738, it received permission from the Honourable Artillery Company to erect a pair of butts at a distance of fifty yards.[1] No reason is given for this unusually short distance: it does not correspond with anything shot competitively, but was perhaps used to refine technique. The pair of butts was duly formed, however, at the northern end of the fields, and a glance at the associated plan of marks extant in 1736 shows them in position, separated by a piece of ground marked "Bogg," evidently not an area the company prized for its own activities. A second pair is also marked on the plan at the extreme northern end, 130 yards apart, a distance that would have been rather more of a challenge.

Butt and target shooting called for heavier shafts than those favored for roving and distance shooting, and, as we shall later note, this form of arrow was to become the norm.

Although arrow making was a flourishing trade during the seventeenth century, fueled by the burst of archery activity initiated through Charles II's obvious interest, by the beginning of the eighteenth century it was once more in the doldrums, and fletchers were in short supply. James Oxley, in his history of the fletchers company, reports that at the end of the seventeenth and commencement of the eighteenth centuries there had been a sharp decline in membership of livery companies generally, and the Worshipful Company of Fletchers, reasonably buoyant during Charles's patronage of the bow and arrow, was no exception. The society's official history suggests that by the end of the seventeenth century, most if not all members had given up arrow making in favor of other work.[2]

That may be so, and there is little doubt that the call for arrows was not great; however, there is documentation that as late as 1758, an apprentice fletcher, young Uriah Streater, was taken on by William Jefferies, a liveryman of the Worshipful Company, and there is no evidence that he was to be taught anything other than arrow making.

Streater was duly indentured to "William Jefferies, Citizen and Fletcher of London to learn his art." The extract from Streater's binding terms and conditions are an interesting reflection of ancient practice and provide an insight into social mores of the time. He was instructed thus:

> . . . He shall not waste the Goods of his Master nor lend them unlawfully to any. He shall not commit fornication, nor contract matrimony within the said term [seven years]. He shall not play at Cards, Dice, Tables or any other unlawful Games whereby his Master shall have any loss. He shall not haunt Taverns or Playhouses nor absent himself from the said Master's Service, day or Night unlawfully. But in all Things as a faithful Apprentice shall behave himself towards his said Master and all his, during the said Term. And the said Master in consideration of one penny [a nominal sum] being the money given with the said Apprentice, his said Apprentice, in the same Art and Mystery which he useth, by the best means that he can, shall teach and instruct, or cause to be taught or Instructed, finding to his said Apprentice Meat, Drink, Apparel, Lodging and all other Necessities according to the Costom of London during the said Term. . . . .

The document was duly signed and sealed, and we must assume that young Uriah ultimately became a knowledgeable fletcher. (It is of incidental interest to see on this document that as late as the reign of George II, in 1758, British monarchs are still shown as rulers of France.)[3]

Although fletcher William Jefferies appears to be an exception, the principle of separate businesses for bows and arrows, established 400 years earlier, seems now to have virtually ceased. Certainly before the century ended, English bowyers were making arrows as a matter of course; while in Scotland this had largely been the arrangement from early times.

Eighteenth-century Scottish bowers and arrow-makers who became burgesses included Bartholomew Pritchard in 1703, and the M'Lean family of George, John, and Thomas later in the century. Those making archery material often did so as a profitable addition to their normal business. Thus David Seton and Daniell Wilson, both of Edinburgh, who were in operation in 1710 and 1712 respectively, were both gun stockers and bowers. Doyen of all Scottish bow and arrow-makers was Thomas Grant, who after completion of his apprenticeship to Robert Jack in 1727, plied his trade until the turn of the century.

As has been noted, arrows as well as bows were habitually made by the few English bowyers who survived during the eighteenth century. The Kelsall family of Manchester was said to be the best in the country, with Samuel Stanway of Northwich, near Chester, and Joseph Wrigley, also of Manchester, being recommended. Thomas Waring the Elder began his bow and arrow business in 1785, and carried it forward until his death in 1806.

An interesting, and so far unresolved question, concerns the manufacture of arrowheads. At some point they ceased to be forged and became brazed. Scottish practice as well as English tradition points to lorimers, who made the metal parts of harnesses, as one of several craftsmen who, for a while, made arrowheads, since their apprentices were required to be able to produce them as part of their training. A member of the Worshipful Company of Lorimers to whom the author has spoken confirmed this. The change from forging to brazing was radical, because at some time during the century, if not earlier, the brazed pile, consisting of a metal point called a "stopping," around which a thin metal sheaf was brazed, came to be the standard arrowhead.[4]

These brazed piles were initially bespoke to the shaft, which was completed first. It was not until the nineteenth century was well advanced that cone lengths and diameters were standardized. A typical dimension for these heads was 1 inch (2.54 centimeters) long and five-sixteenths of an inch (7.94 millimeters) in diameter. Profiles were both cone and parallel.

A pair of eighteenth-century Scottish arrows, believed to have provenance to a member of the Royal Company of Archers, is in the author's possession, and it is apposite to note them now. They are self shafts, each 27 inches (68.58 centimeters) long (which is appropriate for the period) and three-eighths of an inch (9.53 millimeters) in diameter. They are of a dense but so far unidentified wood, and each weighs 740.75 grains (48 grams). Each nock is self, and each is protected by a horn sliver 2 inches (5.08 centimeters) long.

Fletchings are of goose, 4.5 inches (11.43 centimeters) long by three-tenths of an inch (7.62 millimeters) deep, and low triangular in profile. The cock, or leading feather, is grey and placed conventionally at right angles to the string groove, while the shaft feathers are white. They are positioned 1.25 inches (3.17 centimeters) below the string groove. Heads are parallel in profile, of turned brass, and 1 inch (2.54 centimeters) long, terminating in a slight point. Their precise intended purpose is unknown; they would seem unduly heavy for distance shafts and may have been intended for shorter distance butt shooting.

Their provenance, and perhaps their purpose, is suggested by markings on the shaft. The letters "S F" near the fletchings are believed to be the initials of Simon Fraser, writer to the Signet, who was elected to membership of the Royal Company of Archers in 1770. However, fainter initials "H F" are also present, and these may be of a relative, Hugh Fraser, elected in 1749. Accepting this provenance, it is possible that these arrows date from the mid-eighteenth century, and might thus be presumed representative of the style used by

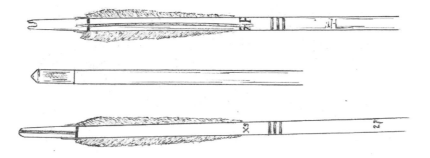

Details of mid to late eighteenth century Scottish arrows in the author's collection. Note the early turned brass head. (Author)

members of the Royal Company of Archers at that time, although a turned brass pile would appear to be unusual.

Other markings appear on each shaft, and interpretation of these offers something of a challenge. The figure "27" is believed to refer to the arrow's length, since it measures 27 inches (68.58 centimeters), while "xs" may be the symbol for ten shillings, the weight against silver coin. These marks would suggest that the practice of weighing and measuring completed arrows by English fletchers mentioned by Randle Holme and noted in the preceding chapter was also practiced in Scotland, and, moreover, that the result was marked on the shaft. The figure "25" is also marked on each shaft, but its meaning is obscure. It is possible this referred to the distance most suited to its shooting, twenty-five yards. We will later see that marking distance on arrows was accepted practice.

Principal among early eighteenth-century English archery societies was the Society of Finsbury Archers, formed in the preceding century. In 1671, its two stewards for that year had designed a target to be shot at by those archers who "most usually shoot at eleven score Pricks or Rovers."[5] This is known to have consisted of concentric colored circles and may represent the first example of that style of target shooting. Eleven score, or 220 yards (201.17 meters) was the statutory distance shot by military archers for practice, and it is interesting that this was the distance the Finsbury archers habitually shot annually until their cessation.[6] The reason for the demise of the Society of Finsbury Archers is not recorded, to the author's knowledge. However, a combination of lack of shooting grounds due to encroachment, and a lessening of interest in archery as a social activity undoubtedly contributed. The last recorded organized meeting appears to have been in 1761, although some individuals may have continued for a while.

The arrangements for shooting at this new target were simple: "All Archers that are pleased to shoot are to Shoot two Rounds [two arrows each Round] at that Standing of Eleven Scores, And then to stand in Ten yards and shoot two Rounds forwards at every Ten yards until they come to Eight score Yards of the Targett, and there to stand shooting Round according to their several Lotts until the Prizes be gotten."

Although we cannot be certain, the arrows used for a 220-yard (201.17-meter) target may have been flight shafts; if so, they were perhaps breasted and a good deal lighter than the weighty Scottish arrows mentioned earlier. However, none are known to the author from this period, so character cannot be confirmed, nor can any maker be identified.

A minor mystery is how there came to be a reduction in length from the 31.5-inch (80-centimeter) military arrow to the 27-inch (68.58-centimeter) recreational arrow now seemingly shot. It can only be assumed that this change took place in the preceding century, and it suggests a change in shooting style involving a shorter draw length. Since most recreational shooting was at distance and no military purpose was served, it would have been sensible to use a lighter shaft. But an interesting question emerges: were military flight arrows, intended to gall and harass rather than kill, usually much lighter and perhaps shorter than the armor-piercing battleshaft? A small number of shorter arrow shafts, 27.5 and 28 inches (69.85 and 71.12 centimeters) long, were recovered from the warship *Mary Rose*, but this number seems relatively insufficient for any real tactical purpose. The matter is enigmatic, and the question remains unanswered.

Although butt, rovers, and target shooting were now socially acceptable to the leisured classes, and a small number of archers kept the practice going through the early and middle years of the eighteenth century, it was not until later in the century that archery became a truly desirable activity. It is generally accepted that the impetus for this burgeoning interest sprang from Prince George, the Prince of Wales (later King George IV), and there is no doubt that his patronage was a significant attraction to those seeking advancement up the social ladder. A claim to have rubbed shoulders with His Royal Highness may well have opened doors hitherto firmly shut. Of those eighteenth century societies that blossomed under his wing, the Royal Kentish Bowmen was among the more prominent. The society was formed in 1786, and its meeting place on Dartford Heath was a model of regally sponsored, organized social archery. Facilities originally consisted of a tent and two rooms in a cottage adjacent to the shooting grounds, which was quite adequate for the original small but select group. Under the benevolent eye of the Prince Regent, the facilities developed into a lodge with adjacent buildings, suitable for the now increased membership, set within a spacious lawn on which were full sets of butts, the whole bordered by a winding terrace.

Notwithstanding the vitality of the society under royal patronage, at least one member yearned for its simpler beginnings. Due to the Napoleonic Wars, the society ceased to exist, and at that time the Reverend William Dodd, its self-styled bard, mourned those earlier times when, after a day's shooting, the original twelve members and a few select guests gathered:

> When the diversions of the day were closed, and all were seated beneath the lowly roof of their simple cottage, around a narrow board and at a plain repast; happy man, said each one to himself, happy moments are ye, while gai-

ety, good humour and rational conviviality prevail. Cribbed and confined as the parties were in their little room yet those were the truly quiet meetings—so pure was the congeniality of the whole that, (to borrow a phrase from the terrific revolution which in a few years after broke out) harmonic merriment became the un-interrupted order of the day; the original small circle of Kentish Bowmen cottoned [harmonized] and combined together by mutual ties of honest freedom and uncontrolled pleasantry.[7]

Those who today mourn the simplicity of their youthful archery will identify with his sentiments. The society was disbanded in 1802.

It is from the notes to Dodd's *Ballads of Archery, Sonnets, Etc.* that we learn a little of the eighteenth century arrow. He tells us that for flight, or distance, shooting, arrows were lighter and longer than those used for butt shooting. He tells us also that "upon every Archer's arrow, just below the feathers, should be painted, not broader than an inch, his Mark, generally the colour of some riband, which each Archer chooses for his colour."[8]

Dodd neatly summarizes his fellow Kentish Bowmen's dress in his ballad "The May Target":

> A feather'd crest, with lightsome play above, his bonnet graces;
> Below, the buskin's [trousers'] neat array, his well-shaped leg embraces.
> Gold buttons on a grass green vest, arranged along the border,
> With cypher'd characters impressed, aptly denote his order.
> Down the right side his arrows see, couched in a belted sling,
> The shafts with marks clear painted, three, good stiff goose feathers wing.[9]

Three major societies contemporary with the Royal Kentish Bowmen survived the Napoleonic era. They were the

Medallion presented by the Royal Kentish Bowman to "the Hon'ble Harry Fitzroy Steward of the Royal Kentish Bowmen" on the occasion of the "Second Grand Annual Meeting of the Archers of Great Britain held on Blackheath 24 May 1790." (*Author*)

London-based Toxophilite Society, formed in 1781 from the rump of the quiescent Finsbury Archers and soon to be raised to royal status through princely patronage; the Loyal British Bowmen of North Wales, formed in 1787, whose elevation was even quicker when they became the Royal British Bowmen; and the Woodmen of Arden, at Meriden, Warwickshire, begun in 1785 under the distinguished guidance of the Earl of Aylesford.

Although the Royal British Bowmen originated at Acton Court, home of Sir Foster and Lady Cunliffe in North Wales, exactly how the society started is a little obscure. But the verses of a ballad composed and sung by a Mr. Hayman, one of the society's self-acclaimed bards, in 1819 (the year the society was re-formed after the Napoleonic Wars), suggests a beginning:

> In tracing the Society, I find it first began,
> like paradise of old, with a woman and a man.
> And contented they did go.

The woman, a "Lady fair," was influenced by a mysterious gentleman:

> He spoke to her of shafts and darts, and numerous stories told
> Of colours "white" and "black" and "red." And then he talked of Gold.
> And a-tempting he did go.

Going into nearby Wrexham, he bought two target bosses and fixed a card on each of them as a mark.

> He then displayed an attitude, well aimed his arrow flew;
> and to her Ladyship's delight he pierc'd the target through.
> And to counting he did go.

The lady (clearly Lady Cunliffe) seemed suitably impressed and wished to take up the activity herself. She attempted to persuade an initially reluctant Sir Foster to join her:

> "Pooh, childish nonsense! No, not I. I'll play with no such toys.
> Such implements are only fit for little girls and boys."
> And a grumbling he did go.

She persevered, however, and,

> His Lady she ne'er heeded this. She made him take a bow,
> and how he has excell'd with it you most of you do know.
> When a shooting he did go.

After this mysterious gentleman had tempted Lady Cunliffe to shoot, and she had later persuaded her reluctant husband to take part, friends were invited to join them at Acton Court. From such beginnings, we are told, was the society formed.[10]

Importantly, perhaps because of its genesis through the persuasive tongue of a woman, it attracted women to its ranks, and they claimed membership on equal terms with their menfolk, taking their turn at the targets. The identity of the mysterious gentleman whose persuasive tongue brought the society into being is not recorded, but there is a clue; for just one year after its formation, the founder member of the Toxophilites, Sir Ashton Lever, was honored by the society, and it is possible his enthusiasm for the bow and arrow was the catalyst.

The Royal British Bowmen survived until 1880, when, after it had mourned the sad death of the son and heir of its patron by drowning, the society ceased to exist.

A feature of the late eighteenth-century societies was their initial size. Of those that exist today, the Toxophilite Society began with fourteen members, of whom at least two were from the rump of the defunct Society of Finsbury Archers, while in 1785, just nine gentlemen formed the Woodmen of Arden. The original composition of the Royal Company of Archers of Scotland is not entirely clear, but eight members of Scottish nobility, and gentlemen, created the original council, supported by a treasurer and clerk. Happily, each society thrives to this day.

We have earlier noted the practice of offering silver arrows for competition in those far off days. These were occasionally purchased by individuals as awards. An example is in the keeping of the author and dates from 1796. A Mr. Perrott, a member of what was then the Toxophilite Society, had it made and presented to his society for competition. The inscription informs us that it was won by a fellow member, a Mr. Shepheard, on August 26, 1796, although for what particular archery expertise is not recorded. The arrow, of London hallmarked silver, is 27.5 inches (69.85 centimeters) long, with silver fletchings 3.5 inches (8.89 centimeters) long and in the low triangular eighteenth-century style. It weighs 10.5 ounces (297.67 grams) and lacks a head.

Pursuit of archery as a pastime for gentlemen inevitably attracted the attention of knowledgeable individuals who occupied themselves by drawing attention to its origins. One such scribe was the Honourable Daines Barrington, a judge and early member of the Toxophilites who contributed an essay to the journal *Archaeologia* in 1785. Although this is largely an understandably biased account of "bowman battles," it does include a comment or two of relevance to our subject. He mentions that "the archers consider an arrow of an ounce weight to be the best for flight or hitting the mark at considerable distance, and that aspen [poplar] is the best material of which they can be made"—an interesting comment and contrary to perceived wisdom in more modern times.

The honourable gentleman continues by mentioning a traditional North Country tale of distance shooting in which an attorney in Wigan is said to have taken just three shots to cover a mile. However, he adds that "he placed himself in a very particular attitude, which cannot be commonly used in this exercise. He is supposed to have sat on a stool, the middle of his bow being fastened to one of his feet, to have elevated to forty-five degrees and drawn the string of a strong bow with both his hands."

This attitude is very similar to the current one in which foot bows are used in distance shooting competitions; our attorney was clearly well ahead of his time.

Assuming the account to be accurate, each arrow flight would have averaged almost 587 yards, a significant distance. The account says nothing of the power of the bow nor of the arrow used, and we can only speculate as to its weight and size. Commenting upon arrow length, Barrington wrote, "A strong man of this size [six feet tall] in the present times cannot easily draw above two inches if the bow is of a proper strength to do execution at a considerable distance." Apparently no such problem faced the Wigan attorney: to gain advantage from the potential of his bow, he may well

Archers at target practice during the eighteenth century. The figure in the foreground is thought to be Sir Ashton Lever, founder of the Toxophilite Society, later the Royal Toxophilite Society. (*Author*)

have used a full 31-inch (78.74-centimeter) shaft. But that is speculation.[11]

We now consider another eighteenth-century writer, Walter Michael Moseley, and what he has to say about the arrow and its uses.

Moseley's essay of 1792 followed much the same path as that of his predecessor; however, from him we learn a little more of the innovative portable target then in use. He tells us that although permanent butts were exclusively of earth and turf, portable butts of straw were then "more in fashion." These were circular, of straw, and little different from the targets in use today. They were about 4.5 feet (1.37 meters) in diameter, and thus twice the length of the 27-inch (68.58-centimeter) arrow in use at that time. The five concentric circles familiar to traditional archers today were marked on cloth, with each circle a fifth of the arrow length wide.

Colors were not then standardized, that refinement was to come later, but the inner circle was covered in either gold or silver leaf, the next circle being red. We are told that each ring could also be subdivided, rather as the international target is subdivided today.

Moseley is also explicit about the straw butt used for short-distance shooting by the Royal Company of Archers in Edinburgh, at the cusp of the eighteenth/nineteenth centuries. This butt was constructed in a different way with straw laid endwise, tightly packed, and cut flat. A permanent fixture, it was protected from weather by a small building.[12]

Arrows used against this butt were armed with bullet-shaped horn heads, known colloquially as "crow's bills" and fashioned after the style of continental shafts also used at short-distance butts. Three modern examples in the author's collection, each self and of *Pinus silvestris*, fashioned by the late master arrow-maker Richard Galloway, replicate this arrow type and the style of head in use.

The lightest, at 310 grains (20.09 grams), is of parallel profile, 0.31 inch (8 millimeters) in diameter, and 26 inches (66.04 centimeters) long, with a self-nock protected by a horn nockpiece. The head is of dark horn, delicately made, and finely pointed.

A second is of similar profile, weighs 425 grains (27.54 grams), and is 27 inches (68.58 centimeters) long, but 0.35 inch (9 millimeters) in diameter, with full nock in light horn and a rather blunter bullet point in dark horn.

The third is altogether more substantial and weighs 550 grains (35.64 grams). It is slightly bob-tailed in profile; from 0.35 inch (9 millimeters) below the fletchings it increases progressively to 0.39 inch (1 centimeter) at the head. It is 26 inches (66.04 centimeters) long, has a full nock in light horn, and terminates in a head of light horn 2 inches (5.08 centimeters) long.

In earlier chapters, we have noted the wish to experiment, albeit on occasion with fatal results. The wish for innovation runs deep and true among archery enthusiasts and Moseley himself succumbed to amiable curiosity.

He explains in his book that the thought had struck him that a gun might be shot remotely by connecting it to a target. Fired with enthusiasm for the venture, he set out to prove his theory, noting as he did that he was not alone in the belief, since he understood "that there are Targets somewhat on the same plan used in Surr[e]y."

Through the center of the target he fixed a tube, within which ran a piece of wood that protruded from the tube, with a card on its end for him to aim at. Behind the target a bracket, holding a lead weight, was supported upon another piece of wood in line with the tube. From the weight ran a line to the trigger of the gun. The gun, fixed behind the target, was then primed and cocked, and all was ready. When Moseley retired thirty paces and shot his arrow at the card, it pushed the wood through the tube, dislodging the wood supporting the bracket; the weight fell, and the trigger was pulled.

Moseley does not say if the gun contained shot. One hopes sincerely that it did not, since the whole arrangement is redolent of danger for any innocent passerby, and it is hoped that with his curiosity now satisfied, Moseley resumed his normal archery practice.[13]

For our part we will now pass to more pressing matters, for chapter 11 will touch upon the Napoleonic era and its effect on the archery idyll.

BUTTS, ROODS, AND WOODMEN

BECAUSE THE LATTER YEARS OF THE EIGHTEENTH CENTURY and the early years of the nineteenth were occupied with the threat of Napoleonic menace, gentlemen of military age who had hitherto gathered to enjoy the pleasures of archery were now occupied with graver matters, and the membership of many societies suffered as a result.

It was a time for roistering patriotic sentiment, and since many of the young gentlemen in the archery societies enjoyed singing, it was inevitable that their songs reflected the popular mood. At its annual ball circa 1798, the provincial Robin Hood Society of Gloucestershire introduced a melody called "The Zodiac," whose verses by "a member" were clear about the national feeling. It was sung to music composed by Hayman Florio and concerned with "Apollo, the god of the bow" as he moves across the sky. The verses of Leo and Aries are relevant to our theme:

> Of the stern British LEO, his Rays scorched the Mane,
> and he bade him be true to John Bull,

"Who's afraid" growled he, rousing, and lay down
again,
"whilst my archers have quivers brimful."
The shaggy old ARIES too treated with scorn,
the insolent foes of the State,
He shook his rough Forehead and swore by his Horn,
their ramparts should yield to his pate.[1]

Sadly, with the need to replace rhetoric with regiment, and with membership depleted by the call to arms, this society lasted no longer than 1802.

As with its contemporaries, the Robin Hood Society of Gloucestershire felt the need for silver arrows as awards, and due to the meticulous housekeeping of its secretary, we know when and where these were purchased and also the cost. They were acquired during May 1796, in London, from Stephen Ivycross of No. 8 Newcastle Street, said to be "near the new church in the Strand." The cost for three was three guineas, or three pounds three shillings.

Three field days were held annually at which shooting took place at 100 yards (91.44 meters). What records we have do not tell us how many arrows were shot, but we know that competition took place from 1 to 3 p.m. A silver arrow was awarded to the captain of the target, ordinarily he who had made the most hits. A gold medal, also obtained from Ivycross, was awarded annually to the captain of numbers: he who had gained the highest score over the three field days.

A certain cavalier attitude toward tradesmen is apparent in the society's dealings. Ivycross submitted an invoice for five guineas for the gold medal, this presumably being his legitimate costs. The society was having none of this rampant inflation, however: five pounds was the sum that had been allocated for the medal, and five pounds was what Ivycross was paid. There is no evidence suggesting that he demurred.

Although the Robin Hood Society failed, Napoleon seems not to have been the direct cause. A reluctance by its members to pay their annual fees appears to have been the rock on which it foundered. On May 5, 1802, a stiff letter was sent by the secretary to each member, pointing out that there was "a considerable debt owing to Mr. John Wallington, of Hunters Hall for the entertainment of the ROBIN HOOD SOCIETY in consequence of Subscriptions not having been regularly paid and to beg that arrears be remitted to me."[2]

This seems not to have had much effect, and the society was duly wound up, those members who remained being offered membership in another society at nearby Kingscote. This society, which one assumes was archery related, is something of a mystery, and its existence and purpose remain to be explored.

Many societies fell by the way, but not all were affected by the national crisis. The Woodmen of Arden continued to hold their annual meetings, and it is with one of these, held in 1802, that we are now concerned, since the winning shafts are in the possession of the author.

One of the principal contests between Woodmen is for their Silver Arrow. This is a magnificent object, weighing 1 pound, 3.5 ounces (552.8 grams). It is 27 inches (68.58 centimeters) long and was presented to the company by the Countess of Aylesford in 1788.[3] It is hotly contested and always shot for at nine-score yards (164.59 meters), each Woodman using what were termed a "pair" of arrows. In 1802, it was won by William Palmer, elected a Woodman in 1786, just a year after the society was formed. The pair of arrows with which he achieved his success are each 27 inches (68.58 centimeters) long, three-eighths of an inch (9.53 millimeters) in diameter, possibly of beechwood, and with two-point footings in a darker wood. Heads are one and one-eighth inches (28.57 millimeters) long, straight, and brazed around a point, or stopping, as was conventional in that period. The self nocks, with 2-inch (5.08-centimeter) protective nockpieces, are three-sixteenths of an inch (4.76 millimeters) wide and one-quarter inch (8.35 millimeters) deep. Helically placed fletches, of grey goose, are 4 inches (10.16 centimeters)

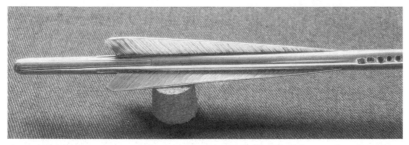

An eighteenth century silver arrow award for excellence in shooting.
(*Author*)

long, and in profile are a shape known as long low triangular.
Weights are identical at 340 grains.

Palmer recorded his win by inscribing the year, 1802, on
each arrow, enabling precise dating. It is, therefore, quite likely they are representative of those in use during the late eighteenth century. No maker's mark is visible, but the Thompson
family of Meriden are known to have been bow- and arrow-
makers to the Woodmen since their formation, and these are
perhaps early examples of their work.

Although records clearly show Palmer to have secured the
Silver Arrow for 1802,[4] there is something of an anomaly.
Fellow Woodman William Gresley is known to have won the
Silver Arrow in 1821, and he likewise recorded the year in
black ink on his arrows, which are also in the author's possession. Strangely, however, both pairs have identical cresting of
blue and gold bands. Palmer and Gresley, therefore, appear to
have shot with arrows identified with the same cresting, and
to which of them this belonged is thus something of a mystery. Like Palmer, Gresley was elected a Woodman in 1786.

Although similar in certain respects, the 1821 shafts are
better finished and suggest either an advance in skill or perhaps a change of Thompson in the workshop. Still 27 inches
(68.58 centimeters) long and of two-point footed beechwood
or similar, they are five-sixteenths of an inch (7.94 millimeters) in diameter and slightly breasted. Their heads are brazed,
straight, and seven-eighths of an inch (0.87 millimeters) long.

Fletches are similar in profile and origin to those of the 1802 pair, but are not helically placed. The nocks are self horn, 2 inches (5.08 centimeters) long. Each arrow weighs 320 grains.

While arrows had been marked with their weights against silver coinage for a century and perhaps more, there was an alternative method of marking that for a while was favored by the Woodmen. This involved writing on the shaft the distance for which it was deemed most suited. Distances then shot were defined in roods, of which there were two competing measurements: 7.5 yards (6.86 meters) and 5.5 yards (5.03 meters). The first, which for convenience we will call the northern rood, was used by the Woodmen. The shorter distance we will call the southern rood.

Distances shot were in multiples of thirty yards, and the shafts were marked accordingly. Thus, at 7.5 yards per rood, "12" would indicate a butt or target distance of 90 yards (82.3 meters), and "16" would be 120 yards (109.73 meters), each a butt or target distance. The author has examples of each in his extensive collection. However, the association of a particular arrow with a specific distance appears to have been arbitrary, based solely on its ability to fly true and to reach the mark. A comparison of three arrows, each dating from the turn of the eighteenth to nineteenth centuries and each marked "12" and thus considered suited to 90 yards, provides the following data:

> Arrow one: weight 375 grains, 26.75 inches (67.94 centimeters) long, self shaft of parallel profile, head 1 inch (2.54 centimeters) blunt tapered.
> Arrow two: weight 310 grains, 26.75 inches (67.94 centimeters) long, self shaft of parallel profile, head 1 inch (2.54 centimeters) sharp tapered.
> Arrow three: weight 365 grains, 27 inches (68.58 centimeters) long, footed shaft (two point) of parallel profile, head 1 inch (2.54 centimeters) parallel.

Clearly there is some variation, particularly in the weights. It may be that each belonged to, and was found suitable by, a different archer with his own distinctive shooting technique.

A weighing balance used by eighteenth and early nineteenth century fletchers to weigh arrows against silver coinage. (*Author*)

Another arrow, marked "16" and thus thought suited to 120 yards, is 27 inches (68.58 centimeters) long, also of parallel profile, footed (two point), and weighs 340 grains.

Penciled notes by Thomas Roberts in his personal copy of *The English Bowman* give a recommended scale of those arrow weights, compared against silver coin, which were generally considered appropriate to distance shooting at the roving marks. Thus, with a self yew bow, for twelve-score yards (109.73 meters), he suggests a three and sixpenny arrow, adding 6d (pence) in weight for every score yards less than that. For 11 score, a four shilling arrow was considered appropriate. Confusingly, for a backed bow of ruby wood and fustic, arrows weighing three and six were recommended for distances between 14 score and 9 score; arrows from six shillings to six and six pence for 9 score to 7 score; and from seven shillings to seven and sixpence for 6 score.[5]

A comparative table of coinage to grain weights may be found in the notes to this chapter. However, to place the weights mentioned above in context, 375 and 365 grains broadly equate to four and threepence in silver, 340 grains to four shillings in silver, and 310 grains to three and ninepence in silver. Finally, to complicate matters, it should be remembered that, subsequent to 1816, the grain scale changed, from 7.74 grains to one penny down to 7.27 grains to one penny.

Should all have now become clear, we will muddy the water yet again, for in *The Book of Archery* (1841), G. A. Hansard recorded the following arrow weights used by archers in Cheshire and Lancashire while shooting at butts:

> At four roods (30 yards, 27.43 meters): five and sixpence.
> At eight roods (60 yards, 54.86 meters): four and sixpence.
> At twelve roods (90 yards, 82.3 meters): three and sixpence.
> At sixteen roods (120 yards, 109.73 meters): three and sixpence.[6]

A peculiarity of Lancashire archers, we are told, was to use two sets of arrows, one set fletched with feathers from the right wing and the other set fletched with left-wing feathers. This practice was known as double pairing, the principle being that the appropriate pair was used when a crosswind blew. One imagines that this dubious practice existed more in the perception than in reality. However, this concept was much discussed by modern archers and coaches in the 1970s on the principle that an arrow would fly better if it revolved into the direction of the side wind. The author is not aware of any experiment that proved or disproved this theory.

A late eighteenth century archery meeting on Blackheath, London, thought to be the Royal Kentish Bowmen. Note the portable target and also the gentlemen's Society uniforms. (*Author*)

Where butts were shot, the targets were known as "papers." These were often round white cards of a size appropriate to the shooting distance. This meant that at four roods, the paper was four inches (10.16 centimeters) in diameter, at eight roods it was eight inches (21.32 centimeters), and as appropriate for twelve and sixteen roods. The Toxophilite Society, however, added a circle in blue around the perimeter of its cards, thus adding two inches (5.08 centimeters) to each diameter, and this feature may have been adopted by other societies.

The Woodmen of Arden shot at the butt and the clout, however, their butt was set at one-hundred yards (91.44 meters), which was neither a northern nor a southern rood distance. This distance had been adopted by the Toxophilite Society (which could now call itself Royal) at the suggestion of its patron, the Prince Regent, one of several made by him and, not surprisingly, quickly adopted by other societies.

When engaged at either butt or clout, Woodmen shot in pairs called butties, a practice hallowed by time, loosing two arrows apiece. We learn from a note, "Casting of Arrows," by

Thomas Roberts that the selection of butties, or who would shoot with whom, was achieved in a rather strange manner. A distinguished member, having taken one arrow from each of the competitors, would stand foursquare and toss them in a loose bundle over his shoulder in the general direction of a mark fixed in the grass. With all the gravitas and deliberation of a fifteenth-century shaman, he then paired as butties those archers in turn whose arrows he deemed to have landed nearest the mark. Naturally, his word was law.

For those interested in the mechanics of clout shooting, rings are marked around the clout at one-and-a-half feet (0.46 meters), three feet (0.91 meters), and six, nine, and twelve feet (1.83, 2.74, and 3.66 meters). The circles are called, respectively, a foot, a half-bow, a bow, a bow-and-a-half, and two bows. Scores are 6 for a hit in the clout, and then progressively through the rings from 5 to 1. An arrow landing adjacent to but not touching the clout is called a thumb. A civilized practice among the Woodmen was to place a decanter of port behind each clout, there, it is said, to reward the winner for his achievement and to inspire the loser to greater effort.

In this form of archery, the distance shot is considerable, and it was, and is, customary for a marker to be engaged to signal the landing place of an arrow, which might not be obvious from a distance. This he does while standing some ten yards away from the side of the clout by displaying a white flag in various positions. A hit on the clout is identified by the marker falling on his back and waving arms and legs in the air rather like an upturned turtle.

Arrows by their nature are dangerous things, of course, and on two memorable occasions, the Woodmen's marker was struck. The first time was in 1889, and by all accounts the sturdy fellow withdrew the arrow from his thigh, wiped off the blood and, stiffening his sinews, signaled a "wide," the very personification of a dutiful servant. Following this event, from 1890, the marker was provided with a pavise, or large protective shield, behind which he might be sheltered until the arrow landed, when he would emerge in order to indicate its whereabouts.[7]

The second time a marker was struck occurred in the late 1900s. On this occasion, he was persuaded to go to the hospital, although he was back on the field within the hour.

To make arrows more visible when in the air, they were occasionally colored dark brown, an arrangement designed to assist the shooter rather than the marker, although the latter may have had reason to appreciate the practice.

It has long been customary to associate the arrow mystically with death; Robert Louis Stevenson's classic tale *The Black Arrow* exemplifies this.[8] At least one English traditional archer has gone to his grave with a black arrow placed on his coffin, and others will surely follow, for the tradition is deep seated.

It is appropriate here to mention that most meaningful of ceremonies, the black *reddendo*. It is said that in olden times when a noble archer went to his Maker, on his coffin was placed one of three black arrows. This went to his grave with him. The remaining two were carried, crossed in saltire with their heads pointing down, by the chief mourner in procession. As the deceased was laid in the earth, these two arrows joined the first. It is also said that the arrows had no string grooves, an acknowledgment that he would not shoot again.[9]

An unusual association of the arrow with death may be found within the little English church at Wreay in Cumbria, where finely carved arrows on the chuch door are thought to commemorate the memory of a military friend of the founder who was killed by an arrow in 1842 while serving in Afghanistan.[10]

A feature of certain early nineteenth-century arrow-makers, notably Thomas Waring the Younger, was the striated shaft. Striations, or shallow parallel grooves, were cut longitudinally into each shaft from the foot for a little over half its length. These were added at the request of customers who believed they helped counter casting, or warping, although Waring is said to have been unconvinced. Striation appears to have been a regular feature of Continental shafts. Examples of arrows for butt and Tir a la perche shooting are each regularly grooved. A modern maker of metal arrows briefly reintroduced striated shafts as offering better flight, but they were quietly dropped after a short time.

Since not all arrow-makers added their names to their products, we do not know the manufacturers of many of the earlier shafts. Although those Woodmen's arrows previously described are likely to have been made on site in the bowyer's workshop at Meriden by whichever of the Thompson family worked there at the time, later examples bearing the name Muir were also made by a member of the Thompson family. This information we have on the authority of James Duff, doyen of North American bow-makers, who tells us that nineteenth-century arrows bearing the name Muir were in fact made by one Dick Thompson, who for sixty years was in Peter Muir's employ.[11]

It would seem from examining a number of late eighteenth- and early nineteenth-century arrows that the manufacture and fitting of heads was peculiar to the maker, since the variations are many. The method was first to create, nock, and fletch the shaft before deciding upon the length and shape of head, the foot being prepared allowing a shoulder for ease when drawing the arrow from the target. A thin sheet of ferrous metal was then cut to fit exactly around the foot of the arrow, and a solid point, or stopping, was positioned within it. The metal sheet and stopping were removed, and the edge of the sheet brazed. The head was then glued into position, and the arrow was complete. The author has been told by an old arrow-maker that he could make a head by this means more speedily than a brass tube could be drilled.

The parallel profile appears to have been favored by those making early heads, the majority perhaps with blunt points

Examples of the progression of the use of horn in nocks (string grooves) from the strengthening insert of the *Mary Rose* replica battleshaft, far left, to the full horn nock of the nineteenth century, far right, still used by traditional recreational archers. (*Author*)

suited to striking straw or earth. Although superseded by turned piles as the century advanced, the brazed head still had many adherents, since when striking a hard object it would split, thus often avoiding damage to the shaft itself, unlike the stronger metal pile, which very often caused the shaft to break upon impact.

Other subtle changes occurred as arrow-makers gained experience. A regular feature of the earlier battleshaft, the self nock, with strengthening horn nockpiece, continued through the seventeenth and eighteenth centuries until it was replaced, first by the half nock, a wider, tapered sliver of horn, between wooden "ears," and finally by the full horn nock, replacing wood entirely with horn, an arrangement that remained in vogue for the rest of the century and even into the next, as we shall later note.

While the practice of footing (piecing) shafts was evidently not universal in the eighteenth and early nineteenth centuries, of those that were footed, two points are believed to have been standard. Examples of footed arrows in the author's possession are carefully executed using wood either similar to or identical with that of the shaft. The footings themselves are 4 inches (10.16 centimeters) long. Footing with a harder or heavier wood was considered undesirable since, unlike present belief, it was thought that this would both unbalance the arrow and, by being significantly stiffer than the rest of the shaft, affect its flight. The prime purpose of footing was to allow a broken arrow to be repaired. Thomas Roberts, in *The English Bowman*,[12] draws attention to the matter when he comments upon the "force of arrows": "A lance-wood arrow of 6s in weight shot at a nine score Mark struck the ground which was much hardened by a drought, and a splinter was driven into the ground with such violence as to require considerable force to extract it."

He continues by questioning the "force" of the arrow, which he decides lies with a combination of velocity and weight, "affording the true criterion." He notes lime tree and deal as "medium wood" and lighter than aspen and lancewood. It is interesting that even in those early days, Prussian deal (alternatively Russian redwood) was said to be the best kind of deal. Roberts describes it as "that wood of which the Turks and English make the most of their ships," adding that an old mast makes excellent arrow wood. Interestingly, in modern times, many types of old wood such as bedsteads, floorboards, and church pews have been utilized for arrows.

From Roberts we learn a little of the wood that eighteenth-century fletchers chose for their arrow shafts. He lists six kinds commonly used, four light: deal, asp, "arbele," and poplar (this last brought in from Flanders), and two heavy: lime and Jamaican lancewood. The Flemish poplar staves were seemingly cut from that part of the tree facing east, it being considered the driest. Arrows from such wood were said to have an excellent reputation.

Roberts claims that both yellow and red deal make very good arrows, although the wood is inclined to splinter. Aspen and arbele are similar in appearance, although the former is stiffer. Lime is a particularly heavy wood, but if too dry it will be brittle. Lancewood is favored for roving and other distance shooting.

In his personal copy of *The English Bowman*, Roberts made a number of penciled notes, and since these reflect late eighteenth century thought concerning the arrow, many are worth examining.

We are told that arrows rubbed in linseed oil, when properly dried with a waxed cloth, will acquire a fine polish and be waterproofed. Additionally, the oil will prevent moth damage to the feather. Arrow wood should be very dry when worked, for if there is sap present, it is liable to warp, or cast. All arrow woods should be baked three or four times in a slack oven (one with a low heat) prior to use. Emphasizing this, Roberts draws attention to a comment by Thomas Waring the Elder that a quantity of ash wood lying dry and exposed to the sun for nine years had still not lost its moisture, and when used warped greatly.

A bowyer/fletcher named Anderson apparently told Roberts that he cut his wood in winter and dried it over an oven. He also mentioned that dry wood that was cut and laid in a heap of fresh dung became "very tough," an interesting concept that may not have been too regularly practiced.

Commenting about fletches, Roberts notes that goose feathers when put on the shaftment were brushed lightly with gum water (gum arabic diluted by a little turpentine). This improved their stiffness and rendered them impervious to moisture without altering their effectiveness.

In the matter of profiles, Roberts's book mentions a preference for breasted shafts by his contemporaries who shot at clout or for distance. However, his penciled note seems to contradict this, since he writes that "arrows tapering from the nock to the pile will not fly far when cast from a wooden bow. With a horn [composite] bow they seem to be the only arrows used, except for the Chase, or in War." He goes on to say that a "taper shaped arrow," by which we may assume he means a bob-tailed profile, needs more elevation than does a breasted arrow, as the weightier end, along with the larger and thus heavier head, makes for a sharper ballistic curve. He considers, however, that a breasted arrow, although it has a propensity to drift, "floats better" and requires less elevation, observations made two centuries before; and since that time the use of such arrows for distance shooting has continued, and is still common practice.

Although barreled and breasted shafts were available and shot during the archery revival of the late eighteenth century, among the limited number of early shafts that the author knows of, profiles vary only between parallel and bob-tailed.

Individual identification of arrows was of obvious importance, and club and society members were exhorted to mark theirs in some suitable way. Originally this merely involved the member's name, inscribed with black ink, although members of the Woodmen of Arden appear to have adopted individual cresting by symbol or color from the outset. Each Woodman's crest is recorded on a roll of vellum, an irreplaceable record from its beginnings and therefore kept by the society under lock and key.

Archery, and in particular the flight of an arrow, has regularly exercised the minds of those concerned with related matters. It is not surprising, therefore, to find a contribution to arrow ballistics from an eminent gunnery officer.

An eighteenth century treatise by Benjamin Robins, *The New Principles of Gunnery*, speculates on the flight of a crooked arrow, that is, one that does not spin true when checked by twirling. In the belief that the more esoterically inclined of my readers will find his conclusions of some interest, I draw this chapter to a close with Robins's considered opinions:

> If a bent arrow, with its wings [fletchings] not placed in
> some degree in a spiral position [i.e., not helically fletched]
> so as to make it revolve around its axis as it flies through

the air, were shot at a mark with a true direction it would constantly deviate from it, in consequence of being pressed to one side by the convex part opposing the air obliquely.

Let us now suppose this deflection in a flight of an hundred yards to be equal to ten yards. Now, if the same bent arrow were made to revolve around its axis once every two yards of its flight, its greatest deviation would take place when it had proceeded only one yard, or made half a revolution; since at the end of the next revolution it would again return to the same direction it had at first; the convex side of the arrow having been once in opposite positions. In this manner it would proceed during the whole course of its flight, constantly returning to the true path at the end of every two yards; and when it reached the mark, the greatest deflection to either side that could happen, would be equal to what it makes in proceeding one yard, equal to a 1/100 part of the former, or 3.6 inches, a very small deflection when compared with the former one.[13]

The author has no wish to spoil the enjoyment of the cognoscenti who seek (in theory or in practice) to test this gentleman's statement, but would remark (before moving to the next chapter) that when an arrow is shot, its fletchings will always cause it to revolve, even when positioned parallel to the shaft, such being the nature of the feather.

THE ROYAL PREROGATIVE

BECAUSE ARCHERY WAS A LARGELY MALE PRESERVE, ITS revival as a recreational activity suffered a setback during the Napoleonic Wars. However, the continued practical interest of the Prince Regent was a stimulant to those societies that had weathered the storm. As we shall see, his attention to target colors, scoring, and distances shot were to be of lasting consequence.

For the arrow, the nineteenth century was a time of change. Tradition had hitherto decreed its length for target shooting to be 27 inches (68.58 centimeters). Why this should be is something of a mystery, although the reason may be related to its purpose. Thomas Roberts tells us that archers of the late eighteenth and early nineteenth centuries considered that when the bow was 5 feet 8 inches (172.72 centimeters) long, the normal height of a man in those far-off days, then the best length for an arrow if used at "less than roving distances" was 27 inches, including the pile, although he does not give a reason.

He adds that for roving and for shooting at "great lengths," it was customary to use 28-, 29-, and even 30-inch (71.12-, 73.66-, and 76.2-centimeter) arrows. For "when the bow is much elevated the archer finds the range and power of his drawing arm much increased."[1] The matter evidently related to style and technique. Examination of etchings of archers of the period shooting at target or butt seem to show the head thrust forward (a modern coach would call that "loading the head"), the shoulder rounded, and the bow arm slightly bent. One gets the impression that a more upright stance would have enabled use of a longer arrow. One has to wonder which influenced which. Did men shoot round-shouldered because they had to in order to accommodate the length of arrow decreed to be correct, or was the arrow length decided by the round-shouldered style of shooting?

As noted earlier, war arrows recovered from the warship *Mary Rose* vary in length, and we learn from that exponent of the bow and arrow, Sir John Smythe, that in his time, it was the practice of archers to choose their first sheaf of arrows and to cut those shorter that they found too long for their use.[2]

Whatever the reason, it appears that at some time, perhaps after 1830, arrow lengths changed and 28 inches (71.12 centimeters) became the standard length. The year is approximate since it is notoriously difficult to date an arrow, it being possible only if there is specific provenance or, unusually, a date inscribed. However, fortuitously, several arrows in the author's collection are marked with a year, prospectively that in which they won awards. Two are marked 1821 and, as previously noted, record success by owner William Gresley at the Woodmen of Arden's Silver Arrow contest of that year. Each arrow is of breasted profile, footed, and with a full, light horn nock, heads are parallel, and each arrow is 27 inches long. An inscribed year is not necessarily that of an arrow's manufacture, but it provides a guide.

Two sets, each of four arrows, made by Robert Braggs of High Holborn, London, are also dated. One set is inscribed "G.H. 1836" in black ink, the other "G.H. 1837." The arrows are all 28 inches (71.12 centimeters) long, of parallel profile, and with the mark 4*9 on them, indicating they weigh four shillings and ninepence against silver coinage. Nocks are full and of black horn. Heads taper to a point and are of a type then known as best sharp. There is no apparent reason for the dating, although 1837 was the year of Queen Victoria's accession to the throne.

If this is indicative of anything at all it is that the change in length occurred sometime between 1821 and 1837. However, we can perhaps be more precise. On August 6, 1830, Henry Ogle of South Saxon Archers won an award, and to commemorate the event he marked the winning arrow with the day and year. This prize arrow is an exceptionally fine barreled self shaft, with tapered sharp pile, and a self nock in buffalo horn, and it measures 28 inches 71.12 centimeters), as does another of his of similar date. If these arrows are representative of the period, this appears to confirm the change of length as some time in the 1820s.

Although there is no maker's name, one shaft is striated in the manner of Thomas Waring the Younger, and each may be from his workshop. It is from Waring that we learn the reason for, if not the date of, the introduction of a longer arrow. He was responsible for an early treatise giving advice on shooting, and he commented that for bows less than 5 feet 9 inches (175.26 centimeters) long, arrows of 27 inches (68.58 centimeters) were appropriate. However, for bows longer than this, 28-inch (71.12-centimeter) arrows might be used. Ladies' arrows should be restricted to 24 inches (60.96 centimeters) when being used with a bow 5 feet (152.4 centimeters) long. Curiously, at no time does the archer's arm length feature in suggestions on arrow length.

He continues with a caution: for bows 5 feet 10 inches (177.8 centimeters) long, no arrow longer than 28 inches (71.12 centimeters) should be shot, although those having bows of greater length might use proportionately longer shafts. For those who may be curious, two men's bows by the younger Waring in the author's collection are each a fraction above 5 feet 9 inches (175.26 centimeters) long, while two

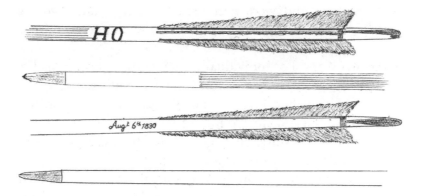

An arrow marked with the initials of Henry Ogle, top, and his prize arrow, bottom, marked with the date when he won a shooting event. If representative of the period, these arrows indicate a change in preference to a shorter overall length. (*Author*)

ladies' bows are 5 feet (152.4 centimeters). A bow by Waring the Elder dating from the late eighteenth century and in the author's possession is, however, 5 feet 11 inches (180.34 centimeters), and it would be instructive to know the length of arrow used with this.

Distances to be shot were now drawing in. The day of the eleven-score (201.17 meter) target, a last fragmentary historic link with the statutory practice distance for military archers, had passed with the demise of the Society of Finsbury Archers, and although the Woodmen of Arden continued with their longer distances, the 120-yard (109.73-meter), or 16-rood, butt was now the longest regularly shot.

Although butt shooting was popular, target shooting was an attractive alternative. This was a forerunner of today's arrangements and particularly approved of by the Prince Regent. He provided a silver bugle horn as an award for members of the Royal Toxophilite Society, and this was avidly contested. Any event patronized by royalty is guaranteed success, and the prince was able to establish shooting rules for this award, and these were meticulously followed. Targets were to be set at 100, 80, and 60 yards (91.44, 73.15, and

54.86 meters) and were four feet, three feet, and two feet (121.02, 91.44, and 60.96 centimeters) in diameter, proportionate to distance.

Arrows were shot individually, each archer loosing his first then giving way to a companion and so on until each member at the shooting line had loosed two. Target faces bore five concentric circles, which counted for nine points, seven, five, three, and one, as Imperial targets do today; these values were called the Prince's Reckoning.

With respect to scoring however, royal authority was challenged by Thomas Waring, whose mathematical mind was concerned with proportion. He notes that "the four-foot target contains 1,750 square inches and is divided into five concentric circles. These are proportionately gold 72 square inches, red 214, inner white (present day blue) 352, black 490, and outer white 626. Dividing the aggregate amount of each circle by its width, 4.75 inches, the circumference of each calculates as gold 15 inches, red 45, inner white 74, black 103, and outer white 132." Thus, he notes, "the gold is one-third the size of the red, half of the inner white, four-fifths of the black, and about one-ninth of the outer white."

He concludes that "the real value of each circle is, therefore, gold 9, red 3, inner white 2, black 1.25 [or a score of five for every four hits] and outer white just 1." Warming to his subject, he then addresses the ladies' smaller target similarly.[3]

There is no evidence that Waring's theoretical pondering influenced the prince in any way, and certainly, having no doubt listened politely, the Royal Toxophilite Society continued to use its patron's reckoning, untrammeled by mathematical logic.

Although arrow lengths were now largely standardized for men and women by those who made them, there was little cohesion between societies concerning distances shot. It had become generally recognized that a man's distance was 100 yards (91.44 meters) and a woman's 60 yards (54.86 meters). For some, the number of arrows to be shot was still at the whim of the club's committee, the weather, the time available, or even the captain of archers for the day. Change was to be gradual, but by the 1840s, certain criteria had been adopted, and gentlemen had now added 80 and 60 yards (73.15 and 54.86 meters) to their target rounds. Butt shooting at 120, 90, 60, and 30 yards (109.73, 87.3, 54.86, and 27.43 meters) had now largely ceased, and the circular target with its colored concentric rings was the order of the day.

The catalyst for uniformity came with the first National Archery Meeting of the nineteenth century at York, when distances, and the number of arrows to be shot at each, were established. The decision to hold such an event was not taken lightly. A general meeting of archers at the Black Swan Inn, York, on May 14, 1844, deliberated a suggestion circulated among societies by the Thirsk Bowmen that "A Grand National Meeting of Archers of Great Britain be held at York during the ensuing Summer." Response was favorable, and it was agreed that the meeting should be held "if 100 Archers shall send in their names as Subscribers before the 1st July next" and that "the design be advertised as soon as that number is attained."[4]

The meeting agreed that the distances to be shot should be 100, 80, and 60 yards (91.44, 73.15, 54.86 meters), known as the prince's lengths. The number of arrows at each distance was to be "settled at a future Meeting of the Subscribers." This meeting was duly held, and it was agreed that a total of twelve dozen arrows would be shot, six dozen at 100 yards, four dozen at 80 yards, and two dozen at 60 yards. Thus was the Gentlemen's National York Round established. Although the 1844 National Meeting was an all-male affair, women were invited to compete at the one held in 1845, when they shot eight dozen arrows at 60 yards. It was not until 1849, at Derby, that the Ladies National Round of four dozen arrows at 60 yards and two dozen at 50 yards was created.

There is discussion between archery historians as to what, or who, influenced the numbers for the York Round, since several societies, including the influential West Berkshire Archers, habitually shot at 100 yards and 80 yards. Thirsk Bowmen, the instigators of the National Meeting, are prime candidates since they regularly shot at all three of the distances set. Their Tuesday Round consisted of nine dozen arrows, four dozen at 100 yards, three dozen at 80 yards, and two dozen at 60 yards.

The National Meeting is notable for one more thing: the substitution of blue for the inner white circle "to prevent mistakes in marking." The origin of the inner white is conjectural, but it may be that it was to accord with heraldic principle, that a metal is not placed upon a metal nor a color upon a color. Thus the outer white (silver, a metal) is followed by black (a color), then inner white (silver), then red (a color), and finally gold (a metal). Originally, the gold was just that—gold leaf.

It is possible that this principle influenced the prince when he decided on his colors, but the suggestion is tentative. As with the York Round itself, however, the new color sequence was maintained and exists to this day.

Providing a target at which to shoot is one thing. Recording the score an arrow makes is another. For a time there were two systems, that which concentrated upon hits and that which recorded both these and their value. Butt shooting at papers was concerned primarily with hits. The paper circle decreased in size from sixteen-inch diameter to four inches as the butt distances shortened, and the skill lay in centering the arrow. Target shooting at the new colored rings allowed a hit even on the outside perimeter circle of the four-foot (121.92-centimeter) diameter boss to count, and the appeal was evident. Hits were still important, but scoring took precedence in many archers' minds. Recording was achieved by a curious combination of "pricking" and scribing. Early nineteenth century archers carried scoring cards to which were attached "prickers"—slim, tapered, pencil-like objects terminating in a metal point. Each card had lines of boxes

A score sheet from the 1845 Grand National Archery Meeting in York.
(*Author*)

colored appropriately to the target colors and with space for a
dozen arrows on each line. The position of individual arrows
was recorded on the scoring card by pricking a hole in an
appropriately colored box. The totals were written in at the
end of the round.

The author possesses a blank, unused, official scoring sheet
for the 1845 National Meeting and notes that they were substantial documents, over twenty inches (50.8 centimeters)
wide and eight inches (20.32 centimeters) deep. Custody of
these was deputed to markers, who were instructed "not to
exhibit the Target Card to any other Parties but those of their
own target and the Judge."[5]

When the round was finished, the number of hits was
totaled and scribed, together with the value of individual
dozens. The whole was then added together and the sheet
handed to the organizing committee, which compared results.
Although the principal prize at the inaugural 1844 meeting
was a silver vase, early awards were largely monetary, that for
the greatest gross score at the 1845 National Meeting being
£100, a significant sum in those days. The creation of nation-

ally recognized target rounds led to their acceptance by local societies, and many subsequently adopted them for their internal competitions.

The profusion of clubs and societies at the middle of the nineteenth century brought with it an increasing need for arrows and put pressure on those who made them. Although some contemporary bowyers also made arrows, others preferred to obtain them elsewhere, either marketing them subsequently as their own or adding their name to that of the maker. A principal manufacturer was Purle, originally of Berners Street, London, a firm with roots in the preceding century and supplier to certain provincial bow-makers, including the popular Henry Bown of Leamington. Other London businesses, such as Burberry's and Gamages, while offering equipment for a variety of country activities also stocked Purle arrows, marked with their own names for the purpose of advertising.

Of those who chose to make their own, Royal Company bowyer Peter Muir of Edinburgh led the field for fifty years. Although his early arrows seem not to be as well finished as his later shafts, they are notable for their quality. In London, umbrella-makers and suppliers of fishing tackle now tried their hands at fletching, and cheap arrows could readily be found in such places. John Cheek, a fishing tackle supplier who traded at the Sign of the Golden Perch, offered self arrows of pine at nine and sixpence a dozen, or others, of "old deal" and footed, for eighteen shillings. Cresting with gold or silver was extra at two shillings a dozen. Abraham Jacobs, who diversified into umbrellas, canes, whips, and fishing tackle as well as archery material, sold his arrows from ten shillings to one pound two shillings and sixpence a dozen.

Umbrellas were fashionable and practical accessories in the early nineteenth century, and manufacturers proliferated. The brothers Freeman, John and David, who were primarily umbrella-makers, also owned an archery business and an archery ground in Abbey Wood, London. In 1847, their business was purchased by entrepreneurs Thomas Aldred, James Buchanan, and Joseph Ainge, and thus was founded an arrow-making dynasty that lasted some eighty years. As we shall later see, Aldred and Buchanan went their separate ways to provide many champion archers with their award-winning arrows.

It is time now to look in a little more detail at arrows available during the early years of the nineteenth century, and five have been selected at random from the author's extensive collection.

It is difficult to identify a maker when no name is marked, but a clue may exist when the owner is known. The first arrow to be examined is inscribed "P. Hesketh Fleetwood" and belonged to the founder of the town of Fleetwood on the northwest Lancashire coast of England. Hesketh Fleetwood was a member of Parliament and a man with liberal leanings who perceived the need for a town to accommodate folk of modest means. His new town, built by the side of the river Wyre, was the first such planned conurbation of the Victorian era.

A prolific fletcher at that time was William Ainsworth of Walton-le-Dale, near Preston, who supplied many of the Lancashire clubs with their equipment, including the prestigious Mersey Bowmen, and this arrow may be by him. Thomas Hastings, author of *The British Archer*, said "his beautiful and excellent arrows are covered with a thin lacquer or varnish."[6]

Hesketh Fleetwood's arrow is 28.625 inches (71.74 centimeters) from its nock to the tip of an exceptionally lengthy brazed and tapered pile. At 2.25 inches (5.71 centimeters) long, this head is unusual and closer to those used for late medieval practice than for contemporary nineteenth-century heads. The weight is not marked, but it registers as 350 grains (22.68 grams).

The shaft is pine with a white (cow horn) self nock and has a two-point beefwood footing. With diameters of 0.30 inches (7.62 millimeters) at the base of the shaftment, 0.35 inches (8.89 millimeters) at point of balance, which is 18 inches (57.72 centimeters) from the nock, and 0.32 inches (8.13 millimeters) at the shoulder of the pile, it is lightly barreled. Fletchings are possibly of goose, 5-inch (12.7-centimeter) triangular in profile, with rounded upper terminals. Cresting is of black and red silk thread.

Next to be examined is a fine example of a ladies' arrow, again with no maker's name. It is 25 inches (63.5 centimeters) long from its nock to the tip of its 1-inch (2.54-centimeter), brazed and tapered head. It is marked 3*3, which should equate to 283.66 grains but is actually 330 grains (21.38 grams). The shaft is of pine, with a black (buffalo horn) self nock and has a two-point beefwood footing. Diameter is consistent at 0.30 inches (7.62 millimeters) throughout its length, and thus the profile is parallel. The point of balance is 14 inches (35.56 centimeters) from the nock. Fletchings are possibly goose, 4.5 inches (11.43 centimeters) triangular, with angled terminals. Provenance is to A. Blundell. No cresting is present.

The two arrows that follow were each marketed by Henry Bown. One is stamped solely with his name, the other is stamped "Bown Leamington," but also marked "Purle."

Each is a man's arrow. The first, perhaps by Bown himself, as there is no additional marking, is 28.25 inches (71.75 centimeters) from its nock to the tip of its 1-inch (2.54-centimeter), brazed, parallel head. Marked on the arrow is 4*9, which should equate to 414.58 grains but is actually 380 grains (24.62 grams). The shaft is of Russian pine with a black (buffalo horn) self nock and has a two-point beefwood footing. The shaft diameter is constant at 0.30 inches (7.62 millimeters) throughout its length, and thus the profile is parallel. Point of balance is 16 inches (40.64 centimeters) from the nock. Fletchings are barred turkey, 5.5 inches (13.97 centimeters) triangular, with slightly angled terminals. The cresting is gold and white interspersed with narrow red circles. There is no provenance.

The second is also 28.25 inches (71.75 centimeters) from the nock to the tip of its 1-inch (2.54-centimeter) brazed, tapered head. The weight is also marked as 4*9, that is, 414.58 grains, but is actually 360 grains (23.33 grams). The shaft is of Russian pine with a black (buffalo horn) self nock and has a two-point footing in a light-colored wood, probably also *Pinus*. The shaft diameter increases exponentially from 0.30 inches (7.62 millimeters) at the base of the shaftment to 0.35 inches (8.89 millimeters) at the pile shoulder. The profile is thus bob-tailed with a point of balance 15.5 inches (39.37 centimeters) from the nock. The fletchings are barred turkey (cock feather) and plain turkey (shaft feathers) 5.5 inches (13.97 centimeters) long, with slightly angled terminals. Cresting is silver and green. There is no provenance.

The final example is by Purle. It is a man's arrow, 27 inches (68.58 centimeters) from the nock to the tip of its brazed, parallel head. Weight is marked as 4*6, that is, 392.76 grains, but is actually 380 grains (24.62 grams). The shaft is Russian pine with a black (buffalo horn) self nock, and it has a two-point footing in beefwood. The shaft diameter increases from 0.30 inches (7.62 millimeters) at the base of the shaftment to 0.345 inches (8.76 millimeters) at the shoulder of the head, and it is therefore lightly bob-tailed. The point of balance is 16 inches (40.64 centimeters) from the nock. Cresting is gold and black. Provenance is to A. P. James, believed to have been a member of Backwell (Somerset) Archery Club.

Terminology changes as custom changes; the arrow and its container exemplify this. Eighteenth century bowmen and women carried their arrows in a leather pouch or cup, suspended from a strap attached to their belt. In the nineteenth century, this was replaced for men by a pocket pouch. Spare

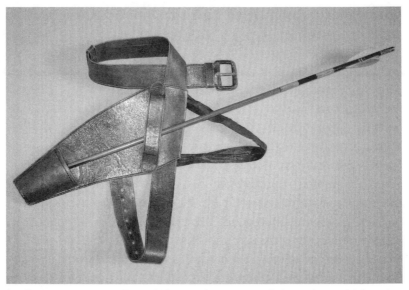

Ladies arrow pouch circa 1825, the forerunner of the quiver which today hangs from her belt. (*Author*)

arrows were kept in a tin quiver put to one side for use as required. These varied in size from the truly impressive 34.5 inches (87.63 centimeters) tall by 5.5 inches (13.97 centimeters) in diameter with separate detachable compartment for strings and things, to the ladies' version, more modest at 25.5 by 3.5 inches (64.77 by 8.89 centimeters).

The thought of carrying a quiver around would have seemed odd indeed to the nineteenth-century archer. It was not until relatively recently that the erstwhile pouch has transmogrified to become the quiver. How strange it would now be if it were suggested that when shooting, one left one's quiver behind.

Nineteenth-century archers acquired their arrows in a wooden box, known technically as a coffin. These varied from simple containers in cheap wood with lid and detachable spacers securing the contents, to elaborate affairs for the discerning bowperson. Each French polished box with dovetailed joints and brass handles opened to reveal velveteen-lined interiors with sophisticated revolving devices to hold arrows in position. Others, known as Wiltshire Boxes, also held arrows in their lids and included small secure compartments for those essentials without which no archer felt himself complete.

Bows were generally kept in tall cupboards called Aschams (in recognition of Roger Ascham, author of *Toxophilus*), and smaller versions of these were marketed for arrows. And so it went, manufacturers vying with each other to solve the perennial problem of what to do with one's arrows when the season has ended. Traveling bow boxes usually included arrow-storage areas, while canvas bags, called poles for some odd reason and used to carry bows, also included pockets for arrows.

Ornamental arrows were created by fletchers in the United Kingdom and on the Continent. Used as awards and known as "prize arrows," they were of exquisite creation and often elaborately endowed with exotic woods of various shades spliced into the shaft at both foot and nock. A particular example was used for many years as a principal award by the Scarborough Archery Society. The term "prize arrow" was, however, also used by arrow-maker F. H. Ayres & Co. of London to describe an arrow having a head that unscrewed to allow insertion or removal of small lead weights, a system designed to alter the point of balance of the arrow and thus, in theory, alter the ballistic traverse.

Altering the arrow's flight to advantage regularly exercised the nineteenth-century mind, none more so than that of the distinguished J. McGrigor Croft, MD. Although his practical association with archery may have been slight, his knowledge of physical theory was unbounded. He was renowned in the middle years of the century for improving the speed and general performance of Her Majesty's private steam yacht *Elfin* by fitting paddles constructed on the Archimedes screw principle, thereby gaining royal approbation. Having given the matter thought, he considered that rotation applied to an arrow in this fashion would result in a better flight.

Convinced of this, in 1863 he had created an arrow with smaller fletchings applied helically, and for this he acquired a patent. He called the result the Alexandra arrow, after a daughter of the queen, and arranged for its marketing by bowyers Philip Highfield, Thomas Aldred, and Messrs. Peters & Son.

There are normally few ripples in the calm waters of traditional archery, but the Alexandra arrow generated a virtual storm. All began well enough in 1864. The national champion lady archer, Mrs. Horniblow, exalted the arrow's properties, as did her immediate predecessor, praising its "superiority" over the "common" arrow in swiftness, lowness, steadiness, and accuracy of flight. It was seemingly less affected by the wind and particularly suited to point-blank shots.[8]

Gentlemen archers, however, largely reserved their judgement during its initial season, but went into print during 1865. Peter Muir, doyen of fletchers, led the debate, claiming that he had made and experimented with the system thirty years earlier and when comparing helically fletched with normally fletched shafts had dismissed them as having no effect upon results. He felt strongly enough about the matter to have a summary of his findings printed and distributed to leading archers of the day.[9]

Although he dismissed the Alexandra arrow as irrelevant in no uncertain terms, Muir was at least genteel in his condemnation, as generally were other male archers who doubted its effect. Former national champion Horace Ford, however, was unnecessarily waspish, ending his diatribe against the offending arrow, "I have the highest veneration for the opinion of the two ladies brought forward so prominently by Dr. Croft when applied to a bonnet string, or a crinoline: but in the discussion of a scientific point, such as that at present under notice, perhaps experience and the male intellect are more to be depended upon."[10]

Predictably, this inflamed the lady archers and did nothing to diminish Ford's reputation for arrogance.

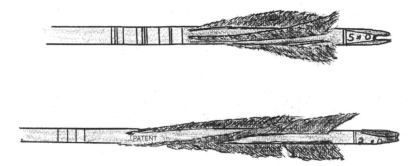

Top, helically fletched arrow by Philip Highfield; bottom, helically fletched "Alexandra" arrow by Thomas Aldred. (*Author*)

The Alexandra arrow was alternatively named the Gomez arrow, for no apparent reason. Charles Gomez was an eccentric London maker of bows and arrows, and of South American extraction. In the 1840s and 1850s, he delighted aficionados (on payment of a small sum) with displays of lassoing on horseback at speed, and javelin throwing, in addition to his undoubted skills with bow and arrow.

The Alexandra arrow stumbled on for a year or two, but like other worthy experiments, it ended in the woodshed of history. And with its passing we will end this chapter.

THE CHOICE OF CHAMPIONS

WITH THE CREATION OF THE TWO NATIONALLY RECOGNIZED target rounds came an increasing interest in competition among male and female archers, both within and outside clubs and societies. Scores had improved markedly since the haphazard advice dispensed by greybeards was replaced by more scientific methods propounded by Horace Alfred Ford, erstwhile national champion and a man who obviously knew what he was doing and, moreover, had clear ideas of why.

Ford's book, *Archery: Its Theory and Practice*, was first published in 1856, following a series of articles in the *Field*, a largely sporting newspaper. It was an instant success and was followed three years later by the second edition. Ford had apparently considered a third edition, but his growing religious scruples caused him to abandon the idea. However, a third edition, an edited version of the second, was published in the United States in 1880 by Dean V. R. Manley, and a fourth edition, titled *The Theory and Practice of Archery by the late Horace Ford* and omitting some material, was edited and produced in England in 1887 by William Butt.[1]

So, what had the great man to say about the arrow? He approached his chosen activity in a thoughtful way, and there is little doubt that his analysis of the shot, the knowledge he gleaned from studying it, and his ability to communicate his findings, both theoretical and practical, had a significant bearing on those aspirant champions who watched him shoot, studied his writings, and practiced his advice. A simple comparison of results, taken from the *Field*, between the first ten scores of men and the first five of women at the National Archery Meetings for 1855 and 1857, would seem to confirm the point.[2]

GENTLEMEN

1855	1857
1st Mr. Ford 809	1st Mr. Ford 1251
2nd Mr. Bramhall 709	2nd Mr. Edwards 786
3rd Mr. Muir 628	3rd Mr. Baynes 771
4th Mr. Wilson 614	4th Mr. Muir 777
5th Mr. Hilton 603	5th Mr. Bramhall 721
6th Mr. Mallory 560	6th Mr. Mules 720
7th Col. Phillips 553	7th Mr. Mason 691
8th Mr. Holland 534	8th Mr. Garnett 667
9th Mr. Farrer 537	9th Mr. Hilton 669
10th Mr. Brown 479	10th Mr. Wilson 658

LADIES

1855	1857
1st Mrs. Davison 570	1st Miss H. Chetwynd 634
2nd Mrs. Horniblow 477	2nd Mrs. Davison 548
3rd Miss Clay 427	3rd Mrs Blaker 496
4th Miss H. Chetwynd 328	4th Miss Cotley 418
5th Miss Leighton 269	5th Mrs. Luard 418

Ford gave considerable thought to the elements that together made up the shot. He studied and acknowledged the phenomenon we know today as the archer's paradox, noting that although the arrow nock lay central to the bow limb as it approached following release and the arrow would therefore be expected to move to the left (given a right-handed archer), paradoxically it did not. We now know that the theoretical flight path alters, since the arrow moves around the bow limb and, straightening, hits the target at which it is aimed.

Ford recognized this phenomenon and knew that in an arrow, stiffness, or as we say today, spine, played a part, however he dismisses this element in just a few words: "To test its strength or stiffness, place the pile on any solid substance, holding it by the nock, and with the other hand press it gently downward in the middle. A very little experience will suffice to tell whether it be sufficiently stiff or not."[3] Later we will note the modern method of spining to determine the whippiness of arrows and its relevance, since this became an exact science and vital to the match of arrow to bow.

With stiffness thus disposed of, Ford concerned himself with other factors related to the shot, first considering the profile of the arrow and its head or pile. He looked at the four different profiles of arrows then in use and carefully considered the ballistic implications of each as they traveled past the bow limb on their way to the target.

Beginning with the chested arrow, used mainly for distance shooting, he saw its shape (a taper from nock to head) as offering a constant deviation toward the left as the shaft passed the bow. Thus, he considered, it had "a greater difficulty in recovering its initial direction, the forces opposed to its doing so being so much increased." Accordingly, he concluded that "the chested arrow has always a tendency to fly left."[4] Modern archers may stroke their metaphorical beards at this suggestion but must recognize that compensatory spining was not then available to Ford.

Turning to the bob-tailed arrow, his opinion was that the converse was true: this profile, he considered, tended to move to the right when released. However, he noted that archers of his day preferred this profile, considering it to be the best with which to shoot straight. Upon reflection, he suggests that the only advantage is to those who, because they draw to the right of their aiming eye, find that their arrows habitually go to the left, and to compensate for the fact choose to shoot an arrow that will fly to the right.

Finally, he examines the barreled shaft, the one most favored today by traditional target archers because it vibrates less than other profiles as it leaves the bow and thus does not lose distance. Ford dismisses this profile because, in his view, the barreling of an arrow, by providing a central high spot on the shaft, does not allow an even passage past the limb of the bow. He saw it as "objectionable as a departure from the straight line." He was unequivocal in his view that "any shape of arrow that causes the centre of its thickness to vary in relation to the edge of the bow is radically bad. Therefore none other than the perfectly straight arrow is recommended."[5] Of course, he failed to recognize that the arrow did not remain in contact with the bow limb as it moved forward.

Horace Ford, twelve times British national champion archer, 1849–1859 and 1867. (*Author*)

Ford was equally forthright about the arrowhead. Since shafts were invariably drawn to the head, any shape that varied from the straight would, he believed, cause a deviation of the shaft. He also dismissed the two forms of "sharp" piles then offered, recommending only those with square shoulders having either blunt or sharp terminals.

Ford was perhaps the most successful archer of his day, so his views were listened to, and it seems that from the time his book was published, arrow-makers concentrated on either straight shafts or those only lightly barreled, each with a straight pile. Whether this was in recognition of his argument or to meet the needs of customers who were convinced the author cannot say.

Ford's principal concern was with aiming, and that is what he will be remembered for. It was a practice hallowed by time to draw the arrow to the ear, along the side of the face. As noted earlier, Shakespeare had King Lear madly berate an imaginary character, "That fellow handles his bow like a crow-keeper; draw me a clothier's yard," clearly a reference to the action of someone measuring cloth. Even Robin Hood, when preparing to loose his shaft, is prompted by the sheriff of Nottingham to "polle het op to they ner" ("pull it up to thine ear").[6] Ford was breaking with well established tradition when he suggested something different; and yet his argument for change was unassailable.

When one aims a gun, he noted, the sight is directly under the eye. What rifleman would hold the gun to the side of his face when aiming? He held the rifle under his eye, lining back and foresight together before squeezing the trigger. Why, therefore, he argued, when aiming an arrow, should the line of sight not be the same?[7] It is from Ford's observations set out in his book that front-of-face draw derives. The aiming eye is directly over the arrow and, given the correct arrow stiffness, or spine, accuracy is greatly improved. There was, moreover, a second advantage to this way of aiming. When shooting at 100 yards (91.44 meters) and drawing to the ear, it was necessary to aim high, since the nock of the arrow was held high. It was measurably less so when the drawing hand, and thus the arrow nock, was below both aiming eye and chin. Thus it was unnecessary to use a heavy draw-weight bow to gain a good trajectory. After Ford's advice, few men's bows exceeded fifty pounds in draw weight. Archers who had hitherto aimed high right when shooting, marking their knuckles or using a pin as an aid to aiming, could now, assuming they had the arrow spine correct, aim directly at the target, and with a significantly improved expectation of hitting it.

Not all nineteenth century revolutionary ideas found favor. One that did not was the Longman target. The standard target face of the time included the center circle covered in real gold leaf, impressive enough when viewed by an admiring spectator, but a nuisance to the archer when flashing in the sun. Charles Longman, a respected archer of impeccable quality and 1883 national champion, took it upon himself to design a replacement, an endeavor given cautious approval by his peers. The result of his deliberations, offered for comment in 1884, was a target face essentially light grey in color with a central black circle.[8] It was presented at a meeting of the Royal Toxophilite Society and was met with, at best, lukewarm enthusiasm. Those who had used it were skeptical of its virtue, pointing out that while the problem of glare had been resolved, it was an advantage to some to see in which color one's arrows landed, and this was impossible with the Longman target. One respected archer, Reverend W. B. Yates Foot of the prestigious West Berkshire Archers, commented that when shooting at it on a foggy day, the grey and black target actually disappeared from view. Others, who sought to pour oil on troubled waters, accepted its virtue but considered this to be outweighed by its disadvantage.

Bloody but unbowed, Longman withdrew his brainchild from view, commenting, a little acidly, in a letter to the *Field* (reproduced in *The Archers Register* of that year), "Timid conservatives need not fear that I shall attempt to spring any violent change upon them, nor that they will be called upon to shoot at the Grand National Meeting at a row of hideous monstrosities whose very outline they are unable to discern."[9]

Although the Longman target joined the Alexandra arrow in the woodshed of history, all was not in vain. Those who pontificated about arrangements at the National Meeting duly considered the original problem and agreed that henceforth the gold center of the target should be in matte paint. And so it is today.

With competitive archery now firmly on the agenda, those organizing the National and other public meetings found themselves with a perhaps unexpected problem. Archery had become a spectator sport, with crowds of onlookers joining the target lines to swell already large contingents of family members there in support of individuals, and noisy betting among them was rife. Although in theory all but those shooting were expected to hold back to allow arrows to be scored and collected, this was honored more in the breach than in the observance, and many were the arrows trodden into the ground. Arrow collection was often a matter for arrow boys, employed to avoid the need for portly gentlemen, and ladies in crinolines, to bend down to pick them up.

There was something of an ambivalent attitude toward these young lads, not all of whom may have been as careful as they should when recovering shafts. An anonymous contributor to the 1886 edition of *The Archer's Register*, writing under the pseudonym Centrum Centrissimum (thought by the author to be Reverend Eyre Hussey), was particularly lacking in Christian charity. He wrote:

> Sometimes the boys who are employed to pick up the arrows that have missed the target get obstreperous, try the patience of the ladies and incur the Judge's reproof. This institution of arrow-boys might very well be dispensed with and a roll of felt, or coconut matting placed twenty feet behind the target might be substituted. The boys are generally strange to the work and know nothing of the tenderness requisite for handling articles of such delicate workmanship as are modern arrows and they often damage them by rough treatment.[10]

This caustic comment brought a poetic response the following year from "Sagittarius" in favor of the lads:

> I am a little arrow boy, and in this year of grace
> As in the shooting of the past, I hope to hold my place,
> It may be I'm presumptuous and avaricious too,
> And value my unvalued self at more than is my due,
> But well I know my business and truly can relate,
> I always very careful am to draw my arrows straight.
> I hope it will not kill us quite, that cruel blow he dealt

And arrow-boys be slaughtered for a lifeless roll of felt.
For there are archers not so young, a large and portly group,
Who shooting 'neath a July sun, don't feel inclined to stoop,
Take heart then boys, and for their shafts move deftly as before,
This is the cry of one and all "To pick 'em up's the bore.[11]

Before leaving the juvenile element, it is appropriate to briefly mention the attention paid to young archers, their arrows, and their purpose. It was an early requirement at Harrow Public School, as with other similar seats of learning, that pupils be equipped with bows and arrows for recreation, and an annual contest took place at Harrow for a silver arrow. This competition continued until 1771, when the disorderly conduct of spectators had become such a nuisance that no further ones were held.[12] Some of the equipment the lads used exists today: twenty-three dilapidated and crudely made self wooden 24-inch (60.96-centimeter) arrows with conical heads and 4.5-inch (11.43-centimeter) low-profile, triangular fletchings. Two are marked "Folkestone," dating them to 1766, when the young Lord Folkestone was a competitor. Their maker is unknown, but a likely candidate must be a member of the Purle family.

The principal arrow-makers each offered juvenile arrows as stock-in-trade; examples by Henry Bown of Leamington are in the author's possession. They are well made, lacquered self shafts of straight profile, 18 inches (45.72 centimeters) long, with 1-inch (2.54-centimeter) parallel piles, self horn nocks, and dark, 2-inch (5.08-centimeter) triangular fletchings. Archery was thought to be a suitable outdoor recreation for young people of the nineteenth century, and bows and arrows were often provided for them to enjoy shooting. Perhaps it was of arrows by Bown that ten-year-old Emily Pepys of Hartlebury, near Worcester, wrote in an August 1844 diary entry, "I got one arrow into the target; I wish I could find the one I lost and mend that which is broken."[13]

With archery firmly established as an acceptable social activity for the leisured class by 1866, the number of societies in Britain had reached about 150, a number that decreased a little toward the end of the decade. Many of these had extensive memberships, sixty to eighty being common, and since casual archery on the lawn was also a favorite pastime, the call for equipment was considerable.

While many of the minor bow-makers of the mid-nineteenth century made and sold arrows, it fell to four principal bowyers to meet the increasing demand for recreational shafts of good quality. Purle, Aldred, Buchanan, and Muir each had their devotees, and in the provinces, Bown of Leamington and Thompson of Meriden supplied local clubs, with Bown in particular calling upon Purle to help satisfy his needs.

Of the four arrow-making firms, Purle and family was the senior. I am indebted to master fletcher Christopher Jury for genealogical research providing evidence of the manufacture of archery equipment by members of the family in the late eighteenth century. Indeed, if we are to believe the firm's letterhead, it had been "making arrows since 1720."

Thomas Aldred and James Buchanan began their archery careers, together with a third partner, Joseph Ainge, when they bought the archery business belonging to brothers David and John Freeman in the mid-1840s. The Freemans sold their firm as a viable concern to allow David the time to concentrate on his Abbey Tavern Archery and Pleasure Grounds at Violet Hill, St. John's Wood, London, located close to Lord's Cricket Ground. It was a successful enterprise, but one fully demanding of David Freeman's time.[14]

The Freeman brothers were ahead of the field in their arrow-making activity, being among the first, if not the first, to introduce cane shafts from Japan. These they offered as the first and only importation of JAPANESE CANES, the growth of which is astonishingly well-suited for Shafts, being desirably formed, very stiff, will not cast, and exceedingly steady in flight. They may be used for any shooting as they vary in weight and shape. Experienced Archers have proved and judge them superior to every other description of arrow.[15]

Curious to put this claim for stiffness to the test, the author placed an antique Japanese cane arrow five-sixteenths of an inch (0.31 millimeters) in diameter (equivalent to an English target arrow of the period) on a deflection meter (spine tester) measuring twenty-eight inches (71.12 centimeters) between points. Using a two-pound (0.9-kilogram) weight, the deflection was just 0.45 inches (11.43 millimeters) from the horizontal, appropriate for a bow of between fifty and fifty-five pounds draw weight. The claim was justified: Freeman's cane shafts would indeed have been stiff enough for target shooting and compare very favorably with those they made from other woods.

With the new owners installed, difficulties were not long in coming. Aldred was fully occupied elsewhere with no time for the new venture, leaving Buchanan and Ainge to deal with day-to-day work. Buchanan quickly tired of the task and left to form his own business. Ainge carried on until 1853, but then he too left, and no more is heard of him. Arrows marked "Ainge and Aldred" are, however, likely to have been his work, or overseen by him, Aldred being otherwise engaged.

Left by himself, Thomas Aldred had to decide whether his future lay in clerical work or in the archery workshop. History confirms the choice he made, and his arrows, together with those of erstwhile partner and now rival Buchanan, became firmly established among the competitive archery element. Equipment made by the latter was particularly favored by national champion Horace Ford.

Sharing the limelight were a number of smaller archery enterprises. Some would have brought in arrows, some would have made their own. Perhaps the most prolific arrow-makers were still the Purle family of Berners Street, London, and Bath, Somerset. They are known to have supplied either shafts, or even finished arrows, to the major bow-makers, while also providing stocks marked with their name to the outdoors sections of such general stores as Gamages, Whiteleys, Burberrys, and Lillywhites.

The personalizing of arrows remained important, and certain of the Woodmen of Arden continued as they had begun, by marking theirs with family crests or heraldic features embodying the predominant tincture from these, where this was appropriate. Those of less august lineage relied on concentric circles of assorted colors for distinction. These were registered with favored suppliers who were thus able to provide replacements correctly marked with personal colors when needed, arrangements maintained up to World War II, during which time all cresting registers seem to have been lost through enemy bombing raids.

During the earlier years of the nineteenth century, tender shoots of archery struggled through in the United States. From these blossomed the United Bowmen of Philadelphia in 1828, and with it a minor curiosity. The earliest members of this prestigious club identified themselves by colors and personal marks (the names of which they used to refer to each other within the club) such as Arrowhead, Crossed Bones, Arrow, Drachm, and Anchor. It is unclear whether these marks appeared on arrows, but when shooting it was customary for each hit on the target to be identified by a small drawing of the personal mark of the bowman who had made it.[16] Curiously, Robert P. Elmer states in his book *Target Archery with a History of the Sport in America* that *The March of Archery*, a print published in London in 1829, shows identical marks in the gold of the target, and he raises the question of which influenced the other.[17] A little perplexing is the fact that the author possesses a copy of this print, and no such marks are visible. Had someone added these to the copy viewed by Elmer?

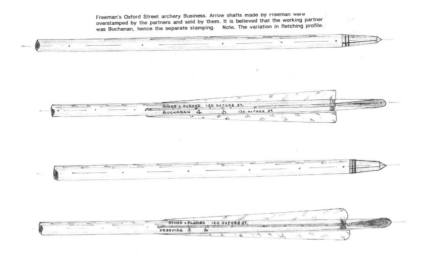

Freeman's Oxford Street archery Business. Arrow shafts made by Freeman were overstamped by the partners and sold by them. It is believed that the working partner was Buchanan, hence the separate stamping.   Note. The variation in fletching profile.

Two rare English recreational arrows bearing the names of their makers: top, head and fletching of an arrow from the workshop of Buchanan, Ainge and Aldred; bottom, head and fletchings of an arrow probably made by Freeman but marked Freeman, Ainge and Aldred, c. 1844. (*Author*)

The later nineteenth century was a period of consolidation for arrows; few innovative features marked its passing. Wood used was now largely *Pinus sylvestris*, with profiles either straight or lightly barreled. Shafts were invariably footed, with beetwood predominating. Two points were the norm, although four were not unusual. Arrowheads (piles) were brazed ferrous metal and straight, although at least one of the minor arrow-makers used horn piles.

Although individual color cresting was confined to the shaftment, below the fletchings, during the latter years of the century, arrows "painted between the feathers" were advertised. Drawing attention to this, bowyer and author James Duff suggests in his book *Bows and Arrows* that perhaps the discovery that paint ground in Japan varnish did not run up the feathers if it accidentally touched them prompted the offer.[18] For some arrows, cresting included gold leaf, increasing the cost.

Perhaps the most noticeable alteration to the nineteenth-century arrow was to the fletching. From time immemorial, the shape of the feather had been long and triangular. The 6-inch (15.24-centimeter) grey goose wing of the mighty English battleshaft had given way to a feather 4.5 to 5 inches (11.43 to 12.7 centimeters) long for men's recreational arrows, and one proportionately shorter for those of the ladies, but all was to change. While shooting one day in the late 1870s, Henry Elliott, from Aston Park Archers and a gun-maker by profession, accidentally broke the forward 3 inches (7.62 centimeters) from one fletching of one of his arrows. To balance the shaft he removed the same amount from the remaining two feathers and noticed to his surprise that with the reduced amount, his arrow flew better and farther. He adapted the new style further by trimming it to a parabolic, or balloon, shape.[19]

Elliott's discovery soon gained credence among principal arrow-makers, and they quickly adopted a shorter profile. To Elliott's parabolic feather was added a shield, or short triangular shape, and it is variations of these two shapes that are used today. The Scottish school, led by Peter Muir, appears to have preferred the shield shape, and the English the parabolic.

Although the turkey provided the majority of nineteenth-century feathers, and barred and plain black or white fletchings from this bird predominated, many women preferred the dusty redness of the peacock, or peahen. These maintain their shape well, and with small quantities becoming available, they became a popular choice.

James Buchanan, who claimed to supply the royal family and the emperors of Russia and Brazil, offered in his 1873 "Reduced Price List" one dozen men's arrows for twenty-four shillings, and a dozen arrows for ladies at twenty-one shillings, each fitted with one of his "registered parallel points." His erstwhile partner and now business rival Thomas Aldred for some reason chose *The Archer's Register* for 1878 to advertise not his arrows but his fishing tackle, claiming to

Progression of fletching profiles for recreational arrows. Left to right, from the eighteenth to the twentieth century. (*Author*)

have supplied it to their Royal Highnesses the Prince and Princess of Wales, Napoleon III of France, the king of the Belgians, and all the principal "Crowned Heads of Europe,"[20] each of whom, one supposes, dangled worms in the water from time to time as a relief from the rigors of royal life.

Footed shafts were now regularly available and *de rigueur* for those concerned with competition. Although two-point footings were the normal choice, four points were popular among some top archers, the quite erroneous view being that they better balanced the stiffness of the shaft. It would be another thirty years before the three-point footing, introduced by American arrow-maker Philip Rownsevelle, became available.

Nocks for all but garden arrows were now largely of full horn spliced into the shaftment, care being taken to provide for the thickness of the string together with its essential central serving, or whipping.

As the century moved into its last quarter, the major archery suppliers began to target the North American market. The firm of Philip Highfield was particularly successful, selling to dealers Peck & Snyder of New York. Highfield's arrows

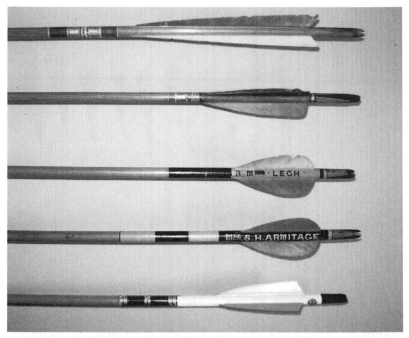

Progression of ladies' recreational target arrows. From top to bottom: early nineteenth century with low triangular fletchings and horn nock; shield shaped fletchings and horn nock, c. 1860; late nineteenth century, balloon shaped peacock feather fletchings with horn nock of Beata Legh; mid twentieth century peacock feather fletching with horn nock of Mrs. S. H. Armitage; late twentieth century shield shaped dyed turkey feather fletching with applied plastic nock. (*Author*)

had attracted the interest of Maurice Thompson. In *The Witchery of Archery*, a contemporary best-selling book, Thompson extolled the virtues of the bow and arrow for recreation.

Peck & Snyder offered a wide selection of shafts in 1878, not all of which were natural English products and therefore probably not made by Highfield. These included Japanese arrows at two dollars a dozen, French arrows 28 inches (71.12 centimeters) long with horn points at five dollars a dozen, and Indian hickory arrows 21 inches (53.34 centimeters) long with steel-pointed heads at eighty cents a dozen.[21]

Encouraged by Maurice Thompson and his brother Will, hunting was a developing North American activity, and "Thompson's Model Hunting Arrows with Indian spear points" were popular among the rapidly increasing hunting fraternity.

Matters moved fast in American archery circles, for in 1879, Maurice Thompson transferred his allegiance to rival firm E. I. Horsman, granting it exclusive right to manufacture the Maurice Thompson Arrow. Maurice wrote that he and Will, the U.S. national champion of 1879, had "tested them in every way" and discovered that they "give a lower trajectory and a more rapid rotary motion, and consequently are less affected by wind than any other kind of arrow." They were available, footed in snake wood, at twelve dollars a dozen for gentlemen and ten dollars a dozen for ladies.[22]

The first Grand Annual Meeting of the American National Archery Association took place in 1879, and we may speculate with some certainty that champion Will used the Maurice Thompson Arrow.[23] The redoubtable team of Peck & Snyder, their stocks of Highfield arrows languishing on the shelves, must have felt upstaged.

And so we move on to chapter fourteen, with even more surprises to tempt the adventurous arrowman . . . or woman!

INNOVATION

THE ARCHER ANTIQUARIAN IS REGULARLY SURPRISED BY THE inventive enthusiasm of archery entrepreneurs, and much of this originated in the United States. During the middle and later years of the nineteenth century, the activity caught the American imagination in a big way, and having finally become an acceptable sporting occupation was thus open to anyone with ideas for its improvement. Foremost among these were the creators of the Royal Bow and Arrow, patented in 1879 and marketed by Perry Mason & Co. of Boston as equipment "Superior to old style archery."[1]

Extolling the virtues of archery in general, the agents explained that it "may be described as walking, lifting, thrusting, leaping, boxing and fencing, with the more violent and objectionable features left out." (Over many years, the author can recall certain bow meetings marked by each of these characteristics, on occasion with the violent features retained.)

From the introductory advice, we learn that the Royal Bow consisted of a "centre made of metal, with a circle containing fixed bearings through which the arrow passes, and two graduated barrels, one on either side, for the reception of two pieces of wood forming the spring of the bow." The Royal

Arrows, it says, "are well made and the wings are made of fine hair cloth instead of feathers and will guide the arrow as well and last much longer than the ordinary ones. The arrows are loaded with metal running two inches into the shaft. This increases the strength and accuracy of the shot."

The arrows were of unspecified wood, parallel in profile, with brass or nickel-plated piles and brass nocks, each innovative for the period. The shaft diameter was designed to fit exactly the hole in the center of the metal handle.[2] Although quite unsuited to the competition circuit, or indeed to regular club archery, these bows and arrows probably found favor as an oddity, and they appear to have enjoyed some modest commercial success.

An activity that quickly gained ground among the younger archery element in the United States was recreational hunting. The pleasures of stalking and killing, or "harvesting," to use its modern euphemism, was introduced to the wider community by the brothers Thompson, through Maurice's ever-popular *Witchery of Archery*, published in 1878.[3] The two had enjoyed the sport from their youth and were eager to pass on the pleasure. The activity they most enjoyed in those early days was bird shooting, and for this they used reed arrows. These were cut when green and left to dry, then straightened over a flame and cut to 38 inches (96.52 centimeters). Nocks were then cut, and tips charred and hardened by fire. This methodology was intriguingly similar to that of Ishi, the California Yana Indian. Finally, when feathered with low fletchings, these shafts, naturally bob-tailed in profile, were considered well suited for bird prey at fifty yards.

For larger game, arrows with broad heads were used, and these were supplied commercially by Horsman of New York and Peck and Snyder of New York. I am indebted to Wade Phillips, owner of the Antique Archery Arsenal & Museum, for presenting me with a copy of his book,[4] thereby sharing his vast knowledge of these and also reminding me of Maurice Thompson's description of his equipment in *Scribner's Monthly* magazine of July 1877.

In his book *Bows and Arrows*, Saxton Pope describes a hunting arrow made by Will Thompson. The shaft, he says, was of red split hickory, 28 inches (71.12 centimeters) long and eleven-thirty-seconds of an inch (8.73 millimeters) in diameter, with a simple nock, red-dyed turkey feathers 2.75 inches (6.98 centimeters) long and three-quarters of an inch (19.05 millimeters) high, with a white cock feather. The blade was of lanceolate steel, 2 inches (5.08 centimeters) long by three-quarters of an inch (19.05 millimeters) wide, and brazed within a thin tubular socket.[5] American archer Howard Hill, whose prowess with bow and arrow is legendary and whose simple philosophy seems to have been "If it moves shoot it," also offers useful advice to those seeking to emulate him, by describing broadheads in his book *Hunting the Hard Way*.[6]

Although nineteenth-century hunting was primarily a masculine activity in the United States, there is some slight evidence for feminine interest. *Scribner's Monthly* of May 1878 includes a drawing of a young girl holding a rabbit she has apparently killed. As the author of the accompanying article remarks, "I think her feat of archery caused her more regret than pleasure, for she declared her intention never again to shoot at a living thing."[7] There are those who echo her sentiments.

Hunting with longbow and arrow in Britain during the nineteenth century was no more than a casual diversion for men of the leisured class, when it happened at all. The sporting crossbow was in evidence, however, for disposing of rooks and vermin among other things, and these were made by certain gunsmiths and bow-makers. Joseph Braggs of 26 High Holborn, London, was one such notable maker.

Arrows, for "Small Game" (distinguished from "Hunting Arrows" by virtue of the size of the heads) were offered during the 1930s by the firms of F. H. Ayres Limited, Thomas Aldred, and Jaques. Ayres offered hunting and small game sets, and prominent within the four arrowheads fitted was the

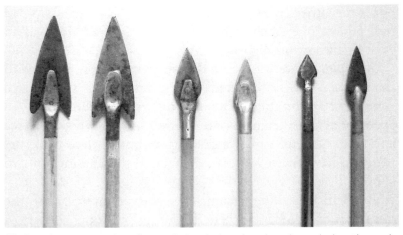

Six hunting arrows showing variation in head and sockets during the early twentieth century. From left to right, 1. American, 2. American, 3. F. H. Ayres, 4. Jaques, 5. F. H. Ayres, 6. F. H. Ayres. (*Author*)

"Saxton Pope." This appears in two forms in the firm's catalogs: In 1933, an exceptionally well made example was offered with a round end socket welded to the barbed head. This was offered again in 1934, but was replaced in 1935 by a similarly welded but flat end socket. Adding a touch of mystery as we shall shortly see are a number of hunting arrows in the author's possession previously belonging to Lieutenant Colonel Jack "Mad Jack" Churchill, a distinctly larger-than-life World War II hero. There is some evidence he acquired them from the United States, and again the method by which the blades are fixed to the sockets varies.

As some will know, Jack Churchill is credited with being the last Englishman to kill an enemy soldier with longbow and arrow. This happened as his regiment made a fighting withdrawal toward Dunkirk in 1940. It is said that in attempting to recover the arrow, he broke off the head. I have one of his hunting shafts without its Saxton Pope blade, and it is apparent that some force has been necessary to remove it from the socket. Could it be that this shaft has a gruesome past? We shall never know.

Of the other Ayres game arrows offered for sale, two had oval points, one smaller than the other, and a third had an even smaller spear-shaped point.

Although there was some British interest in hunting with the arrow, it was never extensive and was always subject to a significant antihunting lobby among archers themselves. An apocryphal tale is told of one aspiring hunter who, by a tree and taking careful aim at a grazing deer, was more than surprised to have an arrow arrive with a dull thud an inch or two above his head.

All British hunting became of academic interest with the Deer Act of 1963 and 1991.[8] Hunting with bow and arrow was outlawed, and an activity that had occupied both lawful and lawless alike for centuries came to an abrupt end.

With United States companies now firmly embedded in the archery market, and without the inhibition of traditional working methods prevalent in Britain to act as a conservative brake on progress, change was inevitable. The twentieth century was to witness the marriage of technology and ingenuity as innovative ideas on arrow design materialized.

An early development that gained some support from archers was the introduction of a strengthening steel core for some 3 inches (7.62 centimeters) into the foot of the arrow, a process patented as early as 1879 by William Wright, who used it in his Royal Archer arrow. Although it would have affected arrow flight by adding forward weight, it fell to the Knight Archery Company of Rome, New York, to successfully market this idea in 1927.

We have already noted the wide use of cane as arrow material, even in Britain, that most conservative of environments. However, it would be a fishing-tackle firm, South Bend Bait Company of Indiana, which developed its potential as an arrow shaft in the 1920s. Their method was to take a thin layer of tonkin cane and glue it to a piece of Lawson cypress. This was then shaped into a triangular section, and six of these sections were glued together to form a hexagonal stele, ready for fletching and the addition of the head. The foot and the nock were strengthened by the omission of cypress at those points. This would have resulted in an exceptionally strong construction, enabling a smaller diameter shaft.[9] The author has not seen an example of this arrow so cannot comment from experience, but it may have proved difficult to produce arrows in varying spines to match bow weights. However innovative the manufacturing concept may have been, it was not successfully marketed, and it failed to displace the traditional wooden shaft. A full decade would pass before that was accomplished.

Although they maintained tradition, the firms of F. H. Ayres and Thomas Aldred were inventive in their way. But Aldred led the field when, in 1908, he introduced the aluminum nock, patent 15328. It was marketed following the Olympic Games, when it was claimed to be a "long-felt want" and, moreover, used by English Olympic champion Queenie Newall, no less. Essentially a protective metal sleeve shaped to cover the nock ears, it did not meet with universal approval, being dismissed by the Thompson family of Meriden as a string cutter, a condemnation that the maker vigorously denied. The full aluminum nock would appear later.

When Thomas Aldred, founder of the firm, died in 1887, after contracting a chill while examining some European yew, his grandson James Izzard assumed responsibility for the business and remained in control until 1918. Diminishing sales following the Great War, however, led to a merger with F. H. Ayres.

A major twentieth-century introduction was the turned metallic pile. Initially of brass but also in ferrous metal and aluminum, and quickly adopted by arrow-makers, it replaced the brazed metal sheath with its stopping, in use since replacement of the forged head nearly three centuries earlier. It was a change particularly welcomed by Ayres, since it allowed the firm to market "matched and tested prize arrows," a somewhat misleading title since they were in every sense

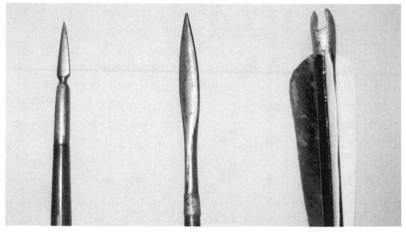

Early twentieth century arrows commissioned by F. H. Ayres (London). Left and center, the arrowheads of two personal commissions made for Col. R. Williams-Thomas, Woodmen of Arden, c. 1930s; right, an unusual bulbous nock made to commission, probably for experimental use with a thumb lock draw. (*Author*)

working shafts. Their brass piles consisted of two halves screwed together, within which were contained a selection of tiny lead weights. By altering the number carried, the balance of the arrow could be altered and the flight path adjusted. The overall weight was adjustable from four shillings and sixpence to five shillings against silver coin, the latter evidently most suited to a shorter distance.[10]

Ayres' company was persuaded to undertake personal commissions from time to time, and these evidently included the fashioning of arrows with bulbous nocks (similar to those of near-Eastern shafts) and grooves designed to take a thick string. The author possesses a pair of these, acquired by exchange from the Pope and Young Museum, in Chatfield, Minnesota. There is now no indication of purpose, or of who may have commissioned their construction, but they have each been carefully made and finished. They are both 28 inches (71.12 centimeters) long and barreled in profile, with a two-point footing and brazed piles. The shaft is 0.28 inches

(7.11 millimeters) in diameter at the base of the shaftment, 0.35 inches (8.89 millimeters) at its deepest section, and 0.32 inches (8.13 millimeters) at the foot. The point of balance is exactly 12 inches (30.48 centimeters) from the point of pile. The weight is 330 grains (21.38 grams).

Fletchings are long triangular, 4 inches (10.16 centimeters) long, and rounded at the nock end. They are set just one-quarter of an inch (6.35 millimeters) from the base of the string groove. The shaftment is painted dark blue between the feathers, with gold and red cresting bands. The nocks are painted gold, with red grooves. The proximity of feather to string groove, and the quarter-inch (6.35-millimeter) width of this groove suggest that these arrows were shot using either a variant of the primary pinch loose or perhaps a thumb lock.

Another commission resulted in the production of a pair of shafts armed with variants of bodkin points. Although the author is aware of who ordered these, his purpose in doing so remains a mystery.

Although occasionally appearing in other societies' calendars, clout shooting was a major event at Forest Hall in Meriden, the shooting ground of the Woodmen of Arden. While arrows for the purpose were generally provided by Thompson, the resident bowyer, demand regularly outstripped supply, and many Woodmen turned elsewhere for their requirements. Ever eager to extend its interests, F. H. Ayres stepped into the breach to create finely made breasted shafts, identified with the crests of individual Woodmen. (Ayres was notable for the diversity of its business interests, ranging from tennis balls, supplied regularly to Wimbledon for the championships, to motor vehicles and cycles. Indeed, abandoned in some deserted barn even today may be the rusting relic of an F. H. Ayres velocipede.)

The early twentieth century was notable for the introduction of international archery matches, offering the opportunity for comparison of traditional styles of arrow. Thus in 1904, a party of English ladies and gentlemen traveled to Le

Touquet, near Calais, France, to take part in what was advertised as "An International Archery Meeting," held under the auspices of Baron de Coubertin, genius behind the Olympic movement. Although as much a social outing as a bow meeting (the dinner menu would not have been out of place in a five-star hotel), there was a modest element of contention in the international competition when 31-inch (78.74-centimeter), horn-tipped, French and Belgian butt shafts met 28-inch (71.12-centimeter) target arrows by Aldred, Buchanan, and Ayres. Arrows were shot individually, in the Continental way, and at their habitual distance of 50 meters (54.68 yards), although oddly, the English gentlemen competitors shot at 60 yards (54.86 meters). It would be ungracious of the author to deny the result, which was a whitewash; he will therefore confine his remarks to noting that 50 meters is shorter by some distance than 60 yards.[11]

An opportunity for gentlemen to redress the results of 1904 came at the London Olympic Games in 1908, when the Double York Round was shot. Unaccustomed to the longer distances and with weaker bows, the French put up a valiant show, but honors fell to the English arrow. Curiously, and out of keeping with contemporary practice, Willie Dod, the gold medalist with 185 hits and 815 scored, chose to use shafts fletched with long, triangular feathers, a choice, incidentally, not shared by brother Anthony or sister Lottie (who achieved silver in the ladies event), each of whom preferred Aldred's shorter parabolic style.

At the separate fifty-meters event (included for the Continental archers), although the English gentlemen decided to shoot, unaccountably all but one chose not to enter competitively. Had they done so, R. O. Backhouse would have won. Instead, in receiving a Special Merit Certificate, he claimed a moral victory, expunging the ignominy of defeat four years earlier.[12]

Arrow development was rapid during the early years of the twentieth century, with every part subject to alteration. We

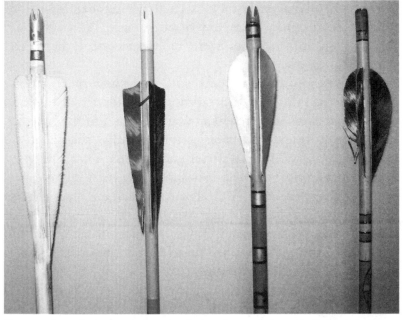

Progression of arrows and nocks during the early twentieth century. From left to right, an American wood shaft with metal nock, an English "Apollo" solid steel shaft with neoprene nock by Accles & Pollock, a duralumin tube shaft with aluminum nock by the Dayton Steel Racquet Company, USA, a steel tube shaft with applied composite nock of unidentified material by SEFFAB, Sweden. (*Author*)

have already noted Aldred's substitution of a metal sleeve for the traditional horn nock; with the American capacity for invention, this was itself replaced in the 1920s by one completely of aluminum, its tapered socket glued to a cone, an arrangement that remained popular until the introduction of neoprene, an early form of plastic.

With the heady scent of revolution in the air, it was not long before entrepreneurs turned their attention to the construction of the shaft from other than natural material. Philip Rounsevelle is credited with introducing the first successful arrow made of duralumin, an aluminum alloy, in 1926,[13] although he was quickly followed by others. The True-Flight target arrow, made of "aeroplane tobing," was advertised in

Sylvan Archer magazine in July 1928, by manufacturer Tru-Flight Metal Arrow Company of Fox Chase, Pennsylvania.[14] These first metal arrows were more successful than early attempts at metal bows.

Although duralumin shafts still held their place among those who had deserted the traditionally made arrow, it was to steel that makers and archers now turned, and to the Swedish firm See Fabriek Aktiebolag, thoughtfully shortened to SEEFAB. With Swedish archer and international champion Henry Kjellson, SEEFAB produced the first viable steel arrow and bow in 1935. Although American engineers were a little further behind, Dayton Steel Racquet Company not only produced a fine example with an aluminum nock, but included patented grooves on the shaftment that were designed to take the fletchings.

While the material of shafts exercised the imagination of some engineers, their profile was of concern to others. The author possesses copies of an exchange of correspondence in 1935 between two Royal Navy captains: Richard Oliver-Bellasis, a member of the Woodmen of Arden who used the wooden arrow, and B. P. Haigh, a naval engineer with an aeronautical responsibility. The exchange took the form of five questions by the former and answers by the latter. I summarize:

Question One: "When the arrow is released where does the maximum bending occur?"

Answer: "The part which is subject to maximum bending moment is about 1/3 from the 'after' end [the foot]. A great deal has been done on taper for aeroplane struts. The best result for giving high load capacity with low resistance to motion and low weight is obtained with the largest section 1/3 from the 'after' end employing a cylindrical section."

Question Two: "What is the best shape for an arrow?"

Answer: "I believe that the largest section fairly well forward would give minimum resistance, so we might regard the cylindrical section as a fair compromise with 1 above."

Question Three: "What is the optimum position for the centre of gravity of an arrow? It would seem that this should be
as far forward as possible so as to require minimum 'steering.'
Is the position of the centre of gravity important? Will a
heavier nosed arrow tend to have a shorter range than one
with the centre of gravity well aft?"

Answer: "Whether a forward C. of G. is desirable is hard as a
subject for me. I doubt if the simpler and more tempting
arguments are really applicable. I would keep it well forward
for first choice but how far forward is a problem too difficult
to define from my experience."

Question Four: "In view of the resistance offered by the feathers, which is the better shape?" [Three shapes are then shown:
short triangular, conventional shield, and reversed shield, that
is with the shape reversed.]

Answer: "I believe that shape A. [short triangular] in which
the height gradually increases is likely to give the greatest
steering force with minimum resistance. The 'blunt end'
[reversed shield] should not go first."

Question Five: "The arrow head is normally parallel but not
particularly symmetrical or smooth, being of bent and brazed
metal. Is it worth having turned points made thus?" [A bullet
point is illustrated.]

Answer: "It is probable that a rounded point would give distinctly better results than a cone shape. I think it would be
steadier as well as less resistant."

Captain Haigh then expresses curiosity about vibration
and noise in flight, commenting that if a shaft were strong
enough to stand the severe force of discharge without collaps-
ing elastically, it would be stable enough to give a definite
vibration where there were eddies around the feathers, and
this would make a noise. He adds that a vibrating arrow is
bound to offer more resistance than one that flies silently
without vibration, a comment that will strike a chord with
those archers who prefer the barreled profile.

Although it was the metal SEEFAB arrow that survived
the war, to be with its steel bow, the preferred shafts of the

serious competitive British archer, those made traditionally of wood, still clung on among certain club archers and were to do so until 1946. That year the Royal Toxophilite Society met with officials of the Grand National Archery Society and "leading archery equipment makers," when steel bows and steel arrows made by Accles & Pollock Limited were introduced to the assembly.[15]

Well made, of high-tensile steel tubing, Apollo arrows, as they were known, quickly began to replace those by SEEFAB. Although initially available just in parallel profile, breasted and barreled shafts soon appeared to extend their range. Typical of the latter were dimensions of 0.22 inches (5.59 millimeters) at the shaftment, 0.26 inches (6.60 millimeters) at the point of balance, 15 inches (38.1 centimeters) from the nock, and 0.21 inches (5.33 millimeters) at the pile. The American equivalent was of parallel profile.

We have already noted the duralumin arrow and its modest impression on American archery. Now it appeared successfully in Apollo's "Championship" mode. Tubular in shape, it featured nylon nocks and helically affixed fletchings "to give additional accuracy," while a light alloy pile was fitted to give a point of balance well forward of center.[16]

With the wooden arrow now totally eclipsed by metal, it depended on a very few enthusiasts for its survival. Even these were troubled, however, as we shall see from one man's archery log from the 1950s.[17] With an engineering background and a sound knowledge of ballistics, John Boulden made a practice of comparing the advertised with the actual weight and spine values of the arrows he purchased, both wooden and metal. The results were not encouraging.

A set of eight wooden practice arrows sold by maker Purle and marked "369 grains" and "60 spine units" varied in actual weight between 373 and 384 grains (24.17 and 24.88 grams), and between 52 and 57 units of spine—clearly at odds with the specification as advertised. When ordering a set of duralumin arrows from supplier Jaques, Boulden was at pains to specify a weight of 370 grains (23.97 grams) and a spine value of between 50 and 60 units as suited to his bow, asking them not to accept the order unless they could supply to his specification. Upon receipt he checked them and found spine variations between 67 and 75 units and no weight lower than 400 grains (29.92 grams). He duly returned them together with a stiff letter, and had his costs refunded.

Sadly, these were not unusual variants from stated specifications. Mr. Boulden's records, kept meticulously across eight years in a small book that is now in the possession of the author, tell the same story. It would seem that makers and retailers alike were either unable or unwilling to meet the needs of a clientele increasingly aware of the importance of arrows matched to bows.

It is appropriate here to mention a subject that diverted the true enthusiast in his quest to match arrow to bow: the resonance, or musical frequency of wood. Convention suggested that wood of a particular stiffness was suited to a bow of particular draw weight as determined by a deflection meter. This revealed by how much an arrow would bend, but gave no clue as to how quickly it would straighten after bending.

Any wooden rod has a natural musical frequency: the longer the rod, the slower its frequency, and the weightier, or denser, the wood, the lower its elasticity and, again, the slower its frequency. When an arrow is put into vibration, a musical note is emitted, the pitch of which is determined by the above characteristics. By comparing these notes, the matching of individual shafts, one to the other, can be determined. Or so it is said.[18] How is this achieved? With his arrow suspended horizontally, its head and nock secured upon posts, the true enthusiast will have acquired a violin bow and by drawing this lightly over the center of the shaft will have produced his musical note. Assuming his ability to distinguish between semitones, it follows that (given compatibility of the elastic modulus) this further test could, at least in theory, more exactly match like with like.

In passing, it is notable that those who make violin bows are conscious of the resonance of the material they use, and the author understands that the optimum choice for the traditionalist is pernambuco wood. Curiously, Roger Ascham dismissed this wood (known by its other name, Brazil wood) as making "dead, heavye, lumpish hobbling shafts," and he did not favor it for arrows.[19]

Returning to the twentieth century, and with shafts now of metal and nocks of plastic, just the feather remained as a final link with nature. But not for long, for as the century advanced, plastic vanes made their appearance. Hard at first, inflexible, and prone to breakage, they were speedily replaced by more supple material, although this, in turn, was prone to biodegrade.

The serious competition arrow was now universally of man-made material. But there was a stirring among the archery fraternity, a feeling that somehow something was missing from their favored sport. A movement began, tenuous at first but growing slowly stronger, seeking to recover something of the romance of the past. Men who had almost lost their skills found them once again, and while technology evolved slim carbon-fiber shafts of unimaginable exactness for ever more accuracy, from workbench and garden shed appeared dowels of cedar, horn nocked, footed, and feathered with turkey.

Across the world, societies are now devoted to traditional shooting, while in England the members of a craft guild formed in 1986 are still making wooden tackle.[20] And so, in the face of technical advance, the simple arrow once more finds its mark in field and forest.

Epilogue

This selective saunter through the world's historic arrows would be incomplete without a glance at their modern Western counterparts. Designed to complement the sophistication of their companion bows, they have evolved to be efficient and purposeful, but sadly are lifeless and devoid of character, mere clones, each of the other. Gone from the modern competitive scene are the warmth of wood, the subtle fusion of footing to shaft, the colored bands denoting pride of ownership, the slim black nocks of horn, and the supple firmness of feather. All have been replaced by advanced technology and engineering wizardry that have enabled the fusion of aluminum sheath and carbon fiber, a coupling for which is claimed accuracy and durability with easier target extraction, but little else.

As one might expect, prices have advanced exponentially with technical progress, and in October 2011, a set of twelve of these aluminum/carbon shafts cost the enthusiastic target archer about $365 (£250). With stainless steel points capable of conversion to give varied forward weight, and barreled profiles to absorb energy and reduce vibration, they must surely be the ultimate target arrows.

One may reflect that a century ago, William Fergie, trained by Peter Muir and then bow-maker to the Royal Company of Archers, offered a dozen arrows "of the very best quality, made and painted to special pattern, price Gents: 30 shillings per dozen, Ladies: 25 shillings per dozen, carriage paid."[1] These would have been matched for weight and made of *Pinus sil-*

vestris. He might also have added that they would have been expertly footed and have finely crafted self horn nocks, brazed metal heads, and be fletched with carefully selected peacock feathers.

For all the importance of technical advance, the creative element has been subverted. Old Mr. Ch'en, with his saw and his glue pot, was especially sought by customers who valued his personalized skill, for the Chinese fletcher's craft was one of dedication. To Mr. Ch'en, the arrow was almost a living thing, an object painstakingly created, each aspect of its making thoughtfully undertaken. When Ishi, the California Indian, or Ötzi, our Alpine archer, made their arrows, a little of themselves went into each, and so it was with unnamed others who through the ages squatted by crackling open fires on cold starlit evenings straightening shafts and reliving their hunting exploits.

A meticulously fashioned flight shaft made by a present-day craftsman fletcher for individual purpose to achieve lasting glory for the greatest distance shot, or a factory-made marvel designed by computers for absolute accuracy and victory at international competition, each is a fulfilment of knowledge gained over millennia, a dichotomy of purpose sharing a common history.

We will leave this book as we began it, remembering Longfellow's ancient unnamed arrow-maker, sitting by his tepee reminiscing:

> Thinking of the great war-parties
> How they came to buy his arrows,
> Could not fight without his arrows.[2]

And with a gentle sigh for bygone days, close its pages.

Glossary

APPLIED NOCK. A nock affixed separately to an arrow.

BARRELLED. An arrow profile which is slightly thicker in its mid section.

BATTLE-SHAFT. An arrow intended for warfare.

BEARING ARROW. An arrow possessing a steady flight.

BIRD BOLT. A blunt-headed arrow intended for hunting birds and small game.

BIRD BOLT BODKIN. A slim arrowhead designed to penetrate mail and plate armor.

BOB-TAILED. An arrow profile which tapers to become thinner at the nock end.

BODKIN. A slim arrowhead designed to penetrate mail and plate armour.

BOLT HEAD. A term once synonymous with arrow head, but now describing the head of a crossbow missile.

BREASTED. An arrow profile which tapers to become thinner at the head.

BROAD ARROW. Descriptive of a military arrow head, often barbed.

BULBOUS NOCK. That end of the arrow with an integral string groove, but which is thicker than the shaft to enable a better grip when a pinch draw is used.

BUTT. An earthen mound on which a target (often a small, usually circular card) was affixed. More recently, the circular straw target used in recreational archery.

BUTT SHAFT. An arrow designed for shooting at a butt.

CLOTHYARD SHAFT. A colloquial term for the military arrow.

CLOUT. A small white target placed on the ground for distance shooting.

COCK FEATHER. The fletching of three that is at right angles to the string groove.

COFFIN. The correct description of a box designed to carry bows.

COMPASS, SHOOTING IN. To shoot an arrow in a curved or parabolic line.

CREASED HEAD. An arrow head having a ridge to enable the archer to feel when he has reached full draw.

CRESCENT HEAD. A military arrow head having a crescent shape. See also forker.

CRESTING. The personalizing of an arrow shaft for identification.

CROSS-NOCK. String grooves cut at right angles to each other.

CROW BILL. A colloquial term for a recreational arrow head made of horn.

CUP NOCK. Alternative description of a bulbous nock (qv).

DRAW. The act of pulling a bowstring preparatory to shooting.

FLETCH. The shaped feather guiding an arrow.

FLETCHING. (n) An alternative name for a fletch. (v) The act of attaching feathers to a shaft.

FLIGHT SHOOTING. The act of shooting for distance.

FLU-FLU. A type of fletching designed to produce more drag and slow the arrow (usually by winding the feathers around the shaft).

FOOTING. Descriptive of wood, usually harder spliced into the fore-end of an arrow shaft to offer protection and to provide forward weight.

FORE-SHAFT. In native arrow making, a separate piece inserted within the main shaft to carry the head.

FORKER. A colloquial term for a crescent or forked broadhead.

GARDEN ARROW. A cheap recreational arrow designed for practicing.

GRAIN WEIGHTS. The table against which recreational arrows were historically weighed using silver coins.

HALF NOCK. Created when a horn piece is inserted and the slot is cut so that two ears of wood remain on either side.

HEAD. A generic term for all arrow heads.

HORN BLUNT. A thickened, hunting arrowhead, usually of horn, with a flat end, designed to kill small game and birds by impact. See bird bolt.

HORN NOCK. A V-shaped piece of horn inserted into an arrow, with a slot cut into it at right angles.

HOYLES. A form of roving archery (qv) conducted at short distances.

MUSKET ARROW. An arrow discharged from a musket or hand gun.

NOCKED. Said of an arrow when it is placed upon the bow string in readiness to be drawn.

NOCK-PIECE. A thin sliver, often of horn, inserted into the arrow end at right angles to the slot and designed to strengthen the string groove.

PAPINGO. An alternative description of tir a la perche (qv) or vertical shooting. See also popinjay.

PARALLEL. Descriptive of an arrow profile which maintains an even diameter along its length.

PILE. Alternative description of an arrow head, more particularly of a recreational or practice head.

POPINJAY. The Scottish term for papingo (qv) shooting.

POUCH. An earlier description of what is now termed a quiver.

PROFILE. The longitudinal shape of an arrow.

RACHIS. The portion of quill to which the feather vanes are attached.

ROOD. A linear measurement of either 7 1/2 or 5 1/2 yards used in earlier times to determine archery distances to be shot.

ROVING. The practice of shooting at defined marks, over a wide area, at either known or unknown distances.

SELF NOCK. A string groove cut directly into an arrow shaft.

SERVING. Thread wound around the center of a bow string for protection from wear.

SHAFT. The arrow before it is nocked, fletched, or headed.

SHAFTMENT (Alt: little shaft). That part of the arrow shaft to which the feathers are affixed.

SHEAF. The collective name for a number of arrows, usually, but not invariably, twenty-four.

SPRITE. A musket arrow (qv).

STANDARD ARROW. Believed to have been a standard issue war arrow.

STELE. An arrow shaft before profiling.

STRAIGHT. An arrow profile. Alt: parallel (qv).

STRIATED SHAFT. An arrow shaft with longitudinal striations along part of its surface.

STRING NOCK. The groove into which the bow string fits. The description is expanded to include the surrounding material.

SWINE BACK. Fletching shaped like the hump of a pig.

TANG. The extension to an arrowhead designed to fit into the arrow.

TILLER (v). To shape a bow stave by observing its curve when drawn back by a tiller bar and shaving off small amounts of wood where necessary to produce an even curve.

TIR A LA PERCHE. A form of archery involving vertical shooting at simulated "birds" on a mast.

VANE. Fletching made of plastic.

WHIPPING. Alt: serving (qv).

Notes

INTRODUCTION

1. Henry Wadsworth Longfellow, *The Song of Hiawatha* (London: G. Routledge, 1856), 105–106.

2. For an overview of Yana culture and archery, including comments upon Ishi's arrow making, see Saxton T. Pope, "Yahi Archery," *University of California Publications in American Archaeology and Ethnology*, vol. 13, no. 3 (March 6, 1918): 103–152. The Yahi were a Native American group of the Yana people of California. "Ishi" means "man" in the Yana language.

3. Mustafa Kani, comp., *Sacred Archery: The Forty Prophetic Traditions* (*Telḫis-i Resâilü'r-rumat*) (Istanbul: Imperial Printing House, 1847); Radhias Shukrulla, trans. (Padstow, England: T. J. International, 2005). The seventeenth *hadith*, or tradition, page 56, says "the casting of arrows is a share and a characteristic of the shares of Islam" and is accompanied, as are all the *haditha*, by its interpretation, illustrating that the practice of archery is considered a form of worship.

CHAPTER ONE: ORIGINS

1. Dorothy A. E. Garrod, "Palaeolithic Spear Throwers," *Proceedings of the Prehistoric Society* 21, no. 3 (1955), 21–35. May be seen at http://www.thudscave.com/npaa/garrod/garrod.pdf.

2. Robert Berg, "Bannerstones and How They Relate to the Atlatl," June 17, 2005, at http://www.thunderbirdatlatl.com/?p-24.

3. Bernal Diaz del Castillo, "*The Truthful History of the Conquest of New Spain*, or, *The Discovery and Conquest of Mexico 1517-1521*" (New York: Farrar, Straus, and Cudahy, 1956).

4. This artifact can be seen at the Pitt Rivers Museum, accession number 1898.75.25, or at the museum's Arms and Armour Virtual Gallery, http://webprojects.prm.ox.ac.uk/arms-and-armour/o/Oceania/1898.75.25/. See also plates in Garrod, "Palaeolithic Spear Throwers," 23, 25, 28.

5. Edouard Lartet and Henry Christy, *Reliquiae Aquitanicae* (Paris: 1865–1875), plates B xix–xx.

6. Garrod, "Palaeolithic Spear Throwers," 21.

7. For use of this weapon, see Ancient Armies of Macedon at http://www.ancient-battles.com/catw/makedon.htm.

8. Acts of the Privy Council N.S.XVI 25, 1588.

9. Sir William Wood, *The Bowman's Glory, or Archery Revived* (London: Published by author, 1682), 58 (repr. Wakefield, England: S. R. Publishers, 1969).

10. D. Starkey, ed., *The Inventory of King Henry VIII*, vol. 1 (London: Harvey Miller, for the Society of Antiquaries, 1998), as quoted in Jonathan Davies, "Military Archery and the Inventory of King Henry VIII," *Journal of the Society of Archer-Antiquaries* 44 (2001), 37n1.

11. For an overview of the use of *flechettes* during World War I, see the periodical *Aeroplanes, Dirigeables, Zeppelins* (Paris: 1915), 211–212; C. G. Carey, ed., *The War Illustrated*, January 23, 1917, 558; and C. G. White and W. Harper, *Aircraft in the Great War* (Chicago: McClurg, 1915), 245.

12. Alf Webb, "Those So Called Arrow Straighteners," *Journal of the Society of Archer-Antiquaries* 38 (1995), 39–40.

13. For more about the modern spear thrower, see The World Atlatl Association at http://www.worldatlatl.org/.

CHAPTER TWO: THE EARLY DAYS

1. J. G. D. Clark, "Neolithic Bows from Somerset, England, and the Prehistory of Archery in North-west Europe," *Proceedings of the Prehistoric Society* 29 (1963), 96.

2. A. Rust, "Die Alte-und Mittelsteinzeitlichen Funde von Stellmoor" (Neumünster: 1943), 189–192, plates 91–96, quoted in Clark, "Neolithic Bows."

3. Clark, "Neolithic Bows," plate 8 c, following p. 64.

4. The following discussion of "Ötzi" is based on Konrad Spindler, *The Man in the Ice* (London: Weidenfeld and Nicolson, 1994).

5. The following discussion of Ishi is based on Saxton Pope, *Hunting with the Bow and Arrow* (New York: G. P. Putnam's Sons, 1925) (repr. of 2nd ed., Prescott, AZ: Wolfe Publishing, 1991).

6. Clark, "Prehistory of Archery," 80.

7. Edward S. Morse, "Ancient and Modern Methods of Arrow Release," *Bulletin of the Essex Institute* 17 (October–December 1885).

8. Walter Hough, "Arrow Feathering and Pointing," in "Arrows and Arrow-makers," *American Anthropologist* 4 (January 1891) (repr. Machynlleth, Wales: Dyfi Valley Bookshop, 2001).

9. Among many writings on the subject of arrowheads, note Noel D. Justice, *Stone Age Spear and Arrow Points of the Midcontinental and Eastern United States* (Bloomington: Indiana University Press, 2009); and William Jack Hranicky, *North American Projectile Points* (Bloomington, IN: AuthorHouse, 2007).

10. W. J. Hoffman, "Poisoned Arrows," in "Arrows and Arrow-makers," *American Anthropologist* 4 (January 1891) (repr. Machynlleth, Wales: Dyfi Valley Bookshop, 2001).

CHAPTER THREE: ÖBERFLACHT AND BEYOND

1. Holger Riesch, "Alamannische Pfeile und Bogen," in *Das Bogenbauer Buch* (Ludwigshaven, Germany: Angelika Hörnig, 2001), 114–116.

2. Wolfgang Menzel, archaeological report of 1847, quoted in Riesch, "Alamannische Pfeile und Bogen," 114.

3. The Archaeologische Landesmuseum in the Schleswig-Holstein Landesmuseum, housed in Schloss Gottorf (Gottorf Castle), presents the archaeology of the region, including ritually sacrificed material from Nydam Moor. See http://www.schloss-gottorf.de/archaeologisches-landesmuseum.

4. E. Mylius's detailed account of the archery material recovered from the Nydam site is in H. Walrond, ed., *The Archer's Register* (London: *Field* newspaper, 1912), 241–246.

5. Snorre Sturlason, *The Norse King Sagas,* Everyman's Library (London and New York: J. M. Dent, 1930), 58.

6. Sturlason, *Norse King Sagas*, 150.

7. Ludvig Holm-Olsen, ed., *Speculum Regale*, 2nd ed. (Oslo: Norsk Historisk Kjeldescrift Institute, 1983). A Norwegian educational text from around 1250, *Speculum Regale* (in Old Norse *Konungs Skuggsja*, or *King's Mirror*) was intended originally for the education of King Magnus Lagaboøte in the form of a dialogue between father and son.

8. Sturlason, *Norse King Sagas*, 258.

9. Richard Hamer, *A Choice of Anglo-Saxon Verse* (London: Faber & Faber, 1970), 48–69.

10. Michael Swanton, ed. and trans., *The Anglo-Saxon Chronicles*, 2nd ed. (London: Phoenix Press, 2000), 198.

11. Sturlason, *Norse King Sagas*, 232.

12. Steve Allely, "Western Indian Bows," in *The Traditional Bowyer's Bible*, vol. 1 (New York: Lyons and Burford, 1992), 183, 185, 187, 188.

13. The following discussion of the Battle of the Wabash is based on a description in Robert van Trees, *Banks of the Wabash* (Fairborn, OH: Van Trees Associates, 1986).

CHAPTER FOUR: OF INDIANS AND INDIA

1. E. G. Heath and Vilma Chiara, *Brazilian Indian Archery* (Manchester, England: Simon Archery Foundation, 1977), 89.

2. Although the Lamas seem to have vanished, the Ticunas (or Tacunas) still survive, living much as they always have, and they have been extensively studied by Dr. Dan James Pantone, editor of the web site Amazon-Indians (http://www.amazon-indians.org/) and founder of the Movement in the Amazon for Tribal Subsistence and Economic Sustainability, a nonprofit organization that is helping indigenous Amazonians so that they themselves can sustain their culture traditionally and independently.

3. Walter Michael Moseley, *An Essay on Archery* (Worcester, England: T & T Holl, 1792), 153–160.

4. "Cherokee Games," Cherokee Heritage Center, accessed October 10, 2011, http://www.cherokeeheritage.org/cherokeeheritage/cherokee_games.html.

5. "Fukiya," Wikipedia, accessed September 29, 2010, http://en.wikipedia.org/wiki/Fukiya. The relevant associations are the International Fukiya Association, the Japan Sport Fukiya Association, and the United States Blowgun Association. Competition rules vary between groups, but internationally the following apply: distance 32.81 feet (10 meters), where thirty darts are discharged at a target having three concentric rings: a central circle 2.36 inches (6 centimeters) in diameter, surrounded by an inner circle 4.72 inches (12 centimeters) in diameter, and an outer circle 7.07 inches (18 centimeters) in diameter. Values are, respectively, seven points, five points, and three points. The height of the central circle from floor level is 62.99 inches (160 centimeters). Six rounds, each of five shots, in twenty-five minutes, constitute a game.

6. Heath and Chiara, *Brazilian Indian Archery*, 60–64, 151–164.

7. Heath and Chiara, *Brazilian Indian Archery*, 62.

8. G. N. Pant, *Indian Archery* (Delhi: Dr. Agam Prasad for Agam Kala Prakashan, 1978), 149.

9. Pant, *Indian Archery*, 151–158.

10. Pant, *Indian Archery*, 125.

11. Pant, *Indian Archery*, 177.

12. Pant, *Indian Archery*, 177.

13. Pant, *Indian Archery*, 180, 181.

14. Ancient guns were of bamboo, and in all European Sanskrit dictionaries, the word *nalika* has been rendered as "stalk, tube, arrow, dart." Both arrow and gun could be referred to as a reed: the arrow is a reed that is discharged as a missile, and a gun is a reed out of which missiles are shot.

15. Thomas Roberts, *The English Bowman* (1802; repr., Wakefield, England: EP Publishing, 1973), 163. The author, in conversation with Lieutenant Commander W. F. Paterson (see note 15), has been informed that the description of an Eastern "returning arrow" may also be found in N. A. Faris and R. P. Elmer, *Arab Archery* (Princeton, NJ: Princeton University Press, 1945), 138–139.

16. W. F. Paterson, "Observation on the Returning Arrow," *Journal of the Society of Archer-Antiquaries* 21 (1978), 14–15.

CHAPTER FIVE: THE ASIAN ARROW

1. Gongar Lhagvasurum, *The Stele of Chinggis Khan* (Ulaanbaatar: Mongolian National Institute of Physical Education, n.d.).

2. Turkish/Saracen flight shooting is a complex subject and unsuited to a book of this nature. Those wishing further study should consult J. D. Latham and W. F. Paterson, *Saracen Archery* (London: Holland Press, 1970); Paul Klopsteg, *Turkish*

Archery and the Composite Bow (Manchester, England: Simon Archery Foundation, 1967); and/or Fred Isles, "Turkish Flight Arrows," *Journal of the Society of Archer-Antiquaries* 4 (1961). Note particularly the presumed effect of the "righting moment" mentioned in *Saracen Archery*, chapter 19.

3. Munkhtsetseg, "Mongolian National Archery," *Instinctive Archer Magazine* (Spring 1999), 49–50. See also Jenni Storey, "What Came First in Mongolia, the Wheel or the Bow?" *Mongol Messenger* (July, 9, 1997), an excellent survey of traditional Mongolian archery.

4. For a detailed discussion of the traditions of Mongolian archery, wrestling, and horse riding, see "Tradition," *Mongolia Today* 1, accessed April 30, 2011, www.mongoliatoday.com/issue/1/.

5. Munkhtsetseg, "Mongolian National Archery," 50–51.

6. Jampa Samten, "An Investigation on Gesar's Arrow Divination," Proceedings of the 6th Seminar of the International Association for Tibetan Studies, Fagernes, Norway, August 21–28, 1992, accessed June 2011, http://www.thlib.org/reference/spt/SPT—FullRecord.php?ResourceId=2482#ixzz1ThjaPL2i.

7. For those interested in the arrow and divination, see Janet Gendall, "Evidence for Archery in Pictish Art," *Journal of the Society of Archer-Antiquarians* 43 (2000), which discusses the Pictish broken-arrow symbol, an enigma demanding a solution.

8. Karma Ura, "Perceptions of Security," *Journal of Bhutan Studies* (Autumn 1999), 117.

9. "Bhutanese Way," Yangphel Archery, http://www.bhutanarchery.com/new/?page_id=41, accessed October 8, 2010.

10. T'an Tan-Chiung, "Investigative Report on Bow and Arrow Manufacture in Chengtu," *Language and History Review* (1951; repr., *Journal of Chinese Art History* 11, July 1981).

11. Stephen Selby, *Chinese Archery* (Hong Kong: Hong Kong University Press, 2000), chapter 4, "The Archery Rituals."

12. T'an, "Investigative Report," 201–204.

13. T'an, "Investigative Report," 204.

14. Selby, *Chinese Archery*, chapter 6, "Examination of Crafts." Within this chapter, see "How the Arrowsmith Makes Arrows," which contains much technical detail on the construction of arrows. It is recommended reading in conjunction with "Investigative Report on Bow and Arrow Manufacture in Chengtu."

15. Selby, *Chinese Archery*, 101–106.

16. T'an, "Investigative Report," 205–207.

17. In the first method of fletching, the cock, or leading feather, was set at right angles to the nock groove, with the shaft feathers each aligned at 120 degrees. In the second method, the leading feather was aligned as above, but the two shaft feathers were spread farther apart, in order to counter yawing. In the third

method, the two shaft feathers followed the nock groove, each at 180 degrees, while the leading feather was conventionally at right angles to the nock groove. One shaft feather came from a left wing and one from a right wing, the belief being that one would cancel out the other. All feathers were low cut and helically fletched.

18. T'an, "Investigative Report," 211–213.

CHAPTER SIX: WARFARE

1. Stephen Pollington, *The English Warrior from Earliest Times until 1066* (Hockwold-cum-Wilton, England: Modern English Anglo-Saxon Books, 2002), 185.

2. Pollington, *English Warrior*, 183. For a full modern English translation see Kevin Crossley-Holland, ed., *The Anglo-Saxon World* (Woodbridge, England: Boydell Press, 2000).

3. Paolo de Vingo, "Personal Equipment and Fighting Techniques among the Anglo Saxon Population in Northern Europe During the Early Middle Ages," University of Torino, Italy, accessed August 27, 2011, http://www.mun.ca/mst/heroicage/issues/6/devingo.html.

4. Lewis Thorpe, *The Bayeux Tapestry and the Norman Invasion* (London: The Folio Society, 1973), 65. See also Jim Bradbury, *The Battle of Hastings* (Stroud, England: Sutton, 1973), 204–205.

5. Joseph Ritson, *Robin Hood Poems, Songs and Ballads: A Collection of All the Ancient Poems, Songs and Ballads, Now Extant, Relative to That Celebrated English Outlaw, to Which Are Prefixed Historical Anecdotes of His Life* (London: John C. Nimmo, 1885), 52.

6. Ritson, *Robin Hood*, 90.

7. Ritson, *Robin Hood*, 25.

8. An ell is an old English measure that, like the foot, was taken from a part of the body, in this case the forearm. It was originally 18 inches (45.72 centimeters), but the measure varied at different times. The English ell of 45 inches (114.3 centimeters) seems to have been introduced from France in the sixteenth century and was used chiefly as a measure for cloth. The Scottish ell was 23 inches (58.42 centimeters), the Flemish ell around 27 inches (66.58 centimeters), and the French ell around 47 inches (119.38 centimeters).

9. Michael Leech, "The Skefington Case of 1298: A Re-assessment of the First Recorded Description of a Medieval Bow and Arrow," *Journal of the Society of Archer-Antiquaries* 53 (2010), 81–82.

10. A. G. Credland, "The Medieval War Arrow," *Journal of the Society of Archer-Antiquaries* 25 (1982), 30.

11. Sir John Dynham was a Devon nobleman who supported Edward IV and the Yorkist cause. For his many acts of military service, he was made a baron in 1461, and elevated to the peerage in 1467. He led the fleet that Edward sent to secure the seas before his invasion of France in 1475. In 1483, Dynham support-

ed the usurpation of the throne by Richard, Duke of Gloucester, and was rewarded with the stewardship of the royal duchy of Cornwall. Dynham also received extensive land grants in autumn 1483, after remaining loyal to Richard III during Buckingham's Rebellion.

12. For an analysis of part of the Arundel Archive, see Janet Gendall, "The Arundel Archive of Arrows and Arrowheads," *Journal of the Society of Archer-Antiquaries* 44 (2001) and 48 (2005).

13. Francis James Child, ed., *English and Scottish Popular Ballads* (Ann Arbor: University of Michigan Library, 2005), accessed August 17, 2011, http://www.sacred-texts.com/neu/eng/child/ch162.htm, stanza 162A.5.

14. The excerpts that follow from the Arundel Archive are from the author's private correspondence with Janet Gendall.

15. James E. Oxley, *The Fletchers and Longbowstringmakers of London* (London: Unwin Brothers, 1968), 16.

16. Geoffrey Chaucer, trans., *The Romance of the Rose* (N.p.: Kissinger, 2004), 28–29, accessed August 27, 2011, http://books.google.com/books?id=KDiJUYW422wC&source=gbs_similarbooks. Chaucer may have translated *Romaunt du Rose* while he was imprisoned in France in 1360, having been captured while skirmishing during the Hundred Years' War. He was subsequently ransomed for fifteen pounds by Edward III.

17. "Dog draw": with a single scenting hound attempting to flush out a deer. Peasants were allowed to have hounds in the forest only if they were tied together in pairs to stop them from chasing deer.

"Stable stand": Standing still with a bow partly drawn and ready to shoot. This derives from a method employed by those attending the king when he hunted: many archers made up a line (known as the stable stand) ready to shoot as the deer were driven toward them.

"Back beround": carrying a deer's carcass on your shoulders.

"Bloody hand": with blood on your hand from cutting up a deer.

18. D. J. Stagg, ed., *New Forest Documents AD 1244–AD 1334*, Hampshire Records Series 3 (N.p.: Hampshire County Council, 1979), 47. A venison plea was the record of the transactions of those who ruled the forest on the king's behalf, particularly with respect to the safety of his deer (venison).

19. Sussex County Archives (Coroners Court), County Hall, Lewes, England, 1267.

20. John Gerard, *The Herball, or the Generall Historie of Plantes*, edited and expanded by Thomas Johnson (London: n.p., 1633).

21. Oxley, *The Fletchers*, 16.

CHAPTER SEVEN: THE TUDOR ARROW

1. Oxley, *Fletchers*, 13.

2. Oxley, *Fletchers*, 13–14.

3. Hugh Soar, "The Bowyers and Fletchers of Bristowe," *Journal of the Society of Archer-Antiquaries* 32 (1989), 27.

4. Soar, "Bowyers and Fletchers," 36.

5. Soar, "Bowyers and Fletchers," 31.

6. Soar, "Bowyers and Fletchers," 30–31.

7. Richard Beadle and Pamela M. King, *York Mystery Plays: A Selection in Modern Spelling* (Oxford: Oxford University Press, 1995, reissued 1999), 138–154. I am indebted to colleague Janet Gendall for drawing my attention to a Cornish mystery play, *The Creacion of the Worlde*, written in 1611, in which author William Jordan tells a tale of Lamech, a story not to be found in the Bible. In Cornish:

> Ow servant, des nes omma, haw gwaracke dro hy genes. My a vyn mos tha wandra bestas gwylls tha asspea hag a vyn gans ow sethaw latgha part anothans y.

> Master da, der tha gymmas me a weall un lodn pur vras hans in bushe ow plattya.

> Bythware them navova dean rag me ny allaf meddra. Set owseth the dennewhan may hallan tenna thotha.

> Now yta an seath compys, tenhy in ban besyn peyll pardel os archer prevys.

> Now yta an seth tennys, han breast sure yma gweskes.

Translated:

> My servant draw close now and bring my bow with you. I will go to seek wild beasts and with my arrows kill some of them.

> Master dear, with your leave I see a very great beast hiding in the bushes, squatting.

> Be sure that it is not a man for I cannot see to aim. Set my arrow on the side of the bow that I may shoot at it.

> Now behold, the arrow is straight, pull her up to the pile, as you are a proven archer.

> Now, behold the arrow is drawn and the beast is surely struck.

Biblical scholars can make of this what they will.

8. Charles E. Whitelaw, *Scottish Arms Makers*, ed. Sarah Barter (London: Arms and Armour Press, 1977).

9. Whitelaw, *Scottish Arms Makers*, 98.

10. Whitelaw, *Scottish Arms Makers*, 99.

11. Whitelaw, *Scottish Arms Makers*, app. 1, 298.

12. The following discussion of arrows, their construction, and their use is based on Roger Ascham, *Toxophilus: The Schole or Partitions of Shootinge* (1544), facsimile of the Wrexham edition of 1788 (Wakefield, England: S. R. Publishers, in collaboration with the Society of Archer-Antiquaries and the Grand National Archery Society, 1968), 160–186.

13. Alexzandra Hildred, ed., *Weapons of Warre: The Armaments of the Mary Rose*, vol. 3 of *The Archeology of the Mary Rose* (Portsmouth, England: Mary Rose Trust, 2011), 674.

14. Ascham, *Toxophilus*, 166. In underhand shooting, the target is visible below the bow hand, resulting in shooting high into the air. Forehand shooting is at a lower trajectory.

15. William Shakespeare, *King Lear*, act 4, scene 6.

16. Personal correspondence with Keith Watson, to whom I am indebted for sharing the results of his research into arrows recovered from the Tudor warship *Mary Rose*.

17. The following discussion of arrows, their construction, and their use is based on Ascham, *Toxophilus*, 168–187.

18. Nottinghamshire Archives (Coroners Court), County Hall, West Bridgford, England, 1562.

CHAPTER EIGHT: SHOOTING FOR DISTANCE

1. Coroner's Office (Records), West Bridgford, Nottingham, as recorded by Hugh D. H. Soar and Veronica-Mae Soar in an unpublished anthology.

2. See Kirsty Rodwell and Robert Bell, *Acton Court: The Evolution of an Early Tudor Courtier's House* (London: English Heritage, 2004) for a full description of the archaeology of this site, including the archery bows and a partial arrowhead.

3. The following incidents are based on coroners' reports noted over several years by the author.

4. Corporation of London Records Office, Letter Book N., folios 169b.–170. CLRO Ref: small ms box 1 no. 11.

5. Roberts, *English Bowman*, 258.

6. Ascham, *Toxophilus*, 215.

7. The following discussion is based on details in an English translation of *L'Art d'Archerie* in *The Archer's Register* (London: *Field* newspaper, 1902–3), 264–277. A French version appeared as an appendix in Henri Stein, *Archers d'Autre Fois: Archers d'Aujourd'hui* (Lille, France: L. Danel, 1925).

8. Statute H.VIII 33 1541–1542, as recorded in Adrian Elliott Hodgkin, *The Archer's Craft* (London: Faber & Faber, 1951), 202, wherein rules for regular shooting practice are laid down, and houses for "unlawful games" played to the detriment of archery are prohibited. A rood was an ancient measurement that in the north of England was 7.5 yards and in the south was 5.5 yards. Distances shot in the south would therefore be divisible by 5.5. The activity was known as "shooting the roods."

9. *L'Art d'Archerie*, 274.

10. Ritson, *Robin Hood*, 70–71.

11. G. Gould Walker, *The Honourable Artillery Company 1537-1947* (Aldershot, England: Gale and Polden, 1954), 2–5.

12. Arthur G. Credland, "Eagle Bowmen," *Journal of the Society of Archer-Antiquaries* 38 (1995), 49–61.

13. Edward Gibbon, *The Decline and Fall of the Roman Empire*, accessed August 27, 2011, http://www.ccel.org/g/gibbon/decline/volume1/chap4.htm. "With arrows, whose point was shaped into the form of a crescent, Commodus often intercepted the rapid career, and cut asunder the long bony neck of the ostrich."

14. Hugh D. H. Soar et al., *Secrets of the English War Bow* (Yardley, PA: Westholme Publishing, 2006), 146.

15. Soar et al., *Secrets of the English War Bow*, 145.

CHAPTER NINE: SIGNIFICANT CHANGES

1. Sir John Smythe, with Humfry Barwicke, *Certain Discourses Military* (1590; repr., *Bow Versus Gun*, Wakefield, England: EP Publishing, 1973), opposite 21. This replica of the original compilation of conflicting sixteenth century arguments concerning the value of military archery contains the challenge by Barwicke (who wanted to see guns replace bows) to Smythe (who wished to retain bows) that he be shot at with arrows to prove his point. See also J. R. Hale, ed., *Certain Discourses Military* (New York: Cornell University Press, 1964) for an analytical discussion of the discourse.

2. William Neade, *The Double Armed Man by the New Invention* (1625; facsimile, York, PA: Shumway, 1970), 25–51.

3. A. G. Credland, "Bow and Pike," *Journal of the Society of Archer-Antiquaries* 29 (1986), 10.

4. R. C., *Mercurius Civicus: Londons Intelligencer, or, Truth Impartially Related from Thence to the Whole Kingdome to Prevent Mis-information*, no. 18 (September 1643). This English Civil War weekly newspaper, published by John Wright and Thomas Bates, appeared on Thursdays from May 4, 1643, to December 10, 1646. Each edition consisted of a quarto sheet and was priced at one penny. It is exceptionally rare, and copies are accessible in the British Library; Bodleian Library, Worcester College, University of Oxford; and Senate House, London.

5. James Mitchell Hill, *Celtic Warfare* (Edinburgh: John Donald, 1986), 48–49. See also David Stevenson, *Highland Warrior: Alasdair MacColl and the Civil Wars* (Edinburgh: John Donald, 1994), 120–128.

6. Randle Holme III, *The Academy of Armory, or, a Storehouse of Armory and Blazon: containing the several variety of created beings, and how born in coats of arms, both foreign and domestick: with the instruments used in all trades and sciences, together with their terms of art: also the etymologies, definitions, and historical observations on the same, explicated and explained according to our modern language. . . .* (Chester, England: printed for the author, 1688), book 3: vol. 1, chap. 3, 105–106; vol. 2, chap. 17, 117–118; vol. 8, chap. 1, 350–351. See also Arthur G. Credland, "The Longbow in the Sixteenth and Seventeenth Centuries," *Journal of the Society of Archer-Antiquaries* 32 (1989), 16–17.

7. City of Bristol Record Office, ref: 1625, no. 30.

8. Whitelaw, *Scottish Arms Makers*, 98.

9. Whitelaw, *Scottish Arms Makers*, 298.

10. James Partridge, *Ayme for Finsburie Archers* (1601; facsimile, STC Reel 2000, Ann Arbor: University of Michigan microfilms), 1.

11. James Partridge, *Ayme for Finsburie Archers* (1628; repr., Royal Leamington Spa, England: W. C. Books, 1998), rule 9.

12. Partridge, *Ayme for Finsburie Archers*, 24.

13. James Balfour Paul, *History of the Royal Company of Archers* (Edinburgh: Wm. Blackwood, 1875), 18–24. See also Major General John Hay Beith [Ian Hay], *The Royal Company of Archers 1676–1951* (Edinburgh: Wm. Blackwood, 1951), 5–7.

14. G. A. Raikes, *History of the Honourable Artillery Company*, vol. 1 (London: R. Bentley and Son, 1878), 154.

15. Ben Hurd, *The Antient Scorton Silver Arrow: The Story of the Oldest Sporting Event in Britain* (London: Society of Archer-Antiquaries, 1972), 50–52.

16. Hugh D. Soar, "Seventeenth Century Archery: Some Notes on the Regulations of Two Seventeenth Century Archery Societies," *Journal of the Society of Archer-Antiquaries* 35 (1992), 8–12.

17. Paul, *History of the Royal Company*, 305–314.

18. *The Ancient Honour of the Famous City of London Restored and Recovered by the NOBLE Sir John Robinson KNIGHT AND BARONET, Lord Mayor for this year 1663 in The truly ENGLISH and Manly Exercises of Wrestling, Archery and Sword and Dagger with The Speeches of Mr William SMEE (Master of the Game pro hoc vice, and Clerk of the Market* [possibly Smithfield]*) upon this Solemn Occasion* (London: printed for R. L., 1663). Located in City of London Record Office.

19. Thomas Smith, *The Complete Soldier* (London: N.p., 1628). Here is the recipe for the contents of the Alnwick fire arrow:

"Powder, bruised, two Parts. [Salt] peter in Roche [rock or crystalline form] one part. Peter in Meele [meal] one part. Sulphur in meele, two parts. Rozin roche, three parts. Turpentine, one part. Linseed oyle, one part. Verdegrease, 1/3rd part. Bole armanack [an astringent, earthy material from Armenia] 1/3rd part. Bay [evaporated salt from the Bay of Biscay] 1/3rd part. Colophomnia [Greek pitch formed from the distillation of turpentine in water] 1/6th prt.

"And if you think it good, you may put thereto of Arsnick 1/8th part. Then coat the same over with this liquid mixture made molten in a pan or coating pot[:] Pitch, four parts. Linseed oyle one part. Turpentine one part. Sulphur one part. Tarre (tar) one part. Tallow one part."

20. H. L., *A New Invention of Shooting Fire-shafts in Long-Bows, wherein besides the maner of making them there is contained a briefe Discourse of the usefulness of them in our moderne Warres by sea and land* (1628; repr., Amsterdam: Walter J. Johnson, 1974), 1–12.

CHAPTER TEN: ROYAL PATRONAGE

1. Raikes, *History of the Honourable Artillery Company*, 302. This request was granted as a favor. It is possible the purpose was to encourage accurate shooting and/or to develop or consolidate technique.

2. Oxley, *The Fletchers*, 22–37.

3. Hugh D. H. Soar, "Uriah Streater: Apprentice Fletcher," *Journal of the Society of Archer-Antiquaries* 42 (1999), 11–12. The original of this indenture was gifted to the Worshipful Company of Fletchers by the descendants of Uriah Streater and is with the company's books and papers at the Guildhall Library.

4. Whitelaw, *Scottish Arms Makers*, 21.

5. *Records of the Society of Finsbury Archers* (1671), unnumbered page. Held in the Guildhall Library, London.

6. Statute of the Realm 33, Henry VIII. Eleven score, or 220 yards, was a statutory distance set down by Henry VIII in 1541 as that appropriate to men older than twenty-one. Shooting at a shorter distance was discouraged by fine. It is interesting to note that this distance, habitually shot in the seventeenth and eighteenth centuries, was established over a century earlier, when archery was still a military tactic.

7. Reverend James William Dodd, *Ballads of Archery, Sonnets, Etc.* (London: R. H. Evans and W. Ginger, 1818), xxii.

8. Dodd, *Ballads of Archery*, 163–164. In an effusive introductory dedication to the Prince Regent, the Reverend Dodd refers to a much earlier success at a match and his subsequent award at the hands of the prince, the society's patron. A silver medallion of the Royal Kentish Bowmen in the possession of the author reads "M[ay] 29 [17]87 J.D.," which may refer to the occasion.

9. Dodd, *Ballads of Archery*, 54.

10. Chris Hassall, "Songs from Bow-Meetings of the Society of the Royal British Bowmen" (computer printout circa 1998), 11–13. This is a transcription and interpretation by Hassall, with contributions by H. D. Soar, from a handwritten book owned by Captain and Mrs. Theo Sax.

11. Daines Barrington, "Observations on the practice of archery in England. In a letter to the Rev. Mr. Norris, Secretary [of the Society of Antiquaries]. By the Honourable Daines Barrington," *Archaeologia* 7 (1785), 46–68.

12. Moseley, *Essay on Archery*, 198–200. Although covering much the same historic ground as Daines Barrington, Moseley introduces some contemporary anecdotes.

13. Moseley, *Essay on Archery*, 201–203.

CHAPTER ELEVEN: BUTTS, ROODS, AND WOODMEN

1. Hugh D. H. Soar, "An Archery Song from Gloucestershire: The Robin Hood Society of Gloucestershire," *Journal of the Society of Archer-Antiquaries* 33 (1990), 23–26.

2. Letter from the secretary of the Robin Hood Society to its members, May 5, 1802, Gloucestershire County Archives, England, accession number D9125/1/2070.

3. *Records of the Woodmen of Arden*, transactions for 1788 (n.p.: privately printed, 1885, for private circulation), 9.

4. *Records of the Woodmen of Arden*, transactions for 1802 (n.p.: privately printed, 1885, for private circulation), 15, 20. On Wednesday, August 25, "W. Palmer won the Arrow by 4 shots in 13 Ends. 30 Woodmen present. 11 competed."

5. Hugh D. H. Soar, "Some Notes to *The English Bowman*," *Journal of the Society of Archer-Antiquaries* 45 (2002), 71.

> Arrows were weighed by their maker on a scale with the arrow on one side and silver coins on the other. This was then marked on the arrow as e.g. 4 * 6 (four shillings and sixpence)
>
> Silver coinage weights appropriate to recreational arrows are shown below in grains
>
> (adjusted to two decimal points) based on the following values
>
> 3 pence = 21.82 grains.   6 pence = 43.63 grains.
> 9 pence = 65.46 grains   1 shilling = 87.27 grains
> 2 * 0 = 174.54 grains.
> 2 * 3 = 196.36 grains.   2 * 6 = 218.17 grains.
> 2 * 9 = 240.00 grains.   3 * 0 = 261.81 grains.
> 3 * 3 = 283.63 grains.   3 * 6 = 305.44 grains.
> 3 * 9 = 327.27 grains   4 * 0 = 349.08 grains.
> 4 * 3 = 370.90 grains.   4 * 6 = 392.73 grains.
> 4 * 9 = 414.54 grains.   5 * 0 = 436.35 grains.
> 5 * 3 = 458.17 grains.   5 * 6 = 479.99 grains.
> 5 * 9 = 501.81 grains.   6 * 0 = 523.62 grains.
>
> Note. This scale of coinage/grains, based upon 7.27 grains to one penny is relevant from 1816. Prior to this year the scale was 7.74 grains to one penny. The arrow marked 9 * 6 and mentioned in Chapter 9 is earlier than 1816 and would thus have weighed 882.36 grains.

6. George Agar Hansard, *The Book of Archery* (London: Longman and Co., 1840), 111.

7. *Records of the Woodmen of Arden*, transactions for 1889 (n.p.: privately printed, 1935, for private circulation), 49. On July 31, "C. W. Digby, having won 2 ends out of 9 was the winner. Mr Digby obtained his first end by a foot, but unfortunately the marker missed sight of the arrow and not being able to get out of the way was shot in the thigh. Fortunately the arrow went through the fleshy part and he was not seriously hurt." Subsequently, at a meeting (which in keeping with ancient tradition they called a wardmote) held in June 1890, the secretary was requested to provide shelter or protection for the markers. There appears to have been an element of levity associated with this arrangement: the author pos-

sesses a set of ten humorous cards printed by William Wood, of Hillside
Studios, Sutton Coldfield, at the behest of a senior Woodman, which illustrate
the marker gesticulating from behind his protective shield as the arrows arrive.
8. Robert Louis Stevenson, *The Black Arrow: A Tale of Two Roses* (New York and
Boston: Books Inc., n.d.).
9. Author's personal correspondence, March 17, 1992, with the late Richard
Galloway, arrow-maker, of Bonnybridge, Allandale, near Falkirk, Scotland.
10. Saint Mary's Church: Symbolism (http://stmaryswreay.org/symbolism.html).
11. James Duff, *Bows and Arrows* (New York: Macmillan, 1927), 96.
12. The following discussion is based on Thomas Roberts, *The English Bowman,
or Tracts on Archery: To Which Is Added the Second Part of the Bowman's Glory*
(London: C. Roworth, 1801), and Soar, "Notes to *The English Bowman,*" *Journal
of the Society of Archer-Antiquaries* 45 (2002), 68–75.
13. Benjamin Robins, *The New Principles of Gunnery* (London: J. Nourse, 1742),
as quoted in Roberts, *English Bowman, or Tracts on Archery,* 149.

CHAPTER TWELVE: THE ROYAL PREROGATIVE

1. Roberts, *English Bowman,* 155.
2. Sir John Smythe, "An Answer to Contrary Opinions Military." This was an
unpublished treatise designed to counter Humfry Barwicke's dismissal of the
bow as an effective tactical military weapon.
3. Thomas Waring (the Younger), *A Treatise on Archery: or, the Art of Shooting
with the Long Bow,* 6th ed. (London: printed by author, 1827), 37–39.
4. Handwritten notification from Thirsk Bowmen's secretaries, Mr. John
Higginson and Mr. Henry Peckitt, to interested parties, including a copy of the
deliberations of a meeting of archers at the Black Swan Hotel, York, on May 14,
1844. Original in the possession of the author. While one hundred archers presumably subscribed, just seventy-two took up their positions at the targets.
Shooting was controlled by a flag bearer who lowered his flag to indicate its
commencement, the band having simultaneously stopped playing.
5. "Rules to be observed by gentlemen competing for the prizes at the Grand
National Archery Meeting York. August 1844," publicity leaflet for the first
National Archery Meeting, in the possession of the author.
6. Thomas Hastings, *The British Archer, or Tracts on Archery* (Newport, Isle of
Wight: J. Rowden, 1831), 84n.
7. Hugh D. H. Soar, "The Scardeburgh Prize Arrow," *Journal of the Society of
Archery-Antiquaries* 42 (1999), 44–45. This arrow is of Continental origin and is
an embellished French or Belgian butt shaft.
8. Robin Ascham [pseud.], "The Alexandra Arrow," *The Archer's Register*
(London: Howell James and Co., 1864), 27–29.
9. Peter Muir, letter dated December 24, 1864, from Archer's Hall, Edinburgh,
addressed to the *Field,* a largely sporting newspaper, and printed by him for cir-

culation to fellow archers. He concludes, "Had Dr. Croft known something of an Arrow, its use and history, he might have saved himself the expense of a Patent."

10. Letter by Horace Ford in response to that of Mrs. Horniblow, the lady champion, the *Field*, January 7, 1865. See also correspondence in the *Field* of December 31, 1864, and January 14, 1865, by Dr. J. McGrigor Croft in response to Peter Muir's letter and to Horace Ford's criticism of his design.

CHAPTER THIRTEEN: THE CHOICE OF CHAMPIONS

1. William Butt, *The Theory and Practice of Archery by the late Horace Ford* (London: Longmans, Green, 1887). Although Butt's omissions are considerable, they do not affect the thrust of Ford's work. His additional material is helpful in providing names and scores of winners and runners-up at major public tournaments from 1844 through 1886.

2. The *Field*, August 1855 and July 1857.

3. H. A. Ford, *Archery: Its Theory and Practice* (London: Buchanan, 1859), 29.

4. Ford, *Archery*, 33.

5. Ford, *Archery*, 35. Today we recognize that an arrow that is too stiff will fly left and one that is too whippy will fly right. Although Ford noted on page 37 that the stronger the bow the stiffer the arrow should be, he did not realize why. Modern longbow archers, by spining their arrows to establish the amount of deflection, are utilizing their knowledge of the bending of an arrow around the bow as it is shot, in order to match arrow with bow for accuracy.

6. Ritson, *Robin Hood*, 90.

7. Ford, *Archery*, 89.

8. C. J. Longman, "The Longman Target," *The Archer's Register* (London: *Field* newspaper, 1884), 70–77.

9. *The Archers Register* (London: *Field* newspaper, 1885), 76–77.

10. Centrum Centrissimum, *The Archer's Register* (London: *Field* newspaper, 1886), 63.

11. Sagittarius, *The Archer's Register* (London: *Field* newspaper, 1887), 73.

12. It is not clear if the final contest took place in 1771. Readers may wish to consult H. Walrond, "Archery as a Pastime," *Archery*, Badminton Library of Sports and Pastimes (London: Longmans, Green, 1894), 165, and draw their own conclusions.

13. Emily Pepys, *The Journal of Emily Pepys* (Otley, England: Prosper Books, 1984), 46. The entry is from August 19, 1844.

14. Fred Lake, "An Archery Pub in St. John's Wood," *The British Archer* 23, no. 5 (March/April 1972), 203.

15. Undated, unnumbered photocopied page, probably from a trade journal, printed by M. A. Fittman, London, and given to the author by a friend many years ago.

16. *The United Bowmen of Philadelphia, 1828–1953*, 125th anniversary book. This privately printed book was limited to two hundred copies. An image opposite page five shows a typical target with the many marks upon it.

17. Robert P. Elmer, *Target Archery with a History of the Sport in America* (New York: Knopf, 1946), 7.

18. Duff, *Bows and Arrows*, 132.

19. C. Hawkins Fisher, "Archery of the Past," *Archery*, Badminton Library of Sports and Pastimes (London: Longmans, Green, 1894), 270. This is a criticism of the innovation, but see also H. Walrond, "The Arrow," 306–307, for further commentary.

20. *The Archer's Register* (London: *Field* newspaper, 1878), 168.

21. An Expert, *The Archer's Complete Guide: Or, Instructions for the Use of the Longbow* (New York: Peck & Snyder, 1878), 14. This instructional book, which included the Peck & Snyder price list, offered forthright advice on preparation for archery: "A gentleman who smokes should never indulge in a cigar or a pipe immediately preceding or during the time of shooting. A lady who wears a tight corset need not hope for much physical benefit from archery, or for that matter from anything else."

22. Maurice Thompson and Will Thompson, *How to Train in Archery* (New York: E. I. Horsman, 1879), 51.

23. Maurice Thompson, "A Review of Archery in America during the Season of 1879," *The Archer's Register* (London: the *Field*, 1880), 180–181. This article includes details of the first Grand Annual Meeting.

CHAPTER FOURTEEN: INNOVATION

1. W. H. Wright and G. L. Thorne. US Patent 213,083, March 11, 1879.

2. Royal Archery advertising booklet and price list (Boston: Perry Mason, 1879), 2.

3. Maurice Thompson, *The Witchery of Archery: A Complete Manual of Archery. With many chapters of adventures by field and flood and an appendix containing practical directions for the manufacture and use of archery implements*, reproduction of 2nd ed., 1879 (Walla Walla, WA: Martin Archery, 1984), 8. The opening lines of chapter two are universally quoted: "So long as the new moon returns in heaven a bent, beautiful bow, so long will the fascination of archery keep hold of the hearts of men."

4. Wade Phillips, *Broadheads 1871-1971: Identification and Rarity Guide for the Most Collectible Antique Archery Broadheads*, 2nd ed. (Boys Town, NE: printed by author, 2004). This book contains images of over two thousand broadheads, with rarities updated.

5. Saxton Pope, *Bows and Arrows* (Los Angeles: University of California Press, 1962), 77.

6. Howard Hill, *Hunting the Hard Way* (London: Robert Hale, 1956).

7. "Merry Days with Bow and Quiver," *Scribner's Monthly* 16, no. 1 (May 1878), 9, 11.

8. The Deer Act, 1991, c. 54, sec. 4. It reads in part: "An Act to provide close seasons for deer, to prohibit the taking of deer by certain devices and at certain times. 31st July 1963. Article 3 1 Subject to Sections 10 and 11 of this Act, if any person . . . c) uses for the purpose of killing or injuring a deer . . . (ii) any arrow, spear or similar missile, he shall be guilty of an offence."

9. Robert P. Elmer, *Target Archery: With a History of the Sport in America* (New York: Knopf, 1946), 27.

10. Ayres archery catalogue, undated advertisement, perhaps 1930.

11. *The Archer's Register* (London: *Field* newspaper, 1905), 259–266. The first English (British) International Archery Medal attained by a lady archer was acquired at this meeting. Mrs. Lewis Weedon of the West Kent Archery Society won the Ladies Double National Round, shooting on July 13 and 15, the scores being aggregated. The medal is in the keeping of the author. Five more international meetings were held at Le Touquet until stopped by the Great War. The 1905 meeting was notable for the presence of Miss Alice Legh, national champion, and is the only known occasion she shot internationally. Five English ladies were challenged by ten of their French counterparts (including two comtesses). Alice Legh gained first place, and her sister, Bea, was second.

12. *The Archer's Register* (London: *Field* newspaper, 1909), 257–259. Mr. Backhouse had the highest number of hits and the second highest score.

13. Elmer, *Target Archery*, 81.

14. Glenn St. Charles, series ed., *Legends of the Longbow*, vol. 2, no. 1 (Lyon, MS: Derrydale, 1993), 20.

15. Ralph Jebb, "Report of a Meeting between Archers and Archery Trade," *Archery News* 26, no. 1 (May 1947), 5.

16. Advertisement, *Archery News* 14, no. 1 (May 1935), unnumbered final page.

17. John Boulden was a member of the Ancient Society of Painswick Bowmen, seemingly so called because all members were elderly. The author has his archery log.

18. K. Ryall Webb, "Spine and Musical Frequency—Vibration Period," *The British Archer* 2, no. 4 (December 1951), 17. See also the letter from J. F. M. Oram in *The British Archer* 5, no. 1 (June/July 1953), 30–31.

19. Ascham, *Toxophilus*, 164.

20. The Craft Guild of Traditional Bowyers and Fletchers was formed in 1986 as a fraternity of bow- and arrow-makers whose work is of proven excellence. It is governed by a warden and a court of six masters, served by a clerk. See www.bowyersandfletchersguild.org.

EPILOGUE

1. Advertisement, *The Archer's Register* (London: The Field and Queen [Horace Cox], 1914), inside back cover.

2. Longfellow, *Hiawatha*, 106.

Bibliography

Acts of the Privy Council N.S.XVI 25 (1588).

Aeroplanes, Dirigeables, Zeppelins. Paris: 1915.

Allely, Steve. "Western Indian Bows." In *The Traditional Bowyer's Bible,* vol. 1. New York: Lyons and Burford, 1992.

Ancient Armies of Macedon. http://www.ancient-battles.com/catw/makedon.htm.

The Ancient Honour of the Famous City of London Restored and Recovered by the NOBLE Sir John Robinson KNIGHT AND BARONET, Lord Mayor for this year 1663 in The truly ENGLISH and Manly Exercises of Wrestling, Archery and Sword and Dagger with The Speeches of Mr William SMEE (Master of the Game pro hoc vice, and Clerk of the Market) upon this Solemn Occasion. London: Printed for R. L., 1663.

The Archer's Register. London: *Field* newspaper, 1878.

————. London: *Field* newspaper, 1885.

————. London: *Field* newspaper, 1905.

————. London: *Field* newspaper, 1909.

————. London: The Field and Queen [Horace Cox], 1914.

Ascham, Robin [pseud.]. "The Alexandra Arrow." *The Archer's Register.* London: Howell James and Co., 1864.

Ascham, Roger. *Toxophilus: The Schole or Partitions of Shootinge,* 1544. Reprint, Wakefield, England: S. R. Publishers, in collaboration with the Society of Archer-Antiquaries and the Grand National Archery Society, 1968.

Barrington, Daines. "Observations on the practice of archery in England. In a letter to the Rev. Mr. Norris, Secretary [of the Society of Antiquaries]. By the Honourable Daines Barrington." *Archaeologia* 7 (1785).

Beadle, Richard, and Pamela M. King. *York Mystery Plays: A Selection in Modern Spelling.* Oxford: Oxford University Press, 1995, reissued 1999.

Beith, John Hay [Ian Hay]. *The Royal Company of Archers 1676–1951.* Edinburgh: Wm. Blackwood, 1951.

Berg, Robert. "Bannerstones and How They Relate to the Atlatl." June 17, 2005. Thunderbird Atlatl. http://www.thunderbirdatlatl.com/ ?p=24.

Bradbury, Jim. *The Battle of Hastings*. Stroud, England: Sutton, 1973.

Butt, William. *The Theory and Practice of Archery by the late Horace Ford*. London: Longmans, Green, 1887.

Carey, C. G., ed. *The War Illustrated*, January 23, 1917.

Centrum Centrissimum. *The Archer's Register*. London: *Field* newspaper, 1886.

Chaucer, Geoffrey, trans. *The Romance of the Rose*. N.p.: Kissinger, 2004. http://books.google.com/books?id=KDiJUYW422wC&source=gbs_si milarbooks.

Cherokee Heritage Center. "Cherokee Games." http://www.cherokee-heritage.org/cherokeeheritage/cherokee_games.html.

Child, Francis James, ed. *English and Scottish Popular Ballads*. Ann Arbor: University of Michigan Library, 2005. http://www.sacred-texts.com/neu/eng/child/ch162.htm.

City of Bristol Record Office. Ref: 1625, no. 30.

Clark, J. G. D. "Neolithic Bows from Somerset, England, and the Prehistory of Archery in North-west Europe." *Proceedings of the Prehistoric Society* 29 (1963), 50–98.

Corporation of London Records Office, Letter Book N., 169b.—170. CLRO Ref: small ms box 1 no. 11.

Credland, Arthur G. "Bow and Pike." *Journal of the Society of Archer-Antiquaries* 29 (1986), 4–14.

———. "Eagle Bowmen." *Journal of the Society of Archer-Antiquaries* 38 (1995), 49–60.

———. "The Longbow in the Sixteenth and Seventeenth Centuries." *Journal of the Society of Archer-Antiquaries* 32 (1989), 9–23.

———. "The Medieval War Arrow." *Journal of the Society of Archer-Antiquaries* 25 (1982), 28–35.

Crossley-Holland, Kevin, ed. *The Anglo-Saxon World*. Woodbridge, England: Boydell Press, 2000.

Davies, Jonathan. "Military Archery and the Inventory of King Henry VIII." *Journal of the Society of Archer-Antiquaries* 44 (2001), 31–38.

De Vingo, Paolo. "Personal Equipment and Fighting Techniques among the Anglo Saxon Population in Northern Europe during the Early Middle Ages." University of Torino, Italy. http://www.mun.ca/mst/heroicage/issues/6/devingo.html.

Diaz del Castillo, Bernal. *The Truthful History of the Conquest of New Spain,* or, *The Discovery and Conquest of Mexico 1517-1521.* New York: Farrar, Straus, and Cudahy, 1956.

Dodd, Reverend James William. *Ballads of Archery, Sonnets, Etc.* London: R. H. Evans and W. Ginger, 1818.

Duff, James. *Bows and Arrows.* New York: Macmillan, 1927.

Elmer, Robert P. *Target Archery: With a History of the Sport in America.* New York: Knopf, 1946.

An Expert. *The Archer's Complete Guide: Or, Instructions for the Use of the Longbow.* New York: Peck & Snyder, 1878.

Fisher, C. Hawkins. "Archery of the Past." *Archery.* Badminton Library of Sports and Pastimes. London: Longmans, Green, 1894.

Ford, H. A. *Archery: Its Theory and Practice.* London: Buchanan, 1859.

Garrod, Dorothy A. E. "Palaeolithic Spear Throwers." *Proceedings of the Prehistoric Society* 21, no. 3 (1955), 21–35.

Gendall, Janet. "The Arundel Archive of Arrows and Arrowheads." *Journal of the Society of Archer-Antiquaries* 44 (2001), 61–62.

———. "Evidence for Archery in Pictish Art." *Journal of the Society of Archer-Antiquarians* 43 (2000), 35–36.

Gerard, John. *The Herball, or the Generall Historie of Plantes.* Edited and expanded by Thomas Johnson. London: n.p., 1633.

Gibbon, Edward. *The Decline and Fall of the Roman Empire.* http://www.ccel.org/g/gibbon/decline/volume1/chap4.htm.

Hale, J. R., ed. *Certain Discourses Military.* Ithaca: Cornell University Press, 1964.

Hamer, Richard. *A Choice of Anglo-Saxon Verse.* London: Faber & Faber, 1970.

Hansard, George Agar. *The Book of Archery.* London: Longman and Co., 1840.

Hassall, Chris. "Songs from Bow-Meetings of the Society of the Royal British Bowmen." Computer printout circa 1998.

Hastings, Thomas. *The British Archer, or Tracts on Archery.* Newport, Isle of Wight: J. Rowden, 1831.

Heath, E. G., and Vilma Chiara. *Brazilian Indian Archery.* Manchester, England: Simon Archery Foundation, 1977.

Hildred, Alexandra, ed. *Weapons of Warre: The Armaments of the Mary Rose.* Vol. 3 of *The Archeology of the Mary Rose.* Portsmouth, England: Mary Rose Trust, 2011.

Hill, Howard. *Hunting the Hard Way.* London: Robert Hale, 1956.

Hill, James Mitchell. *Celtic Warfare*. Edinburgh: John Donald, 1986.

H. L., *A New Invention of Shooting Fire-shafts in Long-Bows, wherein besides the maner of making them there is contained a briefe Discourse of the usefulness of them in our moderne Warres by sea and land*. London: 1628. Reprint, Amsterdam: Walter J. Johnson, 1974.

Hodgkin, Adrian Elliott. *The Archer's Craft*. London: Faber & Faber, 1951.

Hoffman, W. J. "Poisoned Arrows." *American Anthropologist* 4 (January 1891). Reprint, Machynlleth, Wales: Dyfi Valley Bookshop, 2001.

Holme III, Randle. *The Academy of Armory, or, a Storehouse of Armory and Blazon: containing the several variety of created beings, and how born in coats of arms, both foreign and domestick: with the instruments used in all trades and sciences, together with their terms of art: also the etymologies, definitions, and historical observations on the same, explicated and explained according to our modern language: very usefel for all gentlemen, scholars, divines, and all such as desire any knowledge in arts and sciences.* Chester, England: printed for the author, 1688.

Holm-Olsen, Ludvig, ed. *Speculum Regale*, 2nd ed. Oslo: Norsk Historisk Kjeldescrift Institute, 1983.

Hough, Walter. "Arrow Fletching and Pointing." *American Anthropologist* 4 (January 1891). Reprint, Machynlleth, Wales: Dyfi Valley Bookshop, 2001.

Hranicky, William Jack. *North American Projectile Points*. Bloomington, IN: AuthorHouse, 2007.

Hurd, Ben. *The Antient Scorton Silver Arrow: The Story of the Oldest Sporting Event in Britain*. London: Society of Archer-Antiquaries, 1972.

Isles, Fred. "Turkish Flight Arrows." *Journal of the Society of Archer-Antiquaries* 4 (1961), 25–28.

Jebb, Ralph. "Report of a Meeting between Archers and Archery Trade." *Archery News* 26, no. 1 (May 1947), 5.

Jessop, Oliver. "A New Artefact Typology for the Study of Medieval Arrowheads." *Medieval Archaeology* 40 (1996), 192–205.

Jones, David E. *Poison Arrows: North American Indian Hunting and Warfare*. Austin: University of Texas Press, 2007.

Justice, Noel D. *Stone Age Spear and Arrow Points of the Midcontinental and Eastern United States*. Bloomington: Indiana University Press, 2009.

Klopsteg, Paul. *Turkish Archery and the Composite Bow*. Manchester, England: Simon Archery Foundation, 1967.

Lake, Fred. "An Archery Pub in St. John's Wood." *The British Archer* 23, no. 5 (March/April 1972), 23.

L'Art d'Archerie. *The Archer's Register*. London: *Field* newspaper, 1902–3.

Lartet, Edouard, and Henry Christy. *Relique Aquitanacae*. Paris: 1875.

Latham, J. D., and W. F. Paterson. *Saracen Archery*. London: Holland Press, 1970.

Leech, Michael. "The Skefington Case of 1298: A Re-assessment of the First Recorded Description of a Medieval Bow and Arrow." *Journal of the Society of Archer-Antiquaries* 53 (2010), 81–83.

Lhagvasurum, Gongar. *The Stele of Chinggis Khan*. Ulaanbaatar: Mongolian National Institute of Physical Research, n.d.

Longfellow, Henry Wadsworth. *The Song of Hiawatha*. London: G. Routledge, 1856.

Longman, C. J. "The Longman Target." *The Archer's Register*. London: *Field* newspaper, 1884.

"Merry Days with Bow and Quiver." *Scribner's Monthly* 16, no. 1 (May 1878), 1–16.

Mongolia Today 1. "Tradition." www.mongoliatoday.com/issue/1/.

Morse, Edward S. "Ancient and Modern Methods of Arrow Release." *Bulletin of the Essex Institute* 17 (October–December 1885), 1–50.

Moseley, Walter Michael. *An Essay on Archery*. Worcester, England: T & T Holl, 1792.

Munkhtsetseg. "Mongolian National Archery." *Instinctive Archer Magazine* (Spring 1999), 44–51.

Neade, William. *The Double Armed Man by the New Invention*. London: 1625. Facsimile, York, PA: Shumway, 1970.

Nottinghamshire Archives (Coroners Court), County Hall, West Bridgford, England, 1562.

Oram, J. F. M. Letter. *The British Archer* 5, no. 1 (June/July 1953).

Oxley, James E. *The Fletchers and Longbowstringmakers of London*. London: Unwin Brothers, 1968.

Pant, G. N. *Indian Archery*. Delhi: Dr. Agam Prasad for Agam Kala Prakashan, 1978.

Partridge, James. *Ayme for Finsburie Archers*, 1601. Facsimile, STC Reel 2000, Ann Arbor: University of Michigan microfilms.

———. *Ayme for Finsburie Archers*, 1628. Reprint, Royal Leamington Spa, England: W. C. Books, 1998.

Paterson, W. F. "Observation on the Returning Arrow." *Journal of the Society of Archer-Antiquaries* 21 (1978), 4–15.

Paul, James Balfour. *History of the Royal Company of Archers*. Edinburgh: Wm. Blackwood, 1875.

Pepys, Emily. *The Journal of Emily Pepys*. Otley, England: Prosper Books, 1984.

Phillips, Wade. *Broadheads 1871-1971: Identification and Rarity Guide for the Most Collectible Antique Archery Broadheads*, 2nd ed. Boys Town, NE: printed by author, 2004.

Pitt Rivers Museum, Arms and Armour Virtual Gallery, http://web.prm.ox.ac.uk/weapons/.

Pollington, Stephen. *The English Warrior from Earliest Times until 1066*. Hockwold-cum-Wilton, England: Modern English Anglo-Saxon Books, 2002.

Pope, Saxton. *Bows and Arrows*. Los Angeles: University of California Press, 1962.

————. *Hunting with the Bow and Arrow*. New York: G. P. Putnam's Sons, 1925. Reprint of 2nd ed., Prescott, AZ: Wolfe, 1991.

————. "Yahi Archery." *University of California Publications in American Archaeology and Ethnology*, vol. 13, no. 3 (March 6, 1918).

Raikes, G. A. *History of the Honourable Artillery Company*. Vol. 1. London: R. Bentley and Son, 1878.

R.C. *Mercurius Civicus: Londons Intelligencer, or, Truth Impartially Related from Thence to the Whole Kingdome to Prevent Mis-information*. Number 18, September 1643.

Records of the Society of Finsbury Archers, 1671.

Records of the Woodmen of Arden. Transactions for 1788. N.p.: privately printed, 1885.

————. Transactions for 1802. N.p.: privately printed, 1885.

————. Transactions for 1889. N.p.: privately printed, 1935.

Riesch, Holger. "Alamannische Pfeile und Bogen." In *Das Bogenbauer Buch*. Ludwigshaven, Germany: Angelika Hörnig, 2001, 104–124.

Ritson, Joseph. *Robin Hood Poems, Songs and Ballads: A Collection of All the Ancient Poems, Songs and Ballads, Now Extant, Relative to That Celebrated English Outlaw, to Which Are Prefixed Historical Anecdotes of His Life*. London: John C. Nimmo, 1885.

Roberts, Thomas. *The English Bowman*. London: 1802. Reprint, Wakefield, England: EP Publishing, 1973.

————. *The English Bowman, or Tracts on Archery: To Which Is Added the Second Part of the Bowman's Glory*. London: C. Roworth, 1801.

Robins, Benjamin. *The New Principles of Gunnery*. London: J. Nourse, 1742.

Rodwell, Kirsty, and Robert Bell. *Acton Court: The Evolution of an Early Tudor Courtier's House*. London: English Heritage, 2004.

Rust, A. "Die Alte-und Mittelsteinzeitlichen Funde von Stellmoor." Neumünster: 1943.

Sagittarius. Letter. *The Archer's Register*. London: *Field* newspaper, 1887.

Samten, Jampa. "An Investigation on Gesar's Arrow Divination." Proceedings of the 6th Seminar of the International Association for Tibetan Studies, Fagernes, Norway, August 21–28, 1992.

Selby, Stephen. *Chinese Archery*. Hong Kong: Hong Kong University Press, 2000.

Shakespeare, William. *King Lear*.

Smith, Thomas. *The Complete Soldier*. London: N.p., 1628.

Smythe, Sir John. "An Answer to Contrary Opinions Military." Unpublished treatise.

Smythe, Sir John, with Humfry Barwicke. *Certain Discourses Military*, 1590. Reprint, *Bow Versus Gun*. Wakefield, England: EP Publishing, 1973.

Soar, Hugh D. H. "An Archery Song from Gloucestershire: The Robin Hood Society of Gloucestershire." *Journal of the Society of Archer-Antiquaries* 33 (1990), 23–26.

———. "The Bowyers and Fletchers of Bristowe." *Journal of the Society of Archer-Antiquaries* 32 (1989), 27–36.

———. "The Scardeburgh Prize Arrow." *Journal of the Society of Archery-Antiquaries* 42 (1999), 44–45.

———. "Seventeenth Century Archery: Some Notes on the Regulations of Two Seventeenth Century Archery Societies." *Journal of the Society of Archer-Antiquaries* 35 (1992), 8–12.

———. "Some Notes to *The English Bowman*." *Journal of the Society of Archer-Antiquaries* 45 (2002), 64–75.

———. "Uriah Streater: Apprentice Fletcher." *Journal of the Society of Archer-Antiquaries* 42 (1999), 11–12.

Soar, Hugh D. H., with Joseph Gibbs, Chris Jury, and Mark Stretton. *Secrets of the English War Bow*. Yardley, PA: Westholme, 2006.

Spindler, Konrad. *The Man in the Ice*. London: Weidenfeld and Nicolson, 1994.

Stagg, D. J., ed. *New Forest Documents AD 1244–AD 1334*. Hampshire Records Series 3. N.p.: Hampshire County Council, 1979.

Starkey, D., ed. *The Inventory of King Henry VIII*. Vol. 1. London: Harvey Miller, for the Society of Antiquaries, 1998.

St. Charles, Glenn, series ed. *Legends of the Longbow*. Vol. 2, no. 1. Lyon, MS: Derrydale, 1993.

Stein, Henri. *Archers d'Autre Fois: Archers d'Aujourd'hui*. Lille, France: L. Danel, 1925.

Stevenson, David. *Highland Warrior: Alasdair MacColl and the Civil Wars*. Edinburgh: John Donald, 1980.

Stevenson, Robert Louis. *The Black Arrow: A Tale of Two Roses*. New York and Boston: Books Inc., n. d.

Storey, Jenni. "What Came First in Mongolia, the Wheel or the Bow?" *Mongol Messenger* (July 9, 1997) reprinted at http://www.atarn.org/mongolian/mn_nat_arch/messenger.htm.

Sturlason, Snorre. *The Norse King Sagas*. Everyman's Library. London and New York: J. M. Dent, 1930.

Sussex County Archives (Coroners Court), County Hall, Lewes, England, 1267.

Swanton, Michael, ed. and trans. *The Anglo-Saxon Chronicles*, 2nd ed. London: Phoenix Press, 2000.

T'an Tan-Chiung. "Investigative Report on Bow and Arrow Manufacture in Chengtu." *Language and History Review*, 1951. Reprint, *Journal of Chinese Art History* 11 (July 1981), 143–216.

Thompson, Maurice. "A Review of Archery in America during the Season of 1879." *The Archer's Register*. London: *Field* newspaper, 1880.

———. *The Witchery of Archery: A Complete Manual of Archery. With many chapters of adventures by field and flood and an appendix containing practical directions for the manufacture and use of archery implements*, 2nd ed., 1879. Reproduction, Walla Walla, WA: Martin Archery, 1984.

Thompson, Maurice, and Will Thompson. *How to Train in Archery*. New York: E. I. Horsman, 1879.

Thorpe, Lewis. *The Bayeux Tapestry and the Norman Invasion*. London: The Folio Society, 1973.

The United Bowmen of Philadelphia, 1828–1953. 125th anniversary book.

Ura, Karma. "Perceptions of Security." *Journal of Bhutan Studies* 5 (Winter 2001), 113–139.

Van Trees, Robert. *Banks of the Wabash*. Fairborn, OH: Van Trees Associates, 1986.

Walker, G. Gould. *The Honourable Artillery Company 1537-1947*. Aldershot, England: Gale and Polden, 1954.

Walrond, H., ed. *The Archer's Register*. London: *Field* newspaper, 1912.

———. "Archery as a Pastime." *Archery*. Badminton Library of Sports and Pastimes. London: Longmans, Green, 1894.

Waring, Thomas (the Younger). *A Treatise on Archery: or, the Art of Shooting with the Long Bow*, 6th ed. London: printed by author, 1827.

Webb, Alf. "Those So Called Arrow Straighteners." *Journal of the Society of Archer-Antiquaries* 38 (1995), 30–40.

Webb, K. Ryall. "Spine and Musical Frequency—Vibration Period." *The British Archer* 2, no. 4 (December 1951), 17.

White, C. G., and W. Harper. *Aircraft in the Great War*. Chicago: McClurg, 1915.

Whitelaw, Charles E. *Scottish Arms Makers*. Edited by Sarah Barter. London: Arms and Armour Press, 1977.

Wood, Sir William. *The Bowman's Glory, or Archery Revived*. London: Published by author, 1682. Reprint, Wakefield, England: S. R. Publishers, 1969.

World Atlatl Association. http://www.worldatlatl.org/.

Yangphel Archery. "Bhutanese Way." http://www.bhutanarchery.com/new/?page_id=41.

Index

Acknowledgments

I thank my publisher for his forbearance, and my copyeditor for his courteous adjustment of my prose to meet the requirements of an American readership.

I am grateful to Veronica-Mae for her continuing technical support, without which this book would have foundered, and to friends Jan and Lis for their creative encouragement.

I would also like to pay tribute to the many enthusiasts who generously shared their knowledge with me and provided images, including Dr. Jill Brazier, Dr. Alexzandra Hildred, Mr. Peter Dekker, Dr. K.L. Watson, and Mr. Nigel Stevens.